Introduction to
Library Research in
Women's Studies

Other Titles in This Series

Doing Library Research, Robert K. Baker

Introduction to Library Research in French Literature, Robert K. Baker

Aging and the Aged: An Annotated Bibliography and Library Research Guide, Linna F. Place, Linda Parker, and Forrest J. Berghorn

Introduction to Library Research in German Studies: Language, Literature, and Civilization, Larry L. Richardson

Introduction to Library Research in Hispanic Literature, Szilvia E. Szmuk and Angela B. Dellepiane

Also of Interest

**The Underside of History: A View of Women Through Time*, Elise Boulding

International Law and the Status of Women, Natalie Kaufman Hevener

Comparable Worth: The Myth and the Movement, Elaine Johansen

**Women in Third World Development*, Sue Ellen M. Charlton

**The Hidden Sun: Women of Modern Japan*, Dorothy Robins-Mowry

Women in the Cities of Asia: Migration and Urban Adaptation, edited by James T. Fawcett, Siew-Ean Khoo, and Peter C. Smith

Women and Revolution in Iran, edited by Guity Nashat

Social Power and Influence of Women, edited by Liesa Stamm and Carol D. Ryff

Working Women: A Study of Women in Paid Jobs, edited by Ann Seidman

Covert Discrimination and Women in the Sciences, edited by Judith A. Ramaley

Computerized Literature Searching: Research Strategies and Databases, Charles L. Gilreath

*Available in hardcover and paperback

Westview Guides to Library Research
Robert K. Baker, Series Editor

Introduction to Library Research in Women's Studies
Susan E. Searing

    This book fills the need for an introduction to research tools and library services valuable in the investigation of topics related to women. The core of the book is an annotated bibliography that describes selected bibliographies, indexes, catalogs, handbooks, directories, and biographical dictionaries and evaluates the traditional reference aids available in most college libraries in terms of their usefulness in women's studies research. Organized by type of material and general topic, the bibliography is fully indexed by author, title, and specific subject.

    Ms. Searing addresses the general principles of library organization and highlights issues and problems of central concern to researchers in women's studies, such as sexism in card catalog subject headings. The final section of the book illustrates the planning and conduct of systematic literature searches, using sample paper topics, to aid both student and scholar in diving into the interdisciplinary waters of women's studies.

    Susan E. Searing is Women's Studies Librarian-at-Large for the University of Wisconsin System.

Introduction to Library Research in Women's Studies

Susan E. Searing

Westview Press / Boulder and London

Westview Guides to Library Research

All rights reserved. No part of this publication may be reproduced or transmitted in any form or by any means, electronic or mechanical, including photocopy, recording, or any information storage and retrieval system, without permission in writing from the publisher.

Copyright © 1985 by Susan E. Searing

Published in 1985 in the United States of America by Westview Press, Inc., 5500 Central Avenue, Boulder, Colorado 80301; Frederick A. Praeger, Publisher

Library of Congress Cataloging in Publication Data
Searing, Susan E.
    Introduction to library research in women's studies.
    Includes index.
    1. Reference books--Women--Bibliography. 2. Women--Bibliography. 3. Women--Research--Methodology.
4. Women's studies--Bibliography. I. Title.
Z7961.S42 1985 [HQ1206] 016.3054 85-3162
ISBN 0-86531-267-2

Composition for this book was provided by the author
Printed and bound in the United States of America

10 9 8 7 6 5 4 3 2 1

Contents

Preface ix
Acknowledgments xiii

Part I: USING THE LIBRARY
1. What is Women's Studies? 1
2. Research Strategy 5
3. The Catalog 17
4. Beyond the Catalog 29
5. Interlibrary Loan 35
Notes on Part I 36

Part II: THE TOOLS OF RESEARCH
6. Guides to Women's Studies Research and Bibliographies of Reference Sources 37
7. General Women's Studies Bibliographies 41
8. Multidisciplinary Bibliographies and Indexes . 47
   8.1 Books 47
   8.2 Periodical Articles 51
   8.3 Newspapers 59
   8.4 Government Publications 63
   8.5 Conference Proceedings 69
   8.6 Dissertations 73
9. Bibliographies and Indexes in Special Fields . 75
   9.1 Anthropology 77
   9.2 The Arts 81
   9.3 Business, Economics, and Labor Studies . 93
   9.4 Education 101
   9.5 Health and Medicine 107
   9.6 History 111
   9.7 Law and Criminology 119
   9.8 Lesbian Studies 123
   9.9 Linguistics 125
   9.10 Literature 129
   9.11 Minority Studies 139
   9.12 National and Area Studies 145
   9.13 Political Science 161

	9.14 Psychology	167
	9.15 Religion and Philosophy	173
	9.16 Science and Technology	179
	9.17 Sociology	183
10.	Library Catalogs and Guides to Special Collections of Books and Archives	189
11.	Biographical Sources	195
12.	Directories of Organizations and Services	203
13.	Microform Sources	207
14.	Online Sources	211
15.	Periodicals	215
16.	Miscellaneous Guides and Handbooks	221

Appendix A:	The Dewey Decimal System	225
Appendix B:	The Library of Congress System	227
Appendix C:	Review Essays in *Signs*	229

Author Index 235
Title Index 239
Subject Index 253

Preface

This book grew out of my preparations to teach a seminar at Yale in 1981. Titled "Interdisciplinary Research: Women's Studies," the junior-level course was funded by the National Endowment for the Humanities under a curriculum development grant to the fledgling Women's Studies Program.

In designing the syllabus, I faced a major problem -- the lack of a text. The only published research guide in women's studies was out-of-print, and in any case it failed to reflect the latest scholarship and newest tools. More up-to-date bibliographies of bibliographies served only as partial remedies, since they focused on a single type of reference source and did not provide guidance in library research planning or technique. I did what so many women's studies teachers have been forced to do: I pieced together a reading list of articles and chapters in books and placed the materials on reserve. And I substituted hands-on research exercises for classroom discussions.

I later realized that a guide to library research could serve not only as a text for women's studies students, but also as a desk manual for faculty and librarians engaged both in their own projects and in directing student research. My goal, therefore, is to extend two kinds of help to researchers: first, by guiding students in choosing topics and formulating search strategies for term paper assignments; and second, by recommending reference tools that can yield up information about women in a number of disciplines.

Chapters 1 through 5 present the basic facts -- some underlying premises of women's studies as field of inquiry, how libraries are organized, and how researchers can proceed most effectively. I emphasize the challenges involved in seeking information on gender-related subjects, guide the reader in constructing an individualized research plan, and provide guidelines for evaluating the relevance of reference tools to one's inquiry.

In the following chapters the focus shifts from the generalized to the particular, as I describe selected bibliographic resources in light of their usefulness to women's studies. Chapters 6 and 7 treat general bibliographic sources about women. The six sections of chapter 8 focus on multidisciplinary access tools for particular forms of publication: books; periodical articles; newspapers; government documents; conference proceedings; and dissertations.

Chapters 9.1 through 9.17 look at bibliographic resources in various disciplines and fields of study. Each chapter opens with a short introduction to subject headings used in the library catalog and a list of basic research guides, for readers unacquainted with the discipline being treated.

Chapters 10 to 16 discuss additional types of resources -- published library catalogs, biographical sources, directories, microforms, online data bases, periodicals, and handbooks. The appendices provide outlines of the Dewey Decimal and Library of Congress classifications and a full list of review articles in the leading women's studies journal, <u>Signs</u>.

Throughout the book I have provided possible call numbers for the works I cite, insofar as I could determine them from standard cataloging records. Most references include one or two Library of Congress call numbers and a Dewey Decimal number. Readers are cautioned to recheck the numbers in their local catalog if they cannot locate the items under the numbers suggested here.

This guide is selective and by no means covers the full breadth of the reference literature available on women. New sources are constantly being published, and I will be only too happy to learn of better tools that supercede those recommended within these pages.

Although faculty, graduate students, librarians, and independent researchers may all find useful information and encouragement here, undergraduate students are the intended audience. Almost all of the reference tools described are in the English language. Although I enforced no chronological limits, most of the cited sources have been published within the last ten years.

Not all of the sources will be available in every college library, although I have made an effort to avoid obscure works. On the other hand, some of the best sources to date have been self-published or issued by small women's presses; I have not hesitated to discuss such worthy publications.

Information specific to one's own campus library can be obtained from library staff. They are the resident experts on such matters as building layout, special collections, circulation policies, and the like. Reference librarians frequently offer guided tours, free bibliographies, and printed pathfinders.

More importantly, librarians can be counted upon to recommend resources to consult for a particular topic and the proper headings to look under in the catalog. This book, by contrast, generalizes about the patterns of organizing printed materials which are common to most American libraries, and draws the researcher's attention to standard published sources. If one's studies or the vagaries of fate carry her to other campuses, the knowledge and skills gained from reading this book and putting its suggestions into practice will be transferable.

Note on Bibliographic Data

The bibliographic entries in this handbook conform, for the most part, to standard cataloging practice in choice of main entry. Very occasionally I have preferred a title entry over a complicated corporate entry that seemed certain to confuse the reader. Title and imprint information for serials reflects the latest issue.

Library of Congress and Dewey Decimal classification numbers were gathered from several sources, including the National Union Catalog, the OCLC and RLIN data bases, and cataloging-in-publication records.

Acknowledgments

Many people helped in many ways as I labored over this book. Miriam Gilbert at Westview Press struck the initial spark of enthusiasm, provided relentless encouragement, and exhibited patient forbearance as I failed to meet successive deadlines. Series editor Bob Baker was nurturant, perceptive, constructively critical -- and again, patient beyond all reasonable expectation.

Several colleagues read portions of the manuscript and brought their expertise to bear on it. Robert Balay, Barbara Celone, Gerry Hurley, Betsey Patterson, and Michele Sullivan all have my heartfelt appreciation for their contributions. Judith Strasser deserves a special thank you for applying her keen editorial eye to the first five chapters.

To my longsuffering friends and housemates in New Haven and Madison, I owe a debt of gratitude that no amount of home-baked bread can repay. Among my supporters were: Dick Belford, Steve Ela, Carol Gilchrist, Steve Gottlieb, Jackie Kaplan, Catherine Loeb, Steve Ness, and Judith Strasser.

Finally, I am grateful to the children whose daily lives I shared during the completion of this guide: Jed Ela, Nathan Ela, Geoff Gilchrist, and Allie Holly-Gottlieb. Whenever I became despairingly mired in the "how" of feminist scholarship, I looked to them and remembered the "why."

Susan E. Searing
Madison, Wisconsin
November 1984

Part I

Using the Library

1
What is Women's Studies?

The nature of women's studies is still unresolved, although some fifteen years have passed since the first college course about women was offered. Debate even continues over the name for the field. Should it be called "women's studies," "feminist studies," or "gender studies?" The first alternative is most widely used at this writing and is employed throughout this book.

Women's studies is women-centered.

Women's studies is distinguished by its focus on women, women's experiences, and the nature of relationships between the sexes. By placing women at the center of intellectual inquiry, women's studies offers a new perspective on the world.

Further, feminist scholars believe that women's studies must be for women as well as about women. The crux of the need to study women is not merely that they have been ignored by traditional scholarship. Even in fields where researchers have extensively studied women -- psychology and medicine, for example -- the researchers' perspective has been male, and their conclusions have largely served male interests. Feminist critics decry the accepted notion of objectivity in scholarship as a veil for unexamined sexist bias; they see their own work as socially and politically useful. Women's studies has sometimes been labelled the "academic arm of the women's movement," in recognition of the contributions scholars make toward the goal of equality of the sexes.

Women's studies is interdisciplinary.

Women's studies draws upon the accumulated wisdom of many different disciplines, while offering a radical critique of the knowledge and methods of those disciplines. Some research questions are firmly grounded in a traditional field of study. Other queries span several disciplines and require the use of a variety of reference sources. Although bibliographies, indexes, biographical dictionaries, and handbooks devoted to women's studies topics are increasingly available, they generally supplement, rather than replace, the traditional discipline-based sources. Women's studies demands of its practitioners a broad knowledge of reference tools and a familiarity with the concepts and theories of many fields.

Women's studies is still evolving.

Although women's studies is firmly established in the curriculum of many colleges, it is still proper to think of it as a new field, one which is growing and changing. Feminist scholarship took root first in the humanities, finding fertile soil in the fields of literature and history in particular, and it continues to exert a strong and beneficial influence on research in those disciplines. There is ample evidence, however, that women's studies now has affected every branch of the social sciences and the professions, and that its impact is extending to the biological sciences and technology. The expanding scope of feminist inquiry is mirrored in the ever-growing array of specialized reference tools available to the researcher, and in the changing organization and language of the traditional bibliographic sources.

Women's studies is rooted in the women's movement.

Much of the vast and flourishing literature by and about women does not fit the traditional notion of "scholarly" writing. Valuable information and pathbreaking elaborations of theory are often published in activist periodicals, newsletters, and pamphlets, or in paperbacks issued by small feminist presses. Some topics -- for example, the study of the women's liberation movement itself -- may suggest the use of non-traditional materials as sources. In other areas, professors may discount such materials, dismissing them as non-academic or overly subjective. You must be alert to the perspective of the materials you cite. Although you may share a work's bias, you must learn to recognize the particular political perspective from which an author writes.

Researchers must also recognize the diversity of female experience. Works that present only a white, middle-class, heterosexist perspective are common. Such studies are not worthless, but they are biased and their limitations should be noted.

Because women's studies is so tightly tied to the

ongoing struggle for sexual equality, student term papers frequently address current controversies or causes. These very current issues are unlikely to be extensively treated in the academic literature. The lag between the time feminists in the community raise questions and the time those same questions are explored by academic feminists is compounded by the customary delays in getting manuscripts to press and getting published works indexed and cited. The up-to-the-minute nature of many research topics in women's studies places an additional burden on the student to devise innovative strategies for uncovering information.

Women's studies is rewarding.

Despite the obstacles noted above, women's studies research offers considerable compensations. Most students find the subject matter compelling. They often choose term paper topics that relate to their own experiences. Library research can sometimes be a dry, mechanical process, but in women's studies the sense of discovery runs high. The ideas and facts you uncover may shock, enlighten, madden, or amuse you. So don't be discouraged before you even begin. With the help of this handbook, you'll soon learn the tricks of efficient library use.

Given the exciting nature of women's studies -- its interdisciplinary, innovative, political nature -- it is not possible to recommend one single strategy for library research. This handbook attempts to provide a basic foundation of library skills and to suggest ways in which any researcher can structure a sound methodology for a given topic in women's studies.

2
Research Strategy

"I have to write a term paper for my women's history class, and I don't even know where to start!"
"Where do I go now that I've got these numbers?"
"There's nothing in the catalog under SPAIN--WOMEN. Am I doing something wrong?"
"Where are the novels by women? I just want to browse..."

Questions like these are heard every day at the information desks of college and university libraries. You may have posed such queries yourself. Students in all fields commonly experience confusion at the outset of a research project. Students in women's studies are no different. You may find that research in women's studies poses unique challenges. But if you're like most students, you'll also discover that women's studies research is uniquely rewarding.

Before reviewing the basic types of bibliographic publications and the use of the catalog, let's pause to think about "search strategy." Are you used to picking your way through the stacks until you find enough materials for a reading list of credible length? Planning your attack on the library can save you hours of aimless activity. Before your classmates have scratched the surface of the relevant literature, you can be sitting at your desk, surrounded by books and contentedly making notes.

If (like most sincere scholars) you love to browse, the notion of plotting a search strategy in advance may sound dull and regimented. There's no denying the joy of serendipitous discoveries, but unfortunately the odds of making such discoveries are reduced in women's studies. Since feminist scholarship spans the disciplines, relevant materials are disbursed throughout the stacks. It pays to be systematic.

A "search strategy" is nothing more than a logical plan for unearthing information. A classic library search strategy, suitable for a wide range of topics in women's studies and other areas, can be charted as follows:

1. Choose and refine your topic.

2. Gather background information, if necessary.

3. Identify, locate, and read books on the topic.

4. Identify, locate, and read articles on the topic.

5. Identify, locate, and read other materials, such as government documents, conference reports, and pamphlets.

6. Follow up on relevant works cited in the sources you consulted in steps 3, 4, and 5.

7. Fill in the gaps in your knowledge by repeating steps 3, 4, and 5 with any new subject headings, authors' names, etc. that are suggested in your readings.

8. Evaluate and synthesize the literature. Prepare to write.

(This strategy works best for subjects that are well established. Very new topics and issues may require a different approach, as you will soon see.)

In conducting a systematic search, be meticulous. Copy out the full citation for each source you use. For a book, the complete citation includes author, title, place, publisher, and date. For articles, be certain to note the journal title, volume and year, and the author, title, and pages of the article.
Whenever you come upon a promising reference, copy it out precisely. Recording it correctly in your notes the first time can save you from needless bibliographic backtracking later.
Many scholars prefer to use index cards for tracking references. The big cards (4 x 6 inches and larger) can accomodate notes too. In the early stages of your research, cards can be sorted into such pragmatic categories as "not on shelf-look again next week," "examined-not useful," "not in library-try interlibrary loan," and "key source-be sure to quote." If your research is exhaustive, an alphabetically arranged card file can keep you from dashing off to the stacks more than once for the same item. In the final stages of preparing and typing your paper, cards for works to which you've made references can be culled out and put in order for transcribing the concluding bibliography or notes.
With these hints in mind, let's take a closer look at

the steps of a classic search strategy.

Choose and refine your topic.

The first step in any research project is selecting a topic. Let's assume that you're required to write a ten- to fifteen-page term paper. Even if you haven't narrowed your thoughts down to a definite proposal for your paper, you probably have a general idea of what interests you. If that's NOT the case, skimming your textbook, an anthology, or a basic work in the field is one way to identify likely topics. Talking with your professor is another. Reference librarians may be able to give you further suggestions.

Because women's studies brings so many cherished concepts into question -- meanwhile raising a multitude of urgent new issues -- ideas are usually easy to come by. Determining if a topic is workable is more difficult -- especially for new students who may never have faced a research paper deadline before, or returning students whose library and composition skills are tarnished. Unfortunately, not all fascinating ideas can be translated into coherent term papers.

Before committing yourself to a topic, it's wise to do some preliminary research. You may find there's not enough published data to test your thesis or support your argument. For a social anthropology course, for example, you might want to undertake a cross-cultural survey of women's work in the home: how much time is spent cooking, how much caring for children, how much cleaning, and so on. But if comparable data is not available for the particular societies you wish to study, you'll be forced to reconsider your choice of topic. (Even if the data exists, it may be written in a language you can't read.)

Another obstacle will loom if the books and journals you need are not owned by your library. College libraries build collections to meet the needs of academic departments. This reasonable practice can sometimes spell disappointment for researchers in interdisciplinary fields. It also bodes ill for new fields of study. Women's studies, of course, is both cross-disciplinary and innovative.

Imagine that you're planning to research the prevalence of gender-biased language in elementary reading texts and its possible effects on the sex role socialization of pupils in the primary grades. Such a paper might draw on the knowledge bases of several fields -- psychology, sociolinguistics, sociology, and education -- in addition to studies by women's studies specialists. Depending on the curricular emphases of your college, your library may not be well-stocked in all those disciplines.

If you've planned ahead, you can rely on interlibrary loan to satisfy some of your need for items not held locally. You will also have time to rethink your topic and, if feasible, to restructure your paper around the materials and data you have at hand.

On the other hand, you may uncover more material than you can possibly read and synthesize in the time allotted. In that case, you should limit your research to a single aspect of the topic. The psychology of women, for instance, is obviously too general. Even a narrowed focus on women and mental disorders will probably overwhelm you. You might find it advisable to concentrate on, say, women and depression, or on an even more specialized problem -- for example, the emotional crisis mothers are presumed to face when their children grow up and move away from home. Or you might choose to look at alternative therapies for women, at the over-prescribing of mood-altering and anti-depressant drugs (which are administered to women much more frequently than to men), at pre-menstrual symptoms of depression, or at post-childbirth depression. All of these are still large topics, but they could be dealt with in a 15-page paper, depending on the tack you take.

Term paper topics are practically unlimited in women's studies, so there's no need to waste time panicking over a choice of topic. You may decide to refine the focus of your paper, of course, once you've begun your research.

Students are traditionally advised to do some reading before settling on a paper topic. If you don't have an exciting topic in mind, or if you seek to clarify your concept and define it more precisely, this step is critical. The library tools most useful for this initial "getting acquainted" research are encyclopedias, survey texts, anthologies, and handbooks to a discipline. Often these sources provide references, so they can assist you in choosing a topic and then double as your first bibliography.

Whether you're fishing around for an interesting topic in women's studies, or seeking some basic background on an unfamiliar subject, two sources can be especially helpful. One is The Women's Annual, a yearly overview of new scholarship in women's studies. The Women's Annual is valuable not only for its reviews of current publications, but for its attention to pressing issues within the women's movement. Its merged focus on academic and activist progress is refreshing and insightful. Each chapter treats a separate topic and is prepared by an expert in the field. The Women's Action Almanac is also useful for quick background. Its issue-oriented approach to over eighty topics makes the volume an ideal source of ideas and facts for women's studies papers, especially in the social sciences.

Gather background information.

In the process of refining your paper topic you can begin to lay the conceptual foundation for your project by consulting encyclopedias, specialized dictionaries, handbooks, or textbooks for an overview of the field. However, you might still need further background information, and this is the time to look for it. Without it, you may not fully understand the materials you read later.

Suppose, for instance, that you want to explore the experiences of women active in the temperance movement. You can consult any encyclopedia or handbook of American history to verify the dates of the movement's influence, the names of its leaders, and key events. You could read about WCTU president Frances Willard and her colleagues in a biographical source such as Notable American Women. A quick peek into basic reference sources at this early stage will usually suggest key concepts and terms to guide your further research.

Identify, locate, and read books on the topic.

When exploring well-established subject areas, most researchers begin with books. Books usually treat subjects in greater depth and breadth than journal articles can. Moreover, a book-length scholarly study generally outlines and assesses the existing knowledge of or views on the topic.

You can start your search for books at the library's catalog. (In the next chapter, you'll learn how to interpret a typical catalog record and be given some hints to make catalog-based research most efficient.) The advantage of starting with the catalog is that the references you find are (in theory at least) immediately available in your library. Paradoxically, the main disadvantage of the catalog as a bibliographic tool is that it lists only those books owned by your own institution. Even in the largest libraries this may represent only a small percentage of the full universe of writings relevant to your research topic.

The catalog has other drawbacks as a primary tool for research. It lists only books and similar large units of publication -- not smaller works such as individual contributions to anthologies. Furthermore, the catalog gives you no hint as to the worth of the book; you must judge its relevance solely by the title, the date, and perhaps the subject headings assigned to it.

Thus, you would be wise to consult bibliographies even before approaching the catalog. Focused topical bibliographies allow you to tap the subject expertise and critical perception of their compilers. Chapter 4, "Beyond the Catalog," provides an overview of bibliographies and their role in research.

Identify, locate, and read articles.

After digesting the general treatments accorded your topic in books, you should seek more specialized writings in the form of journal articles. Articles serve several purposes in the network of scholarly communication. First, they are perfect for reporting on narrow topics, ranging from the results of a single psychological experiment to the explication of a short story or sonnet. Such topics rarely fill a whole book. Second, articles are a speedier means of disseminating new knowledge, so they are the source for the latest in scholarly opinion and debate, as well as the most recent findings and figures. Third, they are forums for greater intellectual risk-taking. A book must sell a fair number of copies to be profitable to the publisher, and marketability therefore influences what gets published. Journals, on the other hand, are often sponsored by non-profit organizations and targeted at audiences of specialists. Young, unknown scholars usually find readier acceptance for their articles than for full-length book manuscripts. Thus, journal articles form a key link in the chain of scholarly communication.

The number of general and specialized journals in women's studies has grown astonishingly in recent years. Browsing is simply not an effective means of locating journal articles. Therefore, numerous access tools have been developed to help scholars find and use the journal literature. Indexes and abstracts (both discussed in Chapter 4) are the keys to finding useful articles. Subsequent chapters describe indexes and abstracts in many fields of interest to women's studies researchers. Use this handbook for guidance, or ask a librarian to recommend the access tools and journals best suited to your topic.

Identify, locate, and read other materials.

Here's where your imagination must enter in. Books and articles exist on almost every topic, but sometimes they will not provide you with enough information, or with information that is current enough. The additional materials you'll need will depend on your topic. Are you investigating an area that has generated "self-help" materials -- women's health, for example, or women's legal rights? If so, you may want to search in vertical files for pamphlets and clippings that contain down-to-earth practical advice or that espouse a particular viewpoint. ("Vertical files" are collections of timely materials -- such as newspaper articles, booklets, brochures, and articles reprints -- stored in file cabinets rather than on the shelves.) Are you examining an issue related to public policy? Chances are the federal government has an interest in it and has distributed helpful publications. Most scholarly fields generate conference papers, as do professional associations concerned with current social policy. Such papers may be difficult to track down, but they often contain the very latest thinking on a subject.

If you're researching women and the media, you may need audiovisual materials as well as printed sources. A paper on a female composer may require you to track down recordings of her works, in addition to published or manuscript scores. Studies of literary works or popular culture may call for a perusal of reviews. And of course, your investigation may sweep you out of the library entirely, as you turn to interviews, surveys, and field projects to broaden your knowledge of a topic.

Follow up on cited sources.

One hallmark of true scholarship is its reliance on earlier research. New ideas build on previous theories and data -- even when they seek to disprove the results of earlier thinking -- and so researchers are scrupulous in crediting the work of their predecessors. By documenting their sources in footnotes and bibliographies, researchers offer clues to other scholars exploring the same field. At the same time, they buttress their own conclusions with the weight of authority.

As you read, be alert to references worth following up. Copy out the bibliographic data exactly; then track down the most promising works to read yourself.

Fill in the gaps.

No search strategy can be planned perfectly in advance. As you discover new angles and approaches to your topic, you'll inevitably be drawn back to bibliographies, indexes, and the catalog. Often additional subject terms will suggest themselves. Occasionally, you'll recognize certain authors' names being cited repeatedly; you'll decide to make a systematic search for their works. Or you may opt to repeat your basic search strategy using a different set of indexes and bibliographies in another, related discipline.

Evaluate and synthesize the literature. Prepare to write.

Some people find that drawing conclusions from their reading and putting their ideas down on paper are the toughest steps of all. Others consider writing a breeze

compared to the drudgery of library research. If you are
insecure about your ability to organize your thoughts and
express them logically, or if you have questions about
footnote styles and the like, you can look at any of
several guides to writing term papers now on the market.
Inquire at your campus bookstore, or look in the
library's catalog under REPORT WRITING. Kate Turabian's
<u>A Manual for Writers of Term Papers, Theses, and
Dissertations</u> (Chicago: University of Chicago Press,
1973) sets forth a style often recommended by professors,
but you may be instructed to follow a different rule
book. Some research guides in the disciplines also give
hints on term paper composition.

Many campuses offer writing labs or tutoring services
for students struggling with term paper assignments.
Take advantage of such opportunities. Your painstaking
research and brilliant insights are worthless unless you
can communicate them clearly and effectively.

So far, we've sketched a more or less traditional
search strategy. Such an approach is recommended for
topics where a sizeable body of literature exists. Some
examples would be the history of the struggle for
universal suffrage, women's roles in labor organizing,
female managers, the works of Virginia Woolf, and the
image of women in popular film. All of these topics have
generated several books each and numerous journal
articles, plus specialized bibliographies.

Other women's studies topics, however, lack a large
body of literature. Current "hot" issues may trigger
your interest, but they can be frustrating to research
using a traditional method. At this writing, the "gender
gap" in voting behavior, premenstrual syndrome, and women
as writers and consumers of romance fiction are
relatively new interests of women's studies scholars.
Few books exist on these subjects, and specialized
bibliographies, when they are available at all, are
difficult to track down. In other words, there are no
easy short-cuts.

You should have no trouble recognizing "hot" topics
in the current news media. The link between tampons and
toxic shock, for example, was a startling medical
discovery that spurred women's studies students to
explore such matters as product safety testing and
advertising. But when the news was still fresh,
virtually no background materials were available. Other
topics may not be new, but may require a nontraditional
search strategy because they have only recently engaged
the attention of scholars. To use a gruesome example,
women have been beaten throughout history, but only in
the 1970s was the "battered woman syndrome" perceived as
a problem amenable to research and remedy. Your teacher
or librarian can help you gauge the nature of the

literature on a topic and thus guide you in choosing the most effective search strategy.

You shouldn't shy away from new topics -- after all, they can result in the most personally meaningful and educational of papers -- but you should be aware that a modified search strategy is called for. (1) Here's how your approach might be structured:

1. Choose and refine your topic.

2. Identify, locate, and read articles on the topic.

3. Follow up on relevant works cited in the articles.

4. Identify, locate, and read other materials.

5. Identify, locate, and read books on the topic.

6. Identify, locate, and consult sources outside the library.

7. Fill in the gaps by repeating earlier steps with any new subject terms, authors' names, etc. that are suggested in your readings.

8. Evaluate and synthesize the literature. Prepare to write.

As you can see, the basic sub-processes of library research are present in this model, but they have been reordered to reflect the probable nature of the available information.

Choose and refine your topic.

Choosing and refining your topic may be somewhat more challenging in the absence of published overviews or textbook treatments. On the other hand, topics currently in the news are likely to be familiar to you. For these reasons -- the paucity of reference materials and your presumed acquaintance with the subject -- the traditional second step of gathering background data may be inappropriate.

Identify, locate, and read articles on the topic.

If the topic is very new, beginning your research at the library's catalog may be fruitless. Most likely, no books have yet been published on the topic. Even if a handful of pioneering book-length studies are in print and in your library, they may be hard to find through the catalog, since librarians create new subject headings only when a subject is firmly ensconced as a discrete

field of interest.
New issues and emerging academic subjects will appear first in journal articles. Likewise, current public events will be described immediately in the news media, and much later analyzed in scholarly publications.
For a "hot" topic, therefore, indexes and abstracts may prove more reliable research tools than the catalog. Indexes that cover popular magazines -- <u>Readers' Guide to Periodical Literature</u> or the <u>Alternative Press Index</u>, for example -- are quicker to adopt the latest terminology than are more academic sources. Among the scholarly tools, <u>Women Studies Abstracts</u> reflects vocabulary current among feminists much more than do discipline-based abstracts. Thus, you must approach indexes and abstracts -- indeed, all current awareness sources -- with the same caution and creativity that you bring to the catalog.
Many printed indexes are also available online. Computerized databases are more current than their published counterparts. See the chapter devoted to online sources for a fuller discussion of the value of database searching in women's studies.

<u>Follow up on relevant works cited in the articles.</u>

A traditional search strategy begins with the book literature and works forward in time, as the researcher turns from the older classic texts to the latest articles, pamphlets, reports, etc. The model we are now considering moves backwards in time. The current literature will cite older publications that bear on the topic (if any exist). Recent writings may also point to older terms and concepts that you can apply to the catalog, to bibliographies in related fields, and to past volumes of indexes and abstracts.

<u>Identify, locate, and read other materials.</u>

If your library has a vertical file of clippings and pamphlets, look for relevant items in it. Check the latest issues of the <u>Monthly Catalog of Government Publications</u> for new materials from the federal government. Conference proceedings and symposia papers are other sources for up-to-the-minute facts and the latest theories.

<u>Identify, locate, and read books on the topic.</u>

Since you expect most of the information you need to be in articles and other current sources, a systematic search for books can be given a lower priority.

Identify, locate, and consult sources outside the library.

The possibility remains that library materials alone will not satisfy your need for information. You may have to seek further facts and insights from knowledgable individuals or organizations. Action groups and clearinghouses have sprung up on hundreds of women's issues, from sports to pornography, from Chicana rights to re-entry students. A librarian can help you select appropriate organizations to contact. Local agencies and campus women's centers can also put you in touch with resource people and groups. Some representative directories of women's organizations are listed in chapter 12, "Directories of Organizations and Services."

If you live near a feminist bookstore, or a general bookstore with a good women's studies section, scan the shelves for new books and pamphlets from alternative women's presses. Feminist publishers are in the vanguard of the women's movement and play a crucial role in bringing new issues to public attention.

Fill in the gaps.
Evaluate and synthesize the literature. Prepare to write.

The final steps of researching a "hot" topic are the standard closing stages of any library-based research project. Marshal all the references on your topic; read the materials and make notes; analyze, synthesize, and evaluate the content; compose a paper that reveals your thorough exploration of the topic and expresses your own conclusions.

3
The Catalog

　　Most libraries still have card catalogs, but your institution may be one of the pioneers that represents its holdings in an alternative form -- microfilm, microfiche, printed book, computer print-out, or online database. Innovations like these are achieved by using advanced technology to create and maintain library records. Some libraries have two separate catalogs: a card file for older materials; and an online database for more recent acquisitions. Even in traditional card catalogs, you may come across cards that were obviously computer-produced.
　　Regardless of their physical format, library catalogs almost always permit you to look up materials in three different ways -- by author, title, or subject. Some catalogs are "divided" (frequently with subject entries in one section and author and title entries in another), while others, called "dictionary catalogs," interfile all entries in a single alphabetic sequence.
　　A large library system with several branches may have several catalogs, each representing the works in a particular collection. One catalog, housed in the main library, may serve as a "union catalog," with a record for every item owned by any campus library.

<u>The catalog record</u>.

　　A sample record from a traditional card catalog (see next page) will illustrate the usual content and format of the information about an item in the library's collection:

1. <u>The call number</u>. This is the unique number assigned to this book that determines its place on the library's shelves. Be sure to copy it exactly!

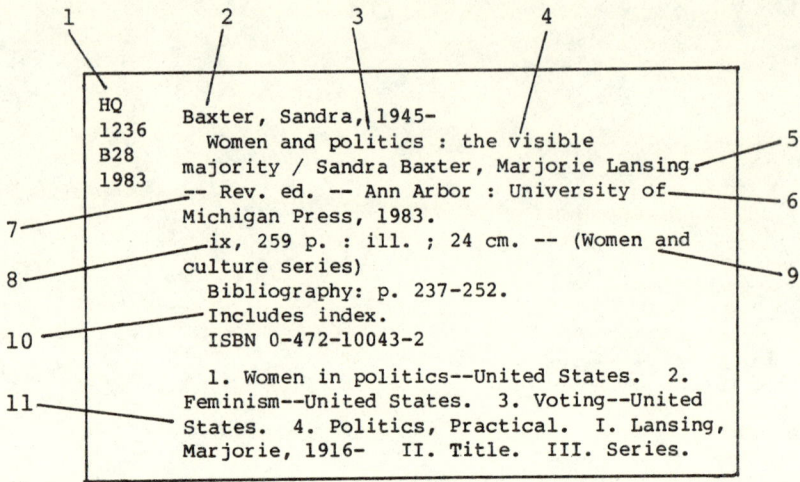

2. The first author or "main entry". If two or more writers share responsibility for the work, the one that appears first on the book's title page will serve as the "main entry." Additional cards will be filed under co-authors' names.

3. The title.

4. The subtitle.

5. The authors. The names of all the authors are listed as they appear in the book.

6. The place, publisher, and date. These facts are called the "imprint" and should be included in any full citation (e.g., a footnote).

7. Edition. Revisions of a work are considered different editions -- second edition, third edition, etc.

8. Description. This line of the catalog record always includes the number of pages (or number of volumes) and the height of the work. Other special physical features, such as illustrations or maps, may also be noted.

9. Series. Some works are part of a larger series. If so, this is noted on the record.

10. Notes. The area in the middle of the catalog record offers additional information of many sorts. Notes

about bibliographies and indexes are common. The International Standard Book Number (ISBN), a unique code number assigned to most books, may also be listed.

11. The "tracings". These are the additional entry points in the catalog for the work. Arabic numerals precede subject entries, while Roman numerals designate "added entries" -- the title, an alternate title, the name of the series, the co-author(s), the editor(s), the organization(s) or "corporate bodies" associated with the work, and so forth. Pay close attention to the tracings -- you can search the catalog under them to locate additional works on the same topics.

Any time you have difficulty interpreting a catalog record, call on a librarian for assistance.

The catalog: author and title.

Finding the catalog entry for a known item should rarely pose problems. Simply look under either the author's name or the title.

Bear in mind, however, that an author need not be an individual human being. The Association for Women in Psychology, for instance, might be deemed the author of its Newsletter. Even an event such as a symposium or conference can be viewed as an author or, to employ the correct jargon, a "main entry." Hence, the International Tribunal on Crimes Against Women, held in 1976, is the creator of its own published proceedings. This concept, called "corporate authorship," is awkward but not illogical. It's a practice worth remembering, because until recently many libraries chose not to clutter their catalogs with cards under such non-specific titles as Journal, Transactions, Report, and Proceedings. Thus older materials may be listed ONLY under the name of the organization that sponsored them. The rules governing corporate entries have varied over the years; when in doubt, try several approaches or ask the librarian to suggest possible forms of entry.

Even with a sophisticated appreciation of how catalogs are constructed, you may occasionally be stymied by an inaccurate citation. If the author's name is misspelled in your source of reference, or if you've transposed the words in the title, it's unlikely you'll unearth the record in the catalog. If you have any reason to doubt the veracity of your source, ask a librarian to help you check the information. Some brilliant professors are notorious for sending their students on wild goose chases through the library, and even the most renowned scholarly texts sometimes contain

garbled footnotes. In most such cases, it's possible to
correct the citation by consulting another bibliographic
source.
    Some of the newer online catalogs offer a powerful
method of retrieving citations called "keyword"
searching. A keyword is any significant word in a given
field in the catalog record -- most often, a word in the
title. Keyword searching is especially helpful when you
are unsure of a book's exact title. It can also
compensate for the vagaries of subject indexing, by
allowing you to search under popular terms and jargon.

The catalog: serials.

    Serials pose special challenges to researchers. The
concept of "serial" encompasses magazines, scholarly
journals, annual reviews, occasional papers with a
running title, published proceedings of yearly events,
newspapers, newsletters and so forth. Defined
succinctly, serials are publications that appear over
time under a single title, with no planned end. A multi-
volume encyclopedia, by way of comparison, is not
considered a serial, although the publisher may take
years to issue the complete set from A to Z.
    Some libraries have separate catalogs or listings for
serials, while others include records for serials in
their main catalog. In either case, individual articles
are almost never represented. You should therefore look
up the title or organizational source of the serial, not
the title or author of the article.

The catalog: subjects.

    Another way of using the catalog is by subject. If
you've nary a clue to the author, editor, or title of a
relevant book, you'll naturally look under the subject of
your paper as your first step. If you've already nosed
out a few promising sources, a subject search can round
out your research and alert you to publications you might
otherwise overlook.
    Subject searching can be a tricky process, especially
in women's studies. A book ought to be recorded in the
catalog under every subject it treats. Seldom, however,
are more than two or three subject heading assigned to a
single work; otherwise library catalogs would grow too
large to be easily consulted. A subject search will
therefore identify only those works which are devoted, in
their entirety or in large part, to the sought-after
subject. For example, studies of American women will be
found under WOMEN--UNITED STATES. By contrast, a book on
Japanese women containing a chapter comparing their
situation to that of their American counterparts will not
be listed that way in the catalog, since WOMEN--UNITED

STATES is not an apt description of the book's overall content.

Becoming skilled at subject searching is somewhat akin to learning a new language. There are rules of syntax and structure in subject headings, which librarians study formally. Like foreigners learning to communicate in a strange country, habitual users of the catalog unconsciously internalize its rules. Reference librarians can be called upon to translate natural language into library-ese for those less fluent. The principles, however, are quickly learned.

First, remember that catalogers use a controlled vocabulary to create subject headings. This means that once a term or phrase is chosen to denote a given topic, that same heading will be used for all books on that topic. For example, would you expect to find a general history of the movies under MOVIES, MOTION PICTURES, FILM, or CINEMA? The heading used by the Library of Congress, and hence by most academic libraries, is the old-fashioned phrase MOVING-PICTURES. Any books on this general subject will be recorded in the catalog under MOVING-PICTURES, regardless of the terms used in the book's title and text.

Specificity is another important factor to bear in mind. A treatise on Hollywood's image of women will not appear under MOVING-PICTURES, but under the more telling heading WOMEN IN MOVING-PICTURES. Likewise, a biography of Katharine Hepburn will be found under her name, since she is the central subject of the book, and not under a broader heading like ACTORS AND ACTRESSES. Defining the scope of your search before you approach the catalog will aid you in selecting the most promising headings. If nothing seems to be listed under the terms you've selected, try to imagine how broader, narrower, and related topics might be worded.

There are two styles of subject headings for works on narrow topics. Consider first the progression of the following subjects:

       WOMEN
       SINGLE WOMEN
       UNMARRIED MOTHERS

In this example each level of specificity is accorded its own straightforward terminology, as the focus narrows from all women, to single women, to single women with children.

The other way librarians analyze the subject of a book is by sub-dividing a broad heading. For example, you might find in the catalog the following sequence of entries:

       WOMEN
       WOMEN--EMPLOYMENT
       WOMEN--EMPLOYMENT--U.S.
       WOMEN--EMPLOYMENT--U.S.--BIBLIOGRAPHY

The first heading, WOMEN, is used for very general works
about the nature and condition of women. By adding the
topical sub-division, EMPLOYMENT, books treating a single
aspect of women's experience are singled out.
Elaborating the heading to read WOMEN--EMPLOYMENT--U.S.
identifies those books specifically on American working
women. The final sub-division, BIBLIOGRAPHY, denotes a
specialized type of publication. Divisions of headings
by place, type of publication, and chronological period
are quite common.
     Inverted headings are also used. In these cases an
adjective-noun phrase, such as JEWISH WOMEN, is turned
about to read WOMEN, JEWISH.
     From the researcher's perspective, the main advantage
of sub-divided and inverted headings is that all the
library's books on a general topic can be grouped
together in the catalog, while their individual themes
are still noted. The major drawback to this arrangement
is that the number of records filed under a subject as
broad as WOMEN may grow to fill several drawers (or many
computer screens), and the refinements of the divisions
and sub-divisions may not be readily apparent when you
first consult the catalog.
     A final caution regarding subject specificity is in
order. Women's studies as a field of inquiry has come of
age quickly, and the recent publishing boom has led to
the devising of more and more sophisticated headings to
maintain some degree of orderliness in library catalogs.
Writings on women that pre-date the "second wave" of
American feminism (that is, before the mid-1960s) were
often given the simple heading WOMAN. Helene Deutsch's
The Psychology of Women (1944), for instance, is entered
under WOMAN, while Phyllis Chesler's Women and Madness
(1972) is more appropriately listed under WOMEN--
PSYCHOLOGY. In larger libraries, subject cards are not
always updated. As a guiding principle, therefore, look
under broader subjects for older materials on women, and
under narrower topics for the most recent publications.
     The growing literature in women's studies has itself
forced changes in subject cataloging, as just noted.
Other reforms have been initiated by librarians sensitive
to sexism in the language of catalog headings. The term
WOMAN was replaced by WOMEN, for example, because the
singular denoted an abstraction or ideal, while the
plural suggests, somewhat more neutrally, a social group.
     WOMEN AS ENGINEERS and WOMEN AS BANKERS were typical
of older headings that implied it was unnatural for women
to fulfill such roles. Such headings have been replaced

by simpler headings without the demeaning "as" -- WOMEN
PHYSICIANS, for example. (At this writing, headings that
single out men are still extremely rare. Men are still
seen as the norm and women as the exception.) A few
other phrases have been replaced or modified -- PILGRIM
FATHERS giving way to PILGRIMS (NEW PLYMOUTH COLONY), for
example. Remember, not all libraries revise the headings
on older records, so you may have to look under the old
biased headings for pre-70s publications.

Don't let the complexities of subject searching
discourage you. Help is built in. Catalogs provide "see
also" references under valid headings, suggesting other
related terms. (E.g., WOMEN'S COLLEGES, see also
EDUCATION OF WOMEN.) Similarly, a "see" reference
directs you from an unused heading to the proper one.
(E.g., BATTERED WIVES, see ABUSED WIVES.)

Most college libraries follow guidelines developed at
the Library of Congress for assigning subject terms. The
Library of Congress Subject Headings, a list of
officially established subject entries, is often placed
in the reference area or near the catalog. At your
library, it may be available as two hefty volumes with
periodic supplements, or as a microfiche set that is
reissued on a regular basis and incorporates all changes
and new headings. Although designed as a tool for
librarians, the LCSH can be invaluable in pointing you to
the correct entry in the catalog for a given topic and
helping you become self-sufficient in the library.

A sample entry from LCSH is reproduced below:

>   Women artists (Indirect)
>   Here are entered works on the attainments
>   of women as artists. Works dealing with
>   women as represented in art are entered
>   under Women in art.
>   sa Women engravers
>   Women painters
>   Women sculptors
>   x Artists, Women
>   Women as artists
>   xx Artists

"Indirect" means that the heading may be modified by
place -- e.g., WOMEN ARTISTS--FRANCE. The "x" instructs
librarians to create a "see" reference from that term to
the accepted one -- in this example, from ARTISTS, WOMEN
to WOMEN ARTISTS. ARTISTS, WOMEN and WOMEN ARTISTS are
synonyms, but WOMEN ARTISTS is the heading used
consistently in the catalog.

The code "xx" instructs librarians to create a "see
also" reference from that term to the accepted one. In
this instance, ARTISTS is a broader term than WOMEN
ARTISTS, and you might find some relevant items under it

as well.

The code "sa" suggests that librarians make a "see also" reference from WOMEN ARTISTS to WOMEN ENGRAVERS and other similar narrower terms. All the headings are used, but they differ in their meaning and scope. As a researcher, you can use the "sa" references to refine your search to more specific headings.

Filing.

Until recently, nearly all card catalogs followed certain conventions for filing that go beyond pure alphabetization. Names beginning with "Mc" and "Mac" were often interfiled; numbers were filed as though spelled out; British and American spellings were interfiled (e.g., labor/labour, center/centre); and certain abbreviations such as "St." and "Dr." were treated as full words. Computers cannot handle such exceptions, so newer catalogs are generally more strict in their alphabetic filing, and entries beginning with numerals may be grouped in a separate sequence before the A's or after the Z's.

In the past, word-by-word filing was almost a universal practice, and this system is still widely followed. Each word in a phrase is treated separately. Word-by-word filing systems use a conventional sequence for sub-divided headings, a sequence that reflects hierarchies of punctuation as well as the alphabet. Thus WOMEN--SOCIAL CONDITIONS comes before WOMEN, JEWISH. An alternate approach is letter-by-letter filing. Letter-by-letter filing ignores punctuation and spaces between words. Below are examples of each filing system.

Word-by-Word	Letter-by-Letter
WOMEN	WOMEN
WOMEN--EMPLOYMENT	WOMEN AND RELIGION
WOMEN--PSYCHOLOGY	WOMEN--EMPLOYMENT
WOMEN--SUFFRAGE	WOMEN, JEWISH
WOMEN, JEWISH	WOMEN JOURNALISTS
WOMEN AND RELIGION	WOMEN--PSYCHOLOGY
WOMEN JOURNALISTS	WOMEN'S CENTERS
WOMEN SENATORS	WOMEN SENATORS
WOMEN'S CENTERS	WOMEN'S STUDIES
WOMEN'S STUDIES	WOMEN--SUFFRACE

Both systems are easy to master, but it's important to know which system is followed in the catalog you are using. Be careful when you switch between filing systems -- for instance, in consulting an index or bibliography that is organized in letter-by-letter fashion and then using a word-by-word catalog to track down the references.

With all the changes and quirks of filing, one truth remains: when a phrase begins with "a," "an," or "the" (or their equivalents in other tongues), that initial article is disregarded.

Call numbers

   A work's call number usually appears in the upper left-hand corner of the catalog record. By assigning call numbers to books, librarians can shelve them by subject to facilitate browsing. The cataloger assigns a call number according to the subject he or she judges to be most salient. Since a book can only occupy one spot in the stacks, the cataloger also creates subject entries for other matters which are treated in the work. For instance, Virginia Woolf's A Room of One's Own has the Library of Congress classification number PN471, placing it firmly in the area of literary history. Catalogers noted its implications beyond the field of literature by recording it under WOMEN--SOCIAL CONDITIONS and WOMEN--ENGLAND, as well as WOMEN AUTHORS, WOMEN IN LITERATURE, and ENGLISH FICTION--HISTORY AND CRITICISM. (This book has five subject entries, an unusually high number.)
   Most American libraries use either the Dewey decimal system or the Library of Congress system to create a unique call number for each book in their collections. Because women's studies cuts across disciplinary borders, neither system is ideally suited for cataloging women's studies materials. Both were invented several decades ago, when women's issues were considered marginal. Consequently, a sizeable body of published work on women has to be squeezed into a rather small corner of the grand plan -- in both systems, tucked awkwardly away with literature on social groupings and the family. Many basic works on women's issues and the feminist movement will be be found between HQ1101 and HQ2030 in libraries using the Library of Congress systemc. Libraries following the Dewey system will shelve these books under 301.4.
   Public libraries and smaller college libraries tend to use the Dewey decimal system, which is purely numerical. All of human knowledge is divided into ten categories, each of which is further divided into ten categories. The main topic of each book is thus represented by a number from 1 to 999. Further refinements are indicated by numbers following a decimal point. For example, the number 301.412 is assigned to Kate Millett's classic study, Sexual Politics. Here's how the call number was constructed from the overall outline:

```
300s      The social sciences
301       Sociology
301.4     Social structure
301.41    The sexes and their relations
301.412   Women
```

A second line, usually derived from the author's name, will be added to the call number to distinguish the book from others on the same subject. Thus the complete call number for <u>Sexual Politics</u> might be 301.412 / M54.

The broad outline of the Dewey system is presented in Appendix A. You needn't understand the finer points of the system to find books on the shelves. Just remember that the numbers preceding the decimal point are arranged numerically and those following the point are arranged decimally. For example:

```
031.1
031.2
301
301.02
301.1
302
```

The Library of Congress system is somewhat more complex and is most often encountered in larger college and research libraries. It is based on a combination of letters and numbers, with 21 major categories. Its basic outline is given in Appendix B. Again, various refinements are used to create a unique number for every book. Call numbers are usually two or three lines long but may be longer. The date of publication is often appended to the call number. A decimal point is printed or implied at the beginning of the second line, indicating that that line and all subsequent lines should be read decimally. For example:

```
HQ1206      HQ1206      HQ1206
.W8         .W854       .W86
```

The grouping of books by subject-specific call numbers makes browsing possible. While enjoyable and often surprisingly rewarding, browsing can never stand alone as a way of locating women's studies books, because the women's studies dimension of a publication may or may not have been considered central by its cataloger. Probably less than a quarter of the materials relevant to women's studies in a library using the Library of Congress system will be shelved in the HQ's.

To illustrate the capricious nature of call numbers, and thus the inadequacy of browsing as a research method, let's examine the treatment of two reference books. Both are dictionaries of quotations by women. <u>The Quotable</u>

Woman carries the Library of Congress call number
PN6081.5, which means that it is shelved next to other
standard quotation sources like Bartlett's Familiar
Quotations. A very similar book, Feminist Quotations,
was given the call number HQ1154, presumably because of
its pro-woman slant. Its neighbors on the shelf include
such resources as Who's Who and Where in Women's Studies
and The Guinness Guide to Feminine Achievements.

This pattern is repeated over and over again in
library collections -- some materials on women will be
found together, and others will be found scattered
throughout the stacks. Therefore, to be sure of locating
all relevant books on any aspect of women's studies, you
must use a subject approach to the catalog in addition to
scanning the library's shelves.

Finding the books.

Every library is laid out differently. It would be
folly to dwell here on the trials of actually finding
books in the stacks. However, there are a few basic
factors to bear in mind, especially if you are using an
unfamiliar library for the first time.

In some libraries, everything is arranged strictly by
call number. Other libraries segregate journals
(generally arranged alphabetically by title) and/or
fiction (commonly shelved by the author's name).
Government documents are sometimes integrated into the
general collection but just as often stored elsewhere
under their own publication numbers. Public libraries
often arrange biographies alphabetically by the names of
their subjects, and may have separate sections for
popular genres such as mysteries and science fiction.
Other kinds of materials -- audiovisual items, pamphlets,
and dissertations, for example -- may also be shelved and
recorded separately. A quick check at the information
desk will reveal how different kinds of materials are
treated in your library.

4
Beyond the Catalog

The catalog can help you locate books. However, information on women is also published in other formats: journal and newspaper articles, government publications, dissertations, conference papers, etc. Sometimes a journal article or two will serve your purposes much better than a book. For example, you may seek up-to-the-minute statistics or the latest opinions on a hotly debated issue; the data and the arguments presented in books will be inaccurate or stale. You may be interested in a fairly narrow topic which is not likely to be accorded full-length book treatment -- for instance, an explication of a single poem by Emily Dickinson. Finally, you may be facing a impending deadline, without the time or patience to wade through a voluminous study.

Since library catalogs list only the largest unit of a publication -- the book but not its chapters, the periodical but not its articles, the proceedings of a meeting but not its individual papers -- you must use one or more bibliographic sources to identify relevant references. Once you have a full citation, you can consult the catalog to locate the publication in which it appears.

What is a bibliographic source? Simply put, it is merely a list of further information sources. The abstract concept of "bibliography" encompasses all sorts of useful guides to published and unpublished works. But in common usage, the word "bibliography" has a narrower connotation, referring to a listing of materials (usually printed materials) with some unifying theme. A bibliography may focus on a particular topic; it may purport to be a complete record of books published in a certain country or during a certain time period; or it may be a definitive record of all editions of an author's works. For non-print forms of information, one finds filmographies, discographies, manuscript inventories, and the like. The principle is the same.

Bibliographic sources are as diverse as the fields

they cover. The majority of the works listed later in this guide are bibliographic sources of one sort or another. Many are published as books. Others are issued regularly as annual, semiannual, quarterly, or even weekly periodicals. What they have in common is their purpose: to point the researcher toward relevant readings.

Unless intended as historical surveys, bibliographies published as books quickly lose their currency. Although publishers occasionally issue new editions and supplements, they rarely promise regular revisions of bibliographies in book form. The same is true, unfortunately, of bibliographies published as articles in journals. On the other hand, some bibliographic sources, known as indexes and abstracts, are designed specifically to provide current information.

Bibliographic sources are not created equal. They vary from each other along several important dimensions. As you use bibliographic sources, be alert to their individual strengths and limitations. To evaluate how useful a source will be to you, ask the following questions:

How detailed is the information?

The amount of information provided in each entry is probably the most obvious measure of a bibliographic source. Indexes usually give only the bare bones of a citation -- that is, just the data necessary to find the publication in a library. The content of the work is neither described nor evaluated. Here is an entry from Readers' Guide to Periodical Literature, an index familiar to most students:

Women bosses. P. O'Toole. il Glamour 81:132+ Mr '83. (2)

The minimal bibliographic data is neatly condensed. The article (which was found under the subject entry WOMEN EXECUTIVES) is titled "Women Bosses." P. O'Toole is its author. The illustrated piece appears in volume 81 of Glamour, the March 1983 issue, starting on page 132.

Other bibliographic sources may be equally spare, or they may be enriched with annotations. An annotation is simply a brief statement about the cited work. Annotations may be either descriptive or critical and may vary greatly in length. Compare the annotated entries below for a single work, taken from three different bibliographies. The work being described is The Sociology of Housework, by Ann Oakley (New York: Pantheon, 1974).

Probes attitudes and working conditions of the
housewife. (3)

This is a sociological study of housework, an
occupation that has been neglected by scholars who
either study women in outside work or else in
relationship to other members of their families. But
here Oakley examines such areas as women's attitudes
about themselves as housewives and their attitudes
about the work itself. (4)

The Sociology of Housework contains a detailed
analysis of Oakley's study of women's attitudes to
housework, based on interviews conducted with London
housewives. She discusses, among other topics,
Images of Housework, Social Class and Domesticity,
Work Conditions, Socialization and Self-Concept, and
Marriage and the Division of Labour. Case-studies of
four housewives, taken from this same study, are
presented in Woman's Work, which also gives
historical and anthropological background on the role
of housewife. (5)

    The first annotation is merely a succinct statement
of the subject of the book. The second annotation
asserts that the study is important because the topic has
been hitherto neglected by scholars. The final
annotation provides more specific details about the
book's contents, refers to the author's methodology
(interviews) and location (London), and cites another
work by the same author. Obviously, there are many ways
to describe the same book, and annotations inevitably
reflect the interests and outlooks of those who compose
them.
    An abstract is more detailed than an annotation and
thus typically more useful. In one or two paragraphs, an
abstract summarizes or condenses the work. A well
written abstract gives the reader an accurate outline of
the work's main thesis and a sense of its perspective --
in other words, enough information to decide whether to
read the original document. The abstract below is taken
from Women Studies Abstracts.

Yogev, Sara. "Judging the professional woman:
changing research, changing values." Psychology of
Women Quarterly 7:219-34 Sp '83.
    A framework is offered for understanding
contradictory findings in the field of the
personality of working and professional women.
Modern theory and research display two patterns: the
early pattern of the 1960s, which viewed professional
women as violating sex stereotypes, lacking
femininity, and having personality disturbances; and

the contemporary view, which emerged during the 1970s
and suggests the possibility of combining career with
family without psychological conflicts and
personality disturbances. A critical appraisal of
the literature in four areas (psychological role
conflict, fear of success, comparison between
housewives and career women, and comparisons between
women in traditional and pioneer occupations)
concludes that little evidence supports the view that
professional women have personality disturbances
because of their career. Possible explanations for
shifting viewpoints and contradictory findings are
presented. Issues and problems professional women
currently face are analyzed and the accessibility of
those issues to empirical study is assessed. (6)

Unfortunately, some sources are only partially
annotated or partially abstracted. Compilers feel
uncomfortable elaborating on items they haven't examined,
yet do not want to omit all such materials from their
lists. Women Studies Abstracts is an example of a partly
abstracted source.

How comprehensive is the coverage?

The scope of coverage is important, but not always
easy to ascertain. Some sources identify a fixed group
of periodicals and cite every article in them. Readers'
Guide to Periodical Literature, Social Sciences Index,
and Humanities Index are representative of this type.
Other sources index journal literature selectively, based
on the subject content of the articles rather than the
journals in which they appear. The PAIS Bulletin is an
example of this approach, as is Women Studies Abstracts.

What types of publications are included?

Some bibliographic sources are devoted exclusively to
certain forms of publications -- The Monthly Catalog of
Government Publications, or Dissertation Abstracts
International, for instance. Other sources are primarily
concerned with subject content, not format, and may
include books, articles, conference papers, research
reports, and even unpublished materials.

In what language(s) are cited works written?

The subjects covered, the background of the
compilers, and the place of publication will all govern
whether a bibliography or index includes works in
languages other than English. Your own abilities and
your research topic will determine whether you want to
find out about foreign-language materials.

What is the time frame?

Every bibliography has a cut-off date. If the date is not explicitly stated in the title or sub-title, it is likely to be noted in the introduction. Some sources also have a start-up date. Women's Periodicals and Newspapers from the 18th Century to 1981, for example, lists publications within a definite time span.

If no clues are given, you can at least infer the currency of coverage from the copyright date. Your need for up-to-date references will depend on the topics you choose to investigate. An exhaustive bibliography on the Equal Rights Amendment was already out-dated when it was published in 1976, for instance, but historians and others interested in the struggle for ratification still find it useful. Indexes and abstracts, by contrast, are examples of bibliographic tools that satisfy the researcher's need for "current awareness" by providing regular access to new publications. Even more recent references can be gleaned from sources that reproduce tables of contents of journals; Management Contents and Feminist Periodicals: A Current Listing of Contents are two examples.

How is the information organized?

Bibliographic sources also differ in their arrangement of references. Some list authors, titles, and subjects in one straightforward alphabetic sequence -- much like a traditional card catalog. Many others use a classified arrangement, which can be likened to the ordering of books by call number. Classified arrangments will vary from discipline to discipline, reflecting the particular perspective and interests of each field. Classified bibliographies can vary in their complexity, from easy-to-use subject categorizations, to intricate outlines of knowledge with multiple sub-divisions. Such sources are frequently enriched by author, title, and subject indexes -- real boons to non-specialists.

How are the entries indexed?

The linguistic factor is of utmost importance, especially in sources organized by subject. Bibliographic sources employ diverse vocabularies, reflecting the different jargons of the academic disciplines. Therefore, it helps to think like a psychologist when using Psychological Abstracts or like a literary critic when consulting the Modern Language Association International Bibliography.

Many sources use a controlled vocabulary -- that is, an established list of subject terms. Occasionally a thesaurus of these terms is separately published. Just as the <u>Library of Congress Subject Headings</u> assists you in searching for subjects in the library's catalog, a thesaurus tells you terms and phrases employed in an index and suggests related terms.

Some sources, especially those produced with the aid of computers, use keywords as subjects. Keywords are words chosen from the title of the work being cited. Keywords work very well as index terms in the hard sciences and fairly well in the social sciences, but are less satisfactory in the humanities, where authors may give their scholarly works titles that are provocative or poetic rather than descriptive.

On the surface, this diversity seems merely to confuse matters and to thwart any attempt at systematic research. How are you to cope with a pool of bibliographic sources that vary so wildly in their content and construction? Comfort yourself with the reminder that any well-wrought bibliographic source is organized in the manner that best suits the materials and the topics it covers. Almost all bibliographies, indexes, and abstracts carry explanatory introductions. If you have trouble understanding how a particular tool is organized or deciding if it really covers your topic adequately, ask a librarian for guidance.

The advent of computers in libraries has added a new twist to the process of bibliographic research. Most academic libraries now offer online retrieval services. Many of the indexes and abstracts available for computer searching are the same ones owned by the library in their printed format. The computer system offers the advantage of combining topics and terms to retrieve citations on very specific subjects in a matter of seconds. Online bibliographic databases are discussed in greater detail in chapter 14.

5
Interlibrary Loan

Your library may not own the publication you need. Women's studies is evolving just as colleges and universities almost everywhere are facing budget crises and as book prices are spiraling upward. Interlibrary loan services are one way libraries have tried to cope with this dilemma.

If you cannot obtain a copy of a work locally, there is a good chance that your library can borrow it from another library. You will be asked to fill out a request form, giving as full a citation as possible, as well as the source of your reference. If the form requires further verification, a librarian will show you how to proceed.

Turn-around time for an interlibrary loan is unpredictable, so don't wait until the last minute to submit your request. Be sure to check with the librarian about restrictions on use -- whether you may remove the book from the library building, if photocopying is allowed, how long a loan period the lending library has specified, and so on.

If you request a journal article, you will probably receive a photocopy of the article rather than the entire volume on loan. Depending on cooperative agreements between your library and others, there may or may not be a charge for the photocopy.

Be sure to ask about charges. Some of the nation's largest libraries are constantly called upon to lend materials to smaller institutions. Many of these larger libraries now charge a fee for loans as well as photocopies to cover staff expenses. Find out in advance if such fees will be passed along to you, or if your library absorbs the cost.

Notes on Part I

(1) I am indebted to Sarah Barbara Watstein and Stan Nash for outlining an alternative search strategy model in their excellent article, "Researching 'Hot' Topics in the Social Sciences," Research Strategies 1 (Spring 1983), p.77-8.

(2) Readers' Guide to Periodical Literature 83 (May 1983), p.532.

(3) Virginia R. Terris, Woman in America: A Guide to Information Sources (Detroit: Gale, 1980), p.124.

(4) Barbara Haber, Women in America: A Guide to Books, 1963-1975 (Boston: G.K. Hall, 1978), p.187.

(5) Esther Stineman, Women's Studies: A Recommended Core Bibliography (Littleton, CO: Libraries Unlimited, 1979), p.545.

(6) Women Studies Abstracts 12, no.2 (Summer 1983), p.18.

Part II

The Tools of Research

6
Guides to Women's Studies Research and Bibliographies of Reference Sources

The sources listed in this chapter serve as general guides to the tools and methods of library research in women's studies. In a sense their purpose is similar to the book you now hold in your hands, although none is so current.

The works by Ballou, Ritchie, and Williamson are pure "bibliographies of bibliographies." When you seek to locate a reading list on a special topic within women's studies, turn to them. They list and describe many bibliographies published as journal articles and mimeographed pamphlets, as well as book-length bibliographies. A ready-made bibliography can be a crucial timesaver, so consult these volumes early in your research.

The other sources listed below cover reference publications of many types. Because each compiler works from her own notion of what a researcher needs to know, you can use such guides to complement this one.

The established disciplines and many of their subfields also have research guides. Many of these are cited in subsequent chapters that focus on special topics. Few discipline-based guides share the perspective of women's studies scholars -- indeed, most of them pay it no heed whatsoever -- but they may still prove useful, especially to someone exploring a topic outside her specialization or major. Research guides usually give practical advice on search strategy, an outline of the organization of the discipline's literature, and a taste of the flavor of writing in the field.

In addition, libraries often make available free booklets describing reference sources in various fields in their collections. Take advantage of any such handouts produced by your library's staff.

Ballou, Patricia K. Women: A Bibliography of
Bibliographies. Boston: G.K. Hall, 1980.   Z7961.A1.
HQ1121.   016.0163054.

This helpful annotated guide lists bibliographies,
bibliographic essays, literature surveys, library
catalogs, and guides to archives and manuscript
repositories -- all useful for tracking down
materials on women. Bibliographies issued as books,
parts of books, pamphlets, journal articles, and
microforms are included. All of the works cited were
published between 1970 and 1979. Entries are divided
into three major groups: publications of one type or
format; geographical subjects; and topical subjects
(the largest group). Further sub-divisions make it
possible to locate bibliographies with limited scope
by first consulting the table of contents.

Lynn, Naomi B., Ann B. Matasar, and Marie Barovic
Rosenberg. Research Guide in Women's Studies.
Morristown, NJ: General Learning Press, 1974.   HQ1206.
301.41.

Despite its title, this book is really a general
introduction to researching and writing papers in the
social sciences. As such, it offers practical
suggestions for selecting a topic and constructing
footnotes, in addition to highlighting reference
sources. Unfortunately, the bibliographic sections
do not cover the wealth of women's studies reference
materials published in recent years. Perhaps the
most valuable feature of this work is its attention
to sources of information outside the library,
including surveys, interviews, government agencies,
and women's organizations.

Ritchie, Maureen. Women's Studies: A Checklist of
Bibliographies. London: Mansell, 1980.   Z7961.A1.
HQ1121.   016.0163054.

An unannotated bibliography of nearly 500
bibliographies "directly relevant to women's studies
that have been published as books, articles,
pamphlets, reports, library lists, or as only a few
stencilled pages." Citations are arranged by
subject.

Schlachter, Gail A. Minorities and Women: A Guide to
Reference Literature in the Social Sciences. Los

Angeles: Reference Service Press, 1977. Z7964.U49.
HQ1410. 016.30145.

This ambitious guide lists reference books on the
"social, educational, psychological, political,
economic, anthropological and historical aspects of
minorities and women in America." American Indians,
Asian Americans, Black Americans, Spanish Americans,
and women are treated in separate sections. Entries
are organized by type of publication: encyclopedias,
handbooks, yearbooks, etc.; statistical compilations;
documents and primary source materials; biographical
sources; directories; and citation sources. Coverage
extends to mid-1976. The long descriptive
annotations are particularly helpful.

Williamson, Jane. <u>New Feminist Scholarship: A Guide to
Bibliographies</u>. Old Westbury, NY: The Feminist Press,
1979. Z7161.A1. HQ1180. 016.30141.

This easy-to-use source lists nearly 400
bibliographies under thirty subject headings.
Approximately half of the entries are annotated; the
annotations are critical and well written. Both
separately published works and bibliographies
appearing as journal articles are included. Author
and title indexes are supplied, along with a
directory of publishers.

7
General Women's Studies Bibliographies

This chapter covers bibliographies that focus solely on women, but from a general or interdisciplinary perspective. These sources can be helpful at all stages of your research, but you will probably find them most valuable when you are first thinking about possible topics for a paper. Using these general guides, you can quickly get a feel for what's available on the subjects that interest you.

Continuing indexes to periodicals in women's studies have been included in chapter 8.2, "Multidisciplinary Bibliographies and Indexes: Periodicals."

Bibliographic Guide to Studies on the Status of Women: Development and Population Trends. New York: UNIPUB, 1983. Z7961. 016.305.

> This volume, sponsored by Unesco, offers separate annotated reading lists on: Africa; the Arab region; Asia; Eastern Europe; Latin America; and the United Kingdom, the United States, and Western Europe. The nearly six hundred entries focus on labor force participation by women, women's role in economic development, education, family and home life, and demographic features. A 39-page introduction surveys the literature and briefly compares leading theories about women's status. Country, subject, and author indexes are provided.

Evans, Mary, and David Morgan. Work on Women: A Guide to the Literature. New York: Methuen, 1980. Z7961. HQ1206. 016.3054.

> This selective bibliography is divided into nine subject-specific chapters, with an additional chapter devoted to bibliographies, journals, and other special forms of publication. Not annotated; groups

of citations are introduced by short texts. This is
a handy guide to the literature of women's studies,
but nowhere near as comprehensive as Esther
Stineman's work (see below).

Haber, Barbara. *Women in America: A Guide to Books, 1963-1975*. Boston: G.K. Hall, 1978.   Z7964.U49.
HQ1410.   016.30141.

This is an exemplary source, compiled by the Curator
of Printed Books at the Schlesinger Library at
Radcliffe, one of the world's largest archives of
women's materials. Only books published between 1963
and 1975 are listed; Haber has carefully selected the
very best. All entries are annotated, and some
representative titles are accorded in-depth reviews.
Arrangement is by subject, covering general areas
such as "The Fine Arts and Popular Culture" and
"Psychology" as well as specific issues such as
"Abortion." A newer paperback edition (Urbana:
University of Illinois Press, 1981) includes an
appendix of bibliographic essays on books published
between 1976 and 1979.

Krichmar, Albert. *The Women's Movement in the Seventies: An International English-Language Bibliography*.
Metuchen, NJ: Scarecrow, 1977.   Z7961.   HQ1154.
016.30141.

As its title indicates, this mammoth bibliography
lists works about the women's movement throughout the
world published in the 1970s. Dissertations, books,
pamphlets, research reports, periodical articles, and
government documents are included. The 8,637
citations are arranged geographically and accompanied
by one-line annotations. There are author and
subject indexes. The excellent coverage of North
America complements the compiler's bibliography on
the women's movement in America prior to 1970, *The
Women's Rights Movement in the United States, 1848-
1970: A Bibliography and Sourcebook* (Metuchen, NJ:
Scarecrow, 1972).

Nordquist, Joan.   *Audiovisuals for Women*.. Jefferson, NC:
McFarland, 1980.   Z7961.   HQ1206.   016.3054.

This source lists 876 16mm films, videotapes,
filmstrips, slides, and recordings of music and the
spoken word, which are by, for, or about women. All
the materials covered are in English and were

produced in the U.S. or Canada. The compiler
excludes materials designed primarily for use in
elementary school classrooms. The arrangement is by
physical medium, with a subject index. Every entry
includes the title, producer and/or distributor,
release date, a technical description, and a brief
annotation citing reviews.

Oakes, Elizabeth H., and Kathleen E. Sheldon. Guide to
Social Science Resources in Women's Studies. Santa
Barbara: ABC-Clio, 1978.   Z7961.   HQ1180.   016.30141.

A selective bibliography aimed at "professors of
introductory interdisciplinary women's studies
courses and those who wish to include material on
women in other courses and in their research." The
fields of anthropology, economics, history,
psychology, and sociology are covered, with an added
chapter on contemporary feminist thought. Book-
length studies and collections of articles are
emphasized. Annotations are long and skillfully
written, describing the contents and thesis of each
work and evaluating its usefulness as an
undergraduate text. Although addressed to teachers,
this bibliography can also serve students as a guide
to reading.

Resources for Feminist Research / Documentation sur la
Recherche Feministe. Toronto: Ontario Institute for
Studies in Education, 1979 to present.   HQ1101.
305.41.

This quarterly publication continues the Canadian
Newsletter of Research on Women (1972-1978) and
emphasizes abstracts of recent publications and
reports of research-in-progress outside the United
States. Also included are book reviews, news of
organizations and projects, reports from conferences,
etc. Often issues are devoted to a single theme. In
recent issues, information is partially organized by
discipline: social sciences and history; humanities,
literature, and the arts; education and women's
studies; social policy and social action; health and
the sciences. This is an up-to-date source on the
development of women's studies in other countries,
especially Canada.

Rosenberg-Dishman, Marie B., and Len V. Bergstrom. Women
and Society: A Critical Review of the Literature with a
Selected Annotated Bibliography. Beverly Hills: Sage

Publications, 1975.   Z7961.   HQ1399.   016.30141.

Een, JoAnn Delores, and Marie B. Rosenberg-Dishman.
Women and Society, Citations 3601 to 6000: An Annotated
Bibliography. Beverly Hills: Sage Publications, 1978.
Z7961.   HQ1399.   016.30141.

These two hefty sources list "works that contribute
to a general understanding of the economic,
political, legal, military, social, moral, religious,
educational, scientific, medical, philosophical,
literary, and artistic aspects of women's roles in
society." Altogether, 6,000 books, pamphlets, and
articles are cited and arranged in detailed subject
categories. There are several indexes. A number of
inaccurate references have been found in these
volumes, but their sheer scope assures their
usefulness nonetheless.

Stineman, Esther.   Women's Studies: A Recommended Core
Bibliography. Littleton, CO: Libraries Unlimited, 1979.
Z7961.   HQ1180.   016.30141.

This bibliography, organized around traditional
disciplines, lists 1,763 books judged to be essential
in libraries supporting undergraduate women's studies
programs. The annotations are evaluative and lively,
often referring the reader to other books on the same
theme. Author, title, and subject indexes are
provided. Because this a selection of basic,
recommended readings, including fiction and
biography, it is an excellent starting point for
research or background reading on almost any topic in
women's studies. A supplement covering 1980 to 1985
is being prepared.

Terris, Virginia R.   Women in America: A Guide to
Information Sources.   Detroit: Gale, 1980.   Z7964.U49.
HQ1426.   016.30141.

This research guide and bibliography covers every
facet of the American woman's experience. Citations
to books, pamphlets, articles, government documents,
and non-print resources are briefly annotated and
arranged in a detailed subject classification.
Unpublished papers and reports are also listed,
usually with a note on availability. Many
publications which do not focus specifically on women
have been deemed relevant by the compiler and
therefore included. Author, title, and subject
indexes are provided. Appendices supply addresses

for research centers, libraries, newsletters, periodicals, and various organizations and societies.

United Nations. Dag Hammerskjold Library. <u>Status of Women: A Select Bibliography</u>. New York: United Nations, 1975.   Z7961.   UN doc. no. ST/LIB/SER. B/20.

This multi-lingual bibliography was prepared for the International Women's Year conference. It covers the political, economic, educational, and social status of women throughout the world. Citations to books, periodical articles, and U.N. documents published between 1965 and 1975 are arranged in subject categories, sub-divided by continent and country.

Wheeler, Helen R. <u>Womanhood Media: Current Resources About Women</u>. Metuchen, NJ: Scarecrow, 1972. <u>Supplement</u>, 1975.   Z7961.   HQ1121.   016.30141.

A general resource guide. Part I is a women's liberation awareness test, now somewhat dated. Part II describes standard reference tools. Part III is a basic bibliography of over 300 books on women's studies, arranged by subject. Part IV lists and annotates non-book materials, including printed matter such as pamphlets and movement periodicals as well as audiovisual resources. Part V is a directory of organizations, publishers, women's groups, etc., far too old to be useful. The supplement updates sections III, IV, and V.

8
Multidisciplinary Bibliographies and Indexes

8.1 BOOKS

This chapter covers two different types of reference materials -- indexes to individual contributions to collected works of nonfiction, and comprehensive records of books that have been published.

Library users often become exasperated when attempting to identify papers that were reprinted or originally published in anthologies. The contents of anthologies are rarely listed separately in the library catalog. Thus, the following two works are indispensible:

Cardinale, Susan. Anthologies By and About Women: An Analytical Index. Westport, CT: Greenwood, 1982. HQ1111. 016.3054.

This interdisciplinary index covers 375 anthologies, most of them published in the 1960s and 1970s. Special issues of journals are excluded. A subject/genre index groups anthologies by broad topic, and a listing by title provides a full table of contents for each volume. The keyword index serves as subject index, using words from the titles of the essays, short stories, plays, and documents contained in the anthologies. Contributor and editor indexes round out the volume.

Essay and General Literature Index. New York: H. W. Wilson, 1900/33 to present. AI3. 016.

This source indexes, by their authors and subjects, essays and articles in collections. The following disciplines are covered: philosophy; religion; social science; political science; economics; law; education; linguistics; sciences; the various arts;

literature; and history. In 1982, this index offered
subject access to 4,101 works included in 315 books.
Issued twice a year, with annual and quinquennial
cumulations. WOMEN is a subject heading, with
various sub-divisions, and there are usually a large
number of essays listed under WOMEN IN LITERATURE.
See also such headings as FEMINISM and SEX ROLES.

The remainder of this chapter is devoted to
publications that can be used to identify books published
in the United States or owned by American libraries.
Because they provide only minimal information (i.e., they
are not annotated) and because they are not selective,
they should not be utilized as a first step in finding
books on a particular topic. Instead, consult a general
bibliography in women's studies or a bibliography in a
relevant discipline.
One special function of the sources listed below is
to verify the existence and facts of publication (author,
title, date and so on) of books that your library does
not own. With a citation from one of these standard
sources, you can request that the item be purchased or
obtained for you on an interlibrary loan.
Librarians often refer to the type of continuing
bibliographies described here as "national and trade
bibliographies." Similar sources exist for most of the
countries or regions of the world. A librarian can point
them out to you and explain their use.

Books in Print. New York: Bowker, 1948 to present.
Z1215.   015.73.

Subject Guide to Books in Print. New York: Bowker, 1957
to present.   Z1215.   015.73.

Books in Print Supplement. New York: Bowker, 1973 to
present.   Z1215.   015.73.

These annual publications are the standard guides to
books currently available from American publishers.
The main set consists of separate volumes for authors
and titles. At the end of the title listing is a
handy list of publishers, with addresses and
telephone numbers. The supplementary Subject Guide
can be helpful in identifying recent works on women's
studies topics. The subject headings used are
usually similar to those employed in the library
catalog. Each entry provides all the information
needed to order the book from a bookseller: author,
title, publisher, price and International Standard
Book Number. Books in Print Supplement is issued

mid-year as an update to the other volumes. Books
announced for publication but not yet on the market
are listed in the bimonthly Forthcoming Books and
Subject Guide to Forthcoming Books, also compiled by
Bowker.

Cumulative Book Index. New York: H. W. Wilson, 1898 to
present.   Z1219.

This publication lists books published in the U.S.
and other countries in one alphabetical sequence of
authors, titles, and subjects. Its aim is to provide
a record of all books published in English. CBI is
issued monthly, with quarterly and annual
cumulations. Because its subject headings are
largely identical to those found in the library
catalog, it is easy to consult.

Paperbound Books in Print. New York: Bowker, 1955 to
present.   Z1033.P3.   017.4.

A semi-annual companion to Books in Print (see
above), providing author, title, and subject access
to books currently available in paperback. Many
paperbound books are also listed in the parent set.
The subject terminology is less specific than in
Books in Print, however. Many works on women are
categorized under GOVERNMENT AND POLITICAL
SCIENCE--MINORITY GROUP STUDIES.

National Union Catalog. Washington: Library of Congress,
1956 to present.   Z881.A1.   018.

The National Union Catalog is an ongoing cooperative
project of the Library of Congress and major
libraries in North America. Each entry duplicates a
library catalog record, with full bibliographic
information, subject tracings, etc. There are coded
indications (in the main listing or in a
supplementary set, the Register of Additional
Locations) of the libraries holding the works. The
NUC is issued monthly, with quarterly, annual, and
five-year cumulations. It is published in microfiche
and paper format both. One set of over 700 volumes
provides a retrospective record for books printed
before 1956. Items are listed under author or main
entry only.

U.S. Library of Congress. <u>Subject Catalog</u>. Washington:
Library of Congress, 1970 to present.   Z881.A1.   017.

   Issed quarterly, with annual and five-year
cumulations, this set replicates the subject catalog
of the nation's largest library. It can be used as a
general topical bibliography, with the advantage of
having the same terminology as your library's
catalog.

8.2 PERIODICAL ARTICLES

Periodical literature is the cutting edge of scholarship. When you want the very latest facts or theories, or when you're investigating a topic too new or too narrow for book-length treatment, an article will probably answer your needs.
This chapter presents four sources of references to articles in women's studies, plus several interdisciplinary indexes that include women's topics. More specialized indexes are presented in the discipline-based sub-chapters of chapter 9. Guides that list current and historical magazines, but do not index articles, are described in chapter 15, "Periodicals."
Be wary of subject terminology when you use any of the sources cited below. Be doubly alert during retrospective searching in older editons, because the vocabulary used to describe women and women's issues is constantly changing.
Many indexes abbreviate the titles of periodicals. Abbreviations are nearly always decoded in the front of the index. If you forget to decipher an abbreviation on the spot and are later puzzled by your notes, Leland G. Alkire's Periodical Title Abbreviations, 4th ed. (Detroit: Gale, 1983) can be a blessing.

SOURCES ON WOMEN

Feminist Periodicals: A Current Listing of Contents. Madison, WI: Office of the Women's Studies Librarian-at-Large, University of Wisconsin System, 1981 to present. 305.4016.

>This quarterly publication reproduces the tables of contents of some seventy women's studies and women's movement periodicals. Although not a subject index, it is useful for surveying recent writing. Many of

the specialized titles covered in **Feminist Periodicals** are published by women's collectives and small presses and are not represented in any other reference sources.

Studies on Women Abstracts. Oxfordshire, England: Carfax, 1983 to present.   HQ1180.   305.4.

This new quarterly service covers both books and journal articles, offering long, non-evaluative abstracts. Each issue has some 250 entries. Unfortunately, the references are grouped in two sections in a most unhelpful manner. References to journal articles are arranged alphabetically by journal title; references to books (including chapters in books) are arranged alphabetically by author. Each issue has an author index and a keyword subject index.

Women: A Bibliography of Special Periodical Issues. Toronto: Ontario Institute for Studies in Education, 1976-78.   2 vols.   Z7962.   HQ1154.   016.3054.

This two-part bibliography singles out some 475 special issues of academic journals "not normally devoted to the study of women" and reprints their tables of contents. Coverage begins with 1960. Entries are grouped by topic, with large sections for arts and literature, education, interdisciplinary social science, and sociology. This source serves as a supplement to the standard periodical indexes. **Women Studies Abstracts** (see below) also lists the contents of thematic issues of journals.

Women Studies Abstracts. Rush, NY: Rush Publishing, 1972 to present.   Z7962.   016.30141.

Until 1983 this was the only journal index devoted solely to women's studies. Articles from both scholarly and popular periodicals are listed, plus selected books, documents, leaflets, and unpublished materials. At present, each quarterly issue offers about 1,000 references. The title is misleading, since most entries are not abstracted. The arrangement is by subject: special issues and publications; education and socialization; sex roles, sex characteristics, differences and similarities; employment; sexuality; family; society and government; finances; religion; mental and physical health; pregnancy, family planning, childbirth and abortion; history; literature and art; media and media reviews; interpersonal relations; women's liberation movement; biography and criticism; and book reviews. There is a detailed subject index in each issue, but unfortunately the indexing is erratic and terminology varies, especially in the early years. Books reviews and bibliographic essays on topics of current interest are occasionally featured, and the tables of contents of special thematic issues of journals are regularly reprinted. Women Studies Abstracts has covered the full range of women's studies topics for over a decade and should be consulted for virtually all research projects.

GENERAL SOURCES

Access. Evanston, IL: John Gordon Burke, 1975 to present. AI3. 016.051.

Published three times a year, this index covers approximately 150 periodicals not covered by Readers' Guide (see below). A number of regional and city magazines are indexed, along with such widely read publications as The Harvard Business Review and TV Guide. Some magazines oriented to women are included (Cosmopolitan, Family Circle, Woman's Day) as are some aimed at men (Playboy, Penthouse). Each issue has separate author and subject sections. A yearly cumulation is published in bound form.

Alternative Press Index. Baltimore: Alternative Press Center, 1969 to present. AI3. 051.016.

This quarterly index to "alternative and radical publications" covers a number of radical feminist periodicals, as well as a wide variety of newspapers and magazines devoted to left-wing politics, the environment, gay rights, etc. A good source for politically-oriented articles on such issues as lesbian culture, women in the peace movement, and racism and class struggle in feminist organizations.

Current Contents: Social and Behavioral Sciences. Philadelphia: Institute for Scientific Information, 1969 to present. Z7163. 016.3.

This weekly alerting service reproduces the tables of contents of more than 1,000 journals in the social sciences. Articles are indexed by their authors and keywords in their titles.

Magazine Index. Los Altos, CA: Information Access Corporation, 1976 to present.

This computer-produced microfilm index is less selective than Readers' Guide (see below). It lists articles, editorials, literary pieces, biographies, and reviews from close to 400 popular American periodicals, employing standard Library of Congress subject headings enriched with current names and terms. Under each subject, the most recent articles are cited first. The index is updated monthly and always provides coverage for the last five years on a single cumulated reel.

Poole's Index to Periodical Literature, 1802-1881. Boston: Houghton, 1891. 1st-5th Supplements, 1882-1907. AI3.

Nineteenth Century Readers' Guide to Periodical Literature, 1890-1899, With Supplementary Indexing, 1900-1922. New York: H. W. Wilson, 1944. AI3. 050.

These two indexes provide access to the English-language periodical press of the nineteenth century. Both popular magazines and academic publications are included; medical, legal, and scientific journals are excluded. A Victorian set of mind is an asset in approaching either source. The indexing in Poole's is largely by subject or keyword-in-title. You should, therefore, try both WOMAN and WOMEN. The Nineteenth Century Readers' Guide combines entries for authors, subjects, and illustrators in one alphabetic list. A controlled subject vocabulary makes it somewhat less cumbersome than Poole's. Note that despite the title, only the final decade of the nineteenth century is covered.

Popular Periodical Index. Collingswood, NJ: Popular Periodical Index, 1973 to present. AI3. 016.05.

A semiannual index to forty magazines, including such popular titles as Rolling Stone. Articles are cited in one alphabetic list of authors and subjects.

Public Affairs Information Service. Bulletin. New York:
Public Affairs Information Service, 1915 to present.
Z7163. 016.3.

Usually referred to simply as PAIS, this is a
semimonthly subject and author index to magazine
articles, reports, government documents, and books on
current public affairs and public policy. Use it to
research the progress of women during the twentieth
century. Subject terms are the same as or similar to
those in the library catalog; there are copious
cross-references. Since 1968, a Foreign Language
Index has also been issued, covering materials in
French, German, Italian, Portuguese, and Spanish.
Retrospective searching is made easier by the
Cumulative Subject Index to the Public Affairs
Information Service Bulletin, 1915-1974 (Arlington,
VA: Carrollton Press, 1977-78).

The compilers of PAIS make a special effort to
list separately published bibliographies and to note
bibliographies that are parts of larger works.
Hence, you should check PAIS early in your search.

Readers' Guide to Periodical Literature. New York: H. W.
Wilson, 1900 to present. AI1. 051.

This old standby should not be overlooked for women's
studies research. Although only the most widely read
general and special-interest magazines are indexed
(Time, Newsweek, Ebony, Scientific American,
Harper's, Ms., Ladies' Home Journal, and about 170
others), Readers' Guide is often the best
bibliographic resource for topics of current
interest. And because it has been published
continuously since the turn of the century, its older
volumes have historical value. For example, Readers'
Guide can lead you to articles reflecting the
opinions of the day on women working between the two
World Wars, or to essays extolling motherhood during
the 1950s.

Among the subject headings currently used are
WOMEN (with numerous sub-headings) and phrases on the
order of WOMEN ATHLETES, WOMEN ENTREPENEURS, and
BLACK WOMEN. The heading WOMEN AND MEN covers both
serious discussions of relations between the sexes
and advice articles on pleasing a boyfriend,
surviving a romantic break-up, and so on.

Readers' Guide is issued twice a month, with
quarterly cumulative issues and annual bound volumes.

Readers' Guide to Periodical Literature. Supplement.
New York: H. W. Wilson, 1907-1919.   AI1.   016.305.

International Index to Periodicals. New York: H. W.
Wilson, 1920-1955.   AI1.

International Index. New York: H. W. Wilson, 1955-1965.
AI1.

Social Sciences and Humanities Index. New York: H. W.
Wilson, 1965-1974.   AI1.

Humanities Index. New York: H. W. Wilson, 1974 to
present.   AI1.   016.0013.

Social Sciences Index. New York: H. W. Wilson, 1974 to
present.   AI1.   016.3.

One notch more scholarly than Readers' Guide (see above), these indexes from the same publisher provide unbroken coverage of the humanities and social sciences since the early part of the century. Today, Humanities Index and Social Sciences Index serve as the standard interdisciplinary indexes to English-language academic journals.

Some 250 periodicals devoted to archeology, folklore, history, language and literature, literary and political criticism, performing arts, philosophy, religion and related subjects are covered by Humanities Index. Entries abound under the subject WOMEN, many of them further qualified by topical or geographic sub-headings. There is much under WOMEN IN LITERATURE in particular.

Social Sciences Index covers another 300 or so journals in the fields of anthropology, economics, environmental sciences, geography, law and criminology, planning and public administration, political science, psychology, social aspects of medicine, and sociology. Most broad subjects, including WOMEN, are sub-divided first by place and then by topic -- e.g., WOMEN--UNITED STATES--PSYCHOLOGY. Both indexes present author and subject entries in a single alphabetic sequence, with a section for books reviews in the back of every issue. Both appear quarterly, with yearly cumulative volumes.

Social Sciences Citation Index. Philadelphia: Institute for Scientific Research, 1973 to present.   Z7163. 016.3.

Arts and Humanities Citation Index. Philadelphia: Institute for Scientific Research, 1977 to present. Z5937.

These sources are produced by computer and provide comprehensive, if somewhat cumbersome, access to scholarly journal literature. They are really indexes to the bibliographic references made in articles, enabling you to identify articles in which known works are cited. If, for example, you needed to find recent critiques of Helene Deutsch's theories on the psychology of women, Social Sciences Citation Index would lead you articles in which her writings are discussed. The subject indexes enhance these works. Each source article (i.e., each article scanned for references) is listed under all the significant words in its title. In Arts and Humanities Citation Index, additional subject words are supplied for articles with non-descriptive titles. Although there are inaccuracies in these sources, their sheer scope makes them invaluable aids in any exhaustive search. Each series is published three times a year, with an annual cumulation. Since the complex organization of these indexes can be intimidating, ask a librarian to explain their use.

8.3 NEWSPAPERS

Newspapers are bountiful primary sources for the study of women. They provide contemporary reporting on events affecting women's lives, are a chronicle of actions by women, and reflect the prevailing opinions of the day. News stories, editorials, featured columns, women's pages, even comic strips reveal underlying assumptions about the place of women in society.

The New York Times has inspired two publications focusing on women:

Women, 1965-1975. Glen Rock, NJ: Microfilming Corporation of America, 1978.   Z7961.   016.30141.

Although the same citations could be culled from the general index to The New York Times (see below), this one-volume tool has the advantage of providing comprehensive coverage of an entire decade. The abstracts of news stories are arranged in a subject outline, with chapters devoted to such topics as apparel, sex and society, the arts, athletics, the labor market, and political and social action. Within each sub-section, abstracts are arranged chronologically. There are four indexes: geographic; subject; organizations; and personal names. A very useful source for information on individual women and on the public lives and personal concerns of American women, during a period when the emerging women's movement was seen as extraordinarily newsworthy.

Women: Their Changing Roles. Edited by Elizabeth Janeway. New York: New York Times/Arno Press, 1973. HQ1426.   301.41.

A potpourri of reprinted news articles, essays, special reports, and advertisements from the 1880s to the early 1970s. Subject and byline indexes.

The sources described above are useful, yet most newspaper research requires careful examination of the papers themselves. Unfortunately, relatively few newspapers are indexed. This may not hinder your investigation of a particular event, since you will probably know, at least roughly, the date it occurred. It is more difficult, however, to trace articles when you have only the topic in mind.
Published indexes are available for some newspapers of national or international importance, at least for recent years. Among them are the following. All are still being issued.

The Chicago Tribune: Newspaper Index. Wooster, OH: Bell & Howell, 1972 to present. AI21. 071. Quarterly.

Index to the Christian Science Monitor. Wooster, OH: Bell & Howell, 1960 to present. AI21. 071. Quarterly.

The [London] Times Index. Reading, England: Newspaper Archives Developments, 1973 to present. AI21. 016.072. Monthly.

For coverage from 1790 to 1905, consult Palmer's Index to the Times Newspaper; from 1906 to 1913, The Annual Index to the Times; and from 1914 to 1972, Index to the Times.

The Los Angeles Times: Newspaper Index. Wooster, OH: Bell & Howell, 1972 to present. AI21. 016.071. Quarterly.

The New Orleans Times-Picayune: Newspaper Index. Wooster, OH: Bell & Howell, 1972 to present. AI21. 016.071. Quarterly.

New York Times Index. New York: New York Times, 1913 to present. AI21. 071. Semimonthly.

The New York Times Index: Prior Series covers the

years 1851 to 1912, but in less depth than the current index.

Wall Street Journal Index. New York: Dow Jones, 1957 to present.   HG1.   332.   Monthly.

Washington Post: Newspaper Index.   Wooster, OH: Bell & Howell, 1972 to present.   AI21.   071.   Quarterly.

Another indexing service covers newspapers from over 100 different American cities. In addition, the service reproduces the articles on microfiche:

NewsBank.   New Canaan, CT: NewsBank, Inc., 1982 to present.   Z6293.   AI3.

NewsBank is a microfiche collection of newspaper clippings, organized by topic: business and economic development; consumer affairs; education; employment; environment; government structure; health; housing and land development; international affairs and defense; law and legal systems; political development; social relations; transportation; welfare and social problems. The key to the clipping file is NewsBank Index, a monthly printed index with quarterly and annual cumulations. There are index entries for WOMEN and WOMEN IN THE WORK FORCE, with sub-headings for narrower topics. COMPARABLE WORTH and SEXUAL HARASSMENT, for example, are two sub-headings under WOMEN IN THE WORK FORCE. WOMEN is also used as a sub-heading under other topics, and the names of women in the news stand alone as subject entries. In addition to the main microfiche set, libraries may purchase two added files, "Review of the Arts" and "Names in the News."

Other papers may be indexed online by local libraries or historical societies. Sometimes a clipping file is maintained, organized by topic. Ask your librarian about resources in your community, or consult the following guide:

Milner, Anita Cheek. Newspaper Indexes: A Location and Subject Guide for Researchers. Metuchen, NJ: Scarecrow, 1977-1982.   Z6951.   016.071.

This three-volume set provides information about card

files and unpublished indexes in libraries, newspaper offices, historical societies, and genealogical societies in the United States.

Because of the paucity of indexes, historical research often entails identifying the paper or papers issued at a given time in a given place and examining them issue by issue. It is tedious work, but it often leads to serendipitous discoveries. The following sources are extremely helpful in this process:

Brigham, Clarence Saunders. <u>History and Bibliography of American Newspapers, 1690-1820.</u> Worcester, MA: American Antiquarian Society, 1947. <u>Additions and Corrections,</u> 1961. Z6951. 016.071.

<u>American Newspapers, 1821-1936: A Union List of Files Available in the United States and Canada.</u> Edited by Winifred Gregory. New York: H. W. Wilson, 1937. Z6945. 016.071.

Both these bibliographies are arranged geographically and furnish some background on the publishing history of each newspaper they cite. Libraries that owned the papers are noted, but this data is sorely out-of-date.

Because newspapers are printed on rough, acidic paper, they deteriorate rapidly. Many libraries conserve backfiles of newspapers only in microform. To determine if a particular paper has been microfilmed, you can consult:

<u>Newspapers in Microform.</u> Washington: Library of Congress, 1973 to present. Z6945. 016.05.

This union list is issued in two parts, <u>United States</u> and <u>Foreign Countries.</u> The original set includes those papers reported between 1948 and 1972, although many were published much earlier. Supplements extend coverage to the present. Newspapers are listed geographically by place of publication, and library locations are given for microform copies of them. This series is useful for identifying papers published in a given city at a given time, and for verifying libraries which might supply microform copies on interlibrary loan.

8.4 GOVERNMENT PUBLICATIONS

The governments of the world have shown considerable interest in women, as evidenced by the wealth of information published through official channels. In this section, the important finding tools for United States federal, state, and local publications are noted, as well as a guide to United Nations materials. If you need documents from another country, begin your search by consulting a librarian, since governmental publishing programs differ so greatly from nation to nation.
   Most libraries choose one of two common methods for organizing U.S. documents. One is to treat federal publications like books, shelving them in the stacks under appropriate call numbers and putting author, subject, and title records for them in the library's catalog. The "author" in most cases is the agency responsible for the publication. For example, the author of <u>A Statistical Portrait of Women in the United States</u> is cited as "United States. Bureau of the Census."
   The other approach, also widely practiced, is to store all federal documents together in a special collection, grouping them by the series numbers assigned by the Government Printing Office. These numbers are referred to as SuDoc numbers -- short for "<u>S</u>uperintendent of <u>D</u>ocuments." Records may be placed in the library's main catalog, or a separate documents catalog or check-in file may be maintained.
   A number of libraries across the country are designated as depository libraries. They are eligible to receive many categories of federal documents free-of-charge, provided they make them available to members of the surrounding community. If your own library is not a depository library, there is sure to be one or more in your state.
   Government publications are a rich source of information on many women's studies topics, ranging from the obvious (women's role in the national economy, demographic statistics, legislation affecting women) to

the unexpected (the psychology of women, continuing
education, women's art). This chapter lists
bibliographies and indexes that will help you ferret out
documents on many different subjects. The U.S.
government has also published many specialized
bibliographies on women's issues; a number of these are
contained in the other chapters of this guide.

American Statistics Index. Washington: Congressional
Information Service, 1973 to present.   Z7554.U5.
016.31.

A master index to statistics contained in all sorts
of federal publications. Monthly issues and annual
bound cumulations follow the same format, with
separate sections for indexes and abstracts. WOMEN
and WOMEN'S EMPLOYMENT are used as subject terms, as
are such specific concepts as SEX DISCRIMINATION,
ABORTION, and MATERNITY. The "Index by Categories"
highlights statistical publications that have
breakdowns by such factors as sex, race, geographic
area, or occupation. Index entries are keyed to
document descriptions, which are organized by issuing
agency in the abstracts section. Detailed
instructions in using ASI are printed in the front of
every edition.

Bibliographic Guide to Government Publications - Foreign.
Boston: G. K. Hall, 1974 to present.   Z7164.G7.   011.

Bibliographic Guide to Government Publications - U.S.
Boston: G. K. Hall, 1974 to present.   Z7164.G7.   015.

These two annual series are based on records
generated by the Library of Congress and the New York
Public Library. Each volume furnishes full catalog-
style records in a single alphabetic sequence of
author, title, subject, and other entries. WOMEN
appears as a heading with many geographic and topical
modifiers. The foreign guide covers international
and intergovernmental bodies, as well as foreign
nations, states, and cities. The U.S. guide includes
federal, state, and city documents, plus many
publications from state-supported universities.

CIS/Index. Washington: Congressional Information
Service, 1970 to present.   KF49.   348.

This monthly guide indexes and summarizes the
official publications of committees of the U.S.

Congress. Each issue is in two parts. The "Index"
section offers various approaches, the most important
being the index by subjects and names. Names include
the witnesses that testified at Congressional
hearings (both private citizens and representatives
of interest groups); subjects include not only the
broad heading WOMEN, but also such specific issues as
ABORTION and WOMEN'S EMPLOYMENT. The index cumulates
quarterly, annually, and quadrennially. The "Index"
section serves as the key to the "Abstracts" section,
which is largely organized by committee and provides
a synopsis of each document, plus its SuDoc number
when known.

CIS U.S. Serial Set Index. Washington: Congressional
Information Service, 1975-1979. 12 vols.   Z1223.Z9.
328.73.

The Serial Set is the official compilation of
Congressional documents. This companion set is a
subject index covering 1789 though 1969, broken down
into twelve chronological segments. Since the
indexing is based on keywords in the titles of the
documents, there are many entries under the word
WOMEN in more recent volumes and under other words
like LADIES and WIDOWS in earlier years. Also
included are indexes by name to Congressional actions
on behalf of individuals, and finding lists arranged
by document number. Look in the front of the volumes
for precise instructions in the use of this valuable
index.

Index to Current Urban Documents. Westport, CT:
Greenwood, 1972 to present.   Z7165.U5.   016.30136.

This quarterly bibliography cites local government
documents of the largest cities and counties of the
United States and Canada. The documents themselves
are available in a microfiche collection from the
same publisher. The index is in two sections, one
geographic and one by subject. The most relevant
subject headings are WOMEN and AFFIRMATIVE ACTION,
EQUAL OPPORTUNITY PROGRAMS. Cumulated annually.

Monthly Catalog of U.S. Government Publications.
Washington: U.S. Government Printing Office, 1895 to
present.   Z1223.A18.   J83.   015.73.   SuDoc no.
GP3.8.

A catalog of documents available from the Government

Printing Office, this is the best general guide to
federal publications, although far from complete.
Entries are arranged by SuDoc number, which amounts
to an arrangement by issuing agency. Current issues
include indexing by author (both personal authors and
divisions of the government), title, subject,
series/report number, stock number, and title
keyword. Subject entries are now based on the
Library of Congress subject headings, though this was
not always so. The indexes cumulate every six months
and yearly. For documents collections arranged by
SuDoc numbers, this series often serves as the
catalog and indicator of shelf locations.

Cumulative Subject Index to the Monthly Catalog of United
States Government Publications, 1900-1971. Washington:
Carrollton Press, 1973-75.   15 vols.   Z1223.
016.328734.

This handy set merges the subject indexes for 71
years of the Monthly Catalog (see above). There are
several pages of entries under WOMEN; because the
sub-divisions are not always logical, one should scan
all the columns. Entries also appear under the names
of agencies -- e.g., WOMEN'S BUREAU, LABOR DEPARTMENT
and WOMEN'S ARMY CORPS.

Monthly Checklist of State Publications. Washington:
U.S. Government Printing Office, 1910 to present.
Z1223.5.A1.   015.73.   SuDoc no. LC30.9.

This nearly complete list of state government
documents is compiled at the Library of Congress.
Entries are arranged alphabetically by state and sub-
arranged by agency. Separate publications and
annuals are covered each month; periodicals are
listed only in June and December. A subject index is
issued annually and helps in identifying items about
women.

UNDOC: Current Index. New York: United Nations, Dag
Hammarskjold Library, 1979 to present.   JX1977.
016.34123.   U.N. no. ST/LIB/SER. M.

Issued ten times a year with an annual cumulation,
this is the official index to United Nations
publications. Citations are displayed in
alphanumeric order by series symbol and session,
which amounts to an arrangement by issuing body
within the U.N. Indexes offer access by subject,

title, and author. (Authors are generally countries
or international organizations, rarely individuals.)
The most relevant headings in the subject index are
WOMEN and WOMEN IN DEVELOPMENT. UNDOC was preceded
by United Nations Documents Index (UNDI), providing
coverage from 1950 to 1973, and UNDEX: United
Nations Documents Index, from 1970 to 1978.

8.5 CONFERENCE PROCEEDINGS

Scholars share new ideas and research findings with their colleagues at professional meetings and symposia. The papers presented at conferences, seminars, colloquia and the like are therefore marvelous resources for women's studies research. Yet tracking them down can sometimes be difficult. Many of these papers never make their way into print. It's not unusual for a limited number of mimeographed copies to be distributed to conference participants, then passed around the community of women's studies scholars, read and debated, and finally credited as "classics" in later studies.

Sometimes the entire proceedings of a conference are published as a book. For reasons of space, quality, and editorial selection, not all of the papers presented at a particular meeting are necessarily included in the final compilation. Some papers may be published later, in identical or substantially altered form, in periodicals or anthologies. A few may be reprinted in pamphlet format by small presses, and still others may eventually surface as microform publications.

Even locating book-length published proceedings can be a challenge. Under the latest cataloging rules commonly agreed upon by American and British libraries, most proceedings are entered in library catalogs under their titles. If they're simply called <u>Proceedings</u>, you'll find a record under P. If they have a distinctive title, as many do, you'll find them under that title. Additional entries may be made under the name of the conference. Under the old rules, however, proceedings were generally entered in the catalog under the official name of the conference. For example: International Symposium on Women and Industrial Relations, Vienna, 1978. <u>Women and Industrial Relations: Working Papers</u>. (Geneva: International Institute for Labor Studies, 1980). Guessing the proper name of a conference -- was it "National Congress of..." or "International Conference on...?" -- can be tiresome.

Some smaller libraries may have revised all the
headings in their catalogs to reflect the new principles,
but larger libraries have tended to apply the new rules
as of January 1981 and to leave old catalog entries as
they are. Check with your reference librarian if you
experience any problems finding conference papers.
 The sources listed in this section are bibliographies
and indexes to published proceedings of conferences.
These sources can be a great help in determining if a
paper was ever published, and if so, how to obtain a
copy.

Bibliographic Guide to Conference Publications. Boston:
G. K. Hall, 1974 to present.   Z5051.   016.06.

 This annual bibliography reproduces cataloging
 records for conference publications acquired by the
 Library of Congress and the New York Public Library.
 Use it as you would your own library's catalog --
 look under the name of the meeting, the sponsoring
 organization, the names of the editors, the title, or
 the subjects.

Directory of Published Proceedings. Series SSH: Social
Sciences/Humanities.   Harrison, NY: InterDok, 1968 to
present.   Z7161.   300.

 This quarterly is "a bibliographic directory of
 preprints and published proceedings of congresses,
 conferences, symposia, meetings, seminars, and summer
 schools which have been held world-wide from 1964 to
 date." Citations are arranged chronologically by the
 date of the conference. The location, the official
 name, and the principal sponsors are given for each
 meeting. In addition to the title of the published
 proceedings, each reference provides the name of the
 publisher or distributor, the price, the series or
 journal (if the proceedings are included in an
 ongoing publication), the editors, and the number of
 pages. The subject index is derived from key words
 in the names of the conferences, the sponsors, and
 the titles. A companion series, Series SEMT:
 Science, Engineering, Medicine, Technology, is issued
 monthly.

Index to Social Science and Humanities Proceedings.
Philadelphia: Institute for Scientific Information, 1979
to present.   Z7163.   H61.   016.3.

 Unlike the two sources noted above, this quarterly

indexes the individual papers presented at conferences. About 1,000 proceedings published as books or as special issues of journals are included each year, for a total of nearly 15,000 papers. The main section of each issue is called "Contents of Proceedings"; it gives full bibliographic and ordering information for published proceedings and then lists the individual papers contained in each. These entries are randomly ordered, so one of the indexes must be consulted first. If you already have a reference to the conference, you can approach it using the "Sponsor Index," the "Author/Editor Index," or the "Meeting Location Index." If you know the name or affiliation of the paper's author, you can use the "Author/Editor Index" or the "Corporate Index." If you are searching more generally for recent meetings on a certain topic, turn to the "Permuterm Subject Index." The "Permuterm Index" takes keywords from the titles of the conferences, the compiled proceedings, and the actual papers. You'll find a number of listings under WOMAN, WOMEN, FEMALE(S), and GIRL(S), as well as the words SEX and GENDER. A companion series, <u>Index to Scientific and Technical Proceedings</u>, has been published since 1978.

8.6 DISSERTATIONS

Why read dissertations? First, they frequently offer in-depth analyses of topics not yet treated in books. Second, most dissertations include comprehensive bibliographies and critical surveys of the literature.

A number of bibliographies have been compiled over the years listing doctoral dissertations in specialized fields, but no comprehensive list of dissertations just on women's studies topics is available. Putting together such a list would be a monumental task, since research on women takes place within so many disciplines. You should therefore rely on the continuing interdisciplinary indexing provided by University Microfilms International, the commercial distributor of most dissertations written in the United States and Canada, as well as at some foreign universities.

Comprehensive Dissertation Index, 1861-1972. Ann Arbor: University Microfilms International, 1973. 37 volumes. Annual supplements. Z5053. AC801. 013.

An attempt to index all dissertations accepted at universities in the U.S. by keywords in their titles and by their authors. In both the main set and the supplements, citations are grouped by field. The author indexes follow the subject groupings. For each dissertation, the complete title and author's name is given, along with the date, university, pagination, and reference to an entry in Dissertation Abstracts International (see below) or some other printed list. If the dissertation can be purchased from University Microfilms, the order number is also noted.

Dissertation Abstracts International. Ann Arbor: University Microfilms International, 1938 to present. Z5505.

Originally called Microfilm Abstracts (1938-1951) and later simply Dissertation Abstracts (1952-1969), this source is essentially a catalog of dissertations available for purchase, in paper copy or microform, from University Microfilms International. Coverage has expanded over the years as more and more universities (over 450 in 1984) adopted this efficient means of distributing their students' dissertations. Dissertation Abstracts International is currently issued in three parts. Section A, covering the humanities and social sciences, and section B, covering the sciences and engineering, both appear monthly. Section C, listing foreign dissertations on all subjects, comes out quarterly. Each section is organized by subject field; within each field, dissertations are listed alphabetically by author. There is now a category called "Women's Studies," although most dissertations on women's topics are classified under other disciplines. Author, title, university, date, and number of pages are given for each entry, along with a half-page abstract. Keyword and author indexes appear in each issue. Nearly all dissertations listed in DAI are available for purchase. Order numbers are given with each entry; refer to the latest issue for the prices currently in effect.

In both Comprehensive Dissertation Index and Dissertation Abstracts International, dissertations relevant to women's studies can best be identified by using the keyword subject indexes.

9
Bibliographies and Indexes in Special Fields

Previous chapters described general bibliographies in women's studies and multidisciplinary bibliographic sources for certain forms of publications. The following chapters, by contrast, highlight bibliographies, indexes, and abstracts in the traditional disciplines and other specialized fields of study.

Some academic fields have reacted to the new scholarship on women by updating their basic reference tools to include sections for women's studies writings. In other fields, feminist scholars have compiled separate compensatory bibliographies to conveniently bring together citations to works by and about women. This section notes both sorts of works. It also draws your attention to sources which make no special allowance for the needs of women's studies researchers, but which must be consulted nevertheless because they are the authoritative bibliographic sources in their specialties. If one is diligent and imaginative in using them, such sources will yield up references to writings about women.

Each disciplinary chapter follows a standard format. First, a brief introduction notes some of the issues posed by women's studies scholars within the discipline and suggests subject headings for searching in the library catalog. Next, selected basic research guides in the field are listed. While these guides rarely devote much attention to women's studies, they can be of great help to researchers working outside their usual area of expertise. Moreover, they are the keys to a wide variety of specialized reference sources which are not mentioned here.

Third, bibliographies focusing on women are cited. In some disciplines, such as literature, these are abundant. In other areas, like science or anthropology, women's studies bibliographies are still rare. The quality of these works varies considerably. Because specialized bibliographies can be such valuable timesavers, I have included a few bibliographies of less-than-ideal accuracy and completeness. Most researchers would agree that a short selective bibliography with occasional errors is, in most instances, better than no bibliography at all. (Sadly, "no bibliography at all" remains the grim fact in many areas of interest to women's studies. By the time this guide is published, new topical bibliographies will surely be available to fill gaps in the scholarly apparatus, while some included here will no doubt be superceded by more impressive publications.)

Finally, indexes, abstracts, and continuing bibliographies are listed. Here I have tried to mention the most basic sources in each field, with hints on how women's studies topics may be searched in each. These ongoing publications are the best (and generally the only) sources of references to recent materials.

Such is the basic outline of each chapter; in a handful of disciplines, other categories appear. Under "Business, Economics, and Labor Studies," for instance, you'll find a separate listing of sources on women anddevelopment. Under literature, bibliographies of writings by women and bibliographies of writings about women authors are differentiated.

Please bear in mind that no works of a non-bibliographic nature appear in chapters 9.1 through 9.17 -- that is, no specialized directories or handbooks, no dictionaries of terms and professional jargon, or their ilk. Also, few retrospective bibliographies or indexes are listed, even those considered basic to their disciplines, since these older works seldom treat women's studies topics.

9.1 ANTHROPOLOGY

Anthropology, traditionally defined as "the science of man," has always studied women. Sexual division of labor, rituals surrounding childbirth, menstrual taboos, the status of women in the community -- all these and much more have been the subject of anthropological fieldwork and theory. Sex is such an ever-present factor that anthropological works focusing on women are not always highlighted with special subject headings. Much relevant literature is buried in library catalogs under the general heading WOMEN -- both as a stand-alone term and modified by place or culture (e.g., WOMEN, MUSLIM). Women may likewise be treated in depth in books found under such broad subject terms as ANTHROPOLOGY and HUMAN EVOLUTION. Conversely, books listed under more specialized headings such as WOMEN (IN RELIGION, FOLKLORE, ETC.) or WOMEN--HEALTH AND HYGIENE may or may not prove useful to anthropologists.

GUIDES TO RESEARCH

Frantz, Charles. The Student Anthropologist's Handbook: A Guide to Research, Training, and Career. Cambridge, MA: Schenkman, 1972. GN42. 301.2.

BIBLIOGRAPHIES ON WOMEN

DeCaro, Francis A. Women and Folklore: A Bibliographic Survey. Westport, CT: Greenwood, 1983. Z5983.W64. GR470. 016.398.

This cross-disciplinary survey emphasizes works in anthropology but also notes materials from the fields of psychology, history, and popular culture. A 45-

page "Essay Guide" highlights such topics as female folk heroes, women's speech, courtship and marriage customs, healers, sexual folklore, and material culture. The essay is keyed to an alphabetical list of 1,664 publications.

Jacobs, Sue-Ellen. <u>Women in Perspective: A Guide for Cross-Cultural Studies.</u> Urbana, IL: University of Illinois Press, 1974. Z7961. 016.30141.

This comprehensive bibliography can be a springboard to research on a wide spectrum of topics. Part I is a geographical listing by country or cultural area; part II is organized by theme. The subjects covered include psychological studies, women and religion, misogyny, suffrage, and many other specialized topics. Not annotated. Author index.

INDEXES AND CONTINUING BIBLIOGRAPHIES

<u>Abstracts in Anthropology.</u> Farmingdale, NY: Baywood Publishing, 1970 to present. GN1. 306.

Abstracts of journal articles on anthropology are classified by broad category: archaeology; physical anthropology; linguistics; cultural anthropology. Each category is sub-divided in a manner that reflects the nature of the field. Cultural anthropology is divided into such topics as economics, kinship, sociocultural change, and symbol systems, with a sub-section for "sex roles" under the heading "Minorities." Because the subject index is inadequate, an approach through the classified arrangement will be most profitable.

<u>Anthropological Literature.</u> South Salem, NY: Redgrave Publishing, 1979 to present. Z5112. GN1. 016.301.

This quarterly index is based on the collection of the Tozzer Library at Harvard. Periodical articles and essays in books are listed by the authors' names under five very broad categories: cultural/social; archaeology; biological/physical; linguistics; and general/method/theory. In each issue there is a joint author index, an archaeological site and culture index, an ethnic and linguistic group index, and a geographic index -- all cumulated annually -- but no detailed subject index that would allow one to single out references about women. The only alternative is to scan the large cultural/social section.

<u>International Bibliography of Social and Cultural Anthropology</u>. Chicago: Aldine, 1955 to present. Z7161. 016.572.

This annual bibliography is sponsored by UNESCO and includes publications in many languages. The basic arrangement is by topic; many of the thematic categories are then sub-divided by geographic area. Subject indexes are provided in both English and French, and many references to women can be found in them. Although lacking annotations, this is a good source with which to begin a search of the international literature in anthropology.

9.2 THE ARTS

The arts are vital both as areas of scholarship in women's studies and as modes for the expression of feminist ideas and values. Courses on women artists and images of women in film, for example, were among the very first women's studies offerings. Interdisciplinary courses with titles such as "Women and Creativity" are also popular.

Despite the trend toward mixed media -- exemplified by the central role of women in the evolving field of performance (or ritual) art -- the reference literature still largely reflects traditional divisions. There are several notable published resources on women in the visual arts, music, and film, while women's theater has yet to receive the bibliographic recognition it deserves. Some of the threads come together in the study of popular culture.

Very general works may be cataloged under FEMINISM AND THE ARTS. Other suggested catalog subject headings introduce each sub-section of this chapter: visual arts; music; film; theater; and popular culture.

THE VISUAL ARTS

For books on the representation of women in works of art, look in the catalog under WOMEN IN ART. For information on women working in the arts, look under such headings as WOMEN ARTISTS and WOMEN PAINTERS.

GUIDES TO RESEARCH

Arntzen, Etta, and Rainwater, Robert. <u>Guide to the Literature of Art History</u>. Chicago: American Library

Association, 1980.   Z5931.   N380.   016.709.

Jones, Lois B. Art Research Methods and Resources: A Guide to Finding Art Information. Dubuque: Kendall/Hunt, 1978.   N85.   707.

Muehsam, Gerd. Guide to Basic Information Sources in the Visual Arts. Santa Barbara: ABC-Clio, 1978.   N7425. 700.

BIBLIOGRAPHIES ON WOMEN

Bachmann, Donna G., and Sherry Piland. Women Artists: An Historical, Contemporary and Feminist Bibliography. Metuchen, NJ: Scarecrow, 1978.   Z7963.A75.   N8354. 016.709.

The first part of this bibliography lists three types of general writings on women artists -- books, periodical articles, and exhibit catalogs. The much larger second part focuses on 161 individual artists. Each artist's entry includes a brief biographical sketch, citations to publications specifically about her or her work, references to information in historical surveys and standard biographical sources, and a list of museum collections in which her work is represented. Women artists of many countries and time periods are included.

Chiarmonte, Paula L., editor. Women Artists: A Resource and Research Guide. Tucson: Art Libraries Society of North America, 1982. (Supplement to Art Documentation, vol. 5, no. 1, October 1982)   Z5937.   Z674.2.   026.

This is a concise guide (24 pp.) to the full range of primary and secondary materials needed by art historians and critics. Print resources are listed, including reference works, historical surveys, contemporary criticism, and exhibition catalogs. Also highlighted are periodicals, archives, organizations, films, slide registries, galleries, and other sources of information.

Tufts, Eleanor. American Women Artists, Past and Present: A Selected Bibliographic Guide. New York: Garland, 1984.   Z7963.A75.   N6505.   016.704.

A bibliography of works by and about 500 women artists, from the 17th century to the present.

Approximately half of the artists covered are still living. Included are articles, books, newspaper articles, reviews of exhibits, catalogs, and references to the artists in standard sources such as biographical dictionaries. Not annotated, but a good place to begin a search for information on an individual American artist.

INDEXES AND CONTINUING BIBLIOGRAPHIES

Art Index. New York: H. W. Wilson, 1929 to present. Z5937.   016.7.

This quarterly index provides access by subject and author to articles on art in some 150 journals, yearbooks, and museum bulletins. All forms and periods of the fine arts are included, plus archaeology, photography, crafts, interior design, and other related subjects. Especially useful for locating write-ups of individual women artists, reviews of their shows, and reproductions of their works.

RILA, Repertoire International de la Litterature de l'Art. Williamstown, MA: Sterling and Francine Clark Institute, 1975 to present.   Z5937.   N7510.   016.7.

Sponsored by the College Art Association, this index is issued twice a year. It includes all varieties of publications -- books, periodical articles, newspaper reports, conference papers, exhibition catalogs, dissertations, and more -- on post-classical European and post-Columbian American art. RILA is noted for its detailed subject indexing and its informative abstracts.

Artbibliographies Modern. Oxford, England: Clio, 1973 to present.   Z5935.   016.709.

This semiannual series is a continuation of LOMA: Literature on Modern Art, which was published between 1969 and 1971. Organized by subject and focusing on the 19th and 20th centuries, it offers abstracts of journal articles, along with references to books, exhibit catalogs, and theses. There is no separate section for women's art.

MUSIC

Books on women in musical professions can be found in the library catalog under WOMEN MUSICIANS and WOMEN COMPOSERS. New works in women's studies may be categorized under FEMINISM AND MUSIC. Recordings may fall under the heading WOMEN--SONGS AND MUSIC.
Although they are not listed below, the reader should be aware that several specialized bibliographies have appeared. Some fine examples are: Keyboard Music by Women Composers: A Catalog and Bibliography (Westport, CT: Greenwood, 1981) compiled by Joan M. Meggett; Contemporary Concert Music by Women: A Directory of Composers and Their Works (Westport, CT: Greenwood, 1981) by Judith Lang Zaimont and Karen Famera; and Women Composers: A Checklist of Works for the Solo Voice by Miriam Stewart-Green (Boston: G. K. Hall, 1980).

GUIDES TO RESEARCH

Druesedow, John E., Jr. Library Research Guide to Music: Illustrated Search Strategy and Sources. Ann Arbor: Pierian Press, 1982. ML111. 780.

Duckles, Vincent. Music Reference and Research Materials. 3rd ed. New York: Free Press, 1974. ML113. 016.78.

BIBLIOGRAPHIES ON WOMEN, INCLUDING DISCOGRAPHIES

Block, Adrienne Fried, and Carol Neuls-Bates. Women in American Music: A Bibliography of Music and Literature. Westport, CT: Greenwood Press, 1979. ML128.W7. 780.

Over two-thirds of the entries in this impressive source are for musical compositions, with references to recordings and reviews. The remaining citations are to writings by and about American women in music. Abstracts are provided. Vernacular music is covered from colonial times to 1920; the coverage of art music extends to the present.

Cohen, Aaron I. International Encyclopedia of Women Composers. New York: Bowker, 1981. ML105. 780.

An alphabetical list of 3,700 women composers from all time periods and seventy countries. In addition to brief biographical data, each entry lists musical compositions and other publications by the composer, plus works about her.

Frasier, Jane. Women Composers: A Discography. Detroit: Information Coordinators, 1983.   ML156.4.W6.   016.7899.

This is an easy-to-use guide to recordings of classical music by over 330 composers. The genres indexed are chamber music, choral music, electronic music, multimedia works, orchestral or band pieces, solo music, stage works, and vocal music.

Hixon, Don L., and Don Hennessee. Women in Music: A Bio-bibliography. Metuchen, NJ: Scarecrow, 1975. ML105.   780.

An index to biographical material on women musicians in over forty music dictionaries and encyclopedias. Limited to classical music, but covers all periods and countries.

Pool, Jeannie G. Women in Music History: A Research Guide. New York: the author, 1977.   ML82.   780.

This self-published pamphlet is a guide to researching women's music and women's role in the history of music. Included are a selective bibliography, a discography, a list of women composers born prior to 1900, and recommendations for research topics.

Skowronski, JoAnn. Women in American Music: A Bibliography. Metuchen, NJ: Scarecrow, 1978. ML128.W7.   016.78.

An annotated bibliography covering 1776 to 1976. Cited are over 1,000 books and articles on women's contributions to every type of American music, from religious to pop, from classical to jazz.

Stern, Susan. Women Composers: A Handbook. Metuchen, NJ: Scarecrow, 1978.   ML105.   780.

An index to information on women composers in books and periodicals. Coverage is limited to women from the United States, Canada, and selected Western

European countries; only classical composers are included.

INDEXES AND CONTINUING BIBLIOGRAPHIES

International Repertory of Music Literature. <u>RILM Abstracts of Music Literature.</u> New York: RILM, 1967 to present. ML1. 780.5.

This quarterly index to writings about music includes books, periodical articles, reviews, dissertations, catalogs, and other materials. Each issue uses a classified subject arrangement, with an annual author/subject index. Look under WOMEN IN MUSIC in the index or under the names of individual composers.

<u>Music Index</u>. Detroit: Information Coordinators, 1949 to present. ML118. 016.78.

A monthly author and subject index to articles appearing in over 300 periodicals. In addition to scholarly studies, the indexing covers books reviews, reviews of performances, and obituaries of famous musicians. A subject heading list is issued annually. WOMEN IN MUSIC and WOMEN IN THE PERFORMING ARTS are among the headings employed.

FILM

Among the subject headings used in the catalog for the portrayal of women in film are WOMEN IN MOVING-PICTURES and WOMEN IN TELEVISION, as well as the broader term WOMEN IN MASS MEDIA. Such headings as WOMEN IN THE MOTION PICTURE INDUSTRY, WOMEN MOTION PICTURE PRODUCERS AND DIRECTORS, and MOVING-PICTURE ACTORS AND ACTRESSES are used for books about cinema artists and businesswomen. FEMINISM AND MOTION PICTURES is a newly approved term.

GUIDES TO RESEARCH

Armour, Robert A. <u>Film: A Reference Guide</u>. Westport, CT: Greenwood, 1980. PN1993.45. 791.43.

Sheahan, Eileen. **Moving Pictures: An Annotated Guide to Selected Film Literature with Suggestions for the Study of Film.** South Brunswick: A.S. Barnes, 1979. Z5784.M9. PN1994. 016.79143.

BIBLIOGRAPHIES ON WOMEN, INCLUDING FILMOGRAPHIES

Dawson, Bonnie. **Women's Films in Print: An Annotated Guide to 800 Films by Women.** San Francisco: Booklegger Press, 1975. PN1998. 016.79143.

A directory of women filmmakers, with annotated lists of their films. Additional features: a list of distributors; a bibliography of relevant books, periodicals, catalogs, and newsletters; and a bibliography of programs from women's film festivals.

Kowalski, Rosemary R. **Women and Film: A Bibliography.** Metuchen, NJ: Scarecrow, 1976. Z5784.M9. PN1995.9.W6. 016.79143.

Provides citations, some annotated, to 2,302 books, articles, catalogs, and reviews. References are arranged in four sections: women as performers; women as filmmakers; images of women; and women columnists and critics. For research on actresses, this source must be used in conjunction with Mel Schuster's **Motion Picture Performers** (Metuchen, NJ: Scarecrow, 1971).

Sullivan, Kaye. **Films For, By, and About Women.** Metuchen, NJ: Scarecrow, 1980. PN1995.9.W6. 791.43.

This impressive annotated filmography supercedes earlier lists of women's films, including **Women's Films in Print** (above). Films are entered alphabetically by title, with indexes for filmmakers and subjects. Sources for rental are included in the entries.

INDEXES AND CONTINUING BIBLIOGRAPHIES

Writers Program, N.Y. **Film Index.** New York: H. W. Wilson, 1941. Z5784.M9. 016.7914.

This comprehensive bibliography was compiled during the Depression as a Works Progress Administration

project, but only volume 1, "The Film as Art," was
ever published. Entries are annotated and arranged
in subject categories. Reviews of individual films
are included under the type of movie -- westerns,
"social films," and so on.

MacCann, Richard Dyer, and Edward S. Perry. The New Film
Index: A Bibliography of Magazine Articles in English,
1930-1970. New York: Dutton, 1975.   Z5784.M9.   011.

Intended as a supplement to Film Index (above), this
bibliography cites approximately 12,000 articles on
278 different topics. Most entries are briefly
annotated; reviews are excluded. A few items
relating to women's studies are listed under
STEREOTYPES and FILM CONTENT AS A REFLECTION OF
SOCIETY.

Batty, Linda. Retrospective Index to Film Periodicals,
1930-1971. New York: Bowker, 1975.   Z5784.M9.
791.43.

Designed to bridge the gap between Film Index (above)
and International Index to Film Periodicals (below),
this index uses the same subject terms as the latter.
Coverage is strongest after 1950. References are
placed in three sections: individual films; subjects;
and book reviews.

International Index to Film Periodicals. London:
Federation Internationale des Archives du Film, 1972 to
present.   Z5784.M9.   016.79143.

This annual publication indexes about 60 periodicals
which are devoted exclusively to the film. "Women
and the Cinema" appears as a sub-category of "Society
and Cinema" in the classified arrangement of
citations. Indexes facilitate searching by author,
topic, or director.

Film Literature Index. Albany, NY: Film and Television
Documentation Center, 1973 to present.   Z5784.M9.
791.43.

This computer-produced author/subject index has two
advantages over the International Index to Film
Periodicals (above). First, it is issued quarterly,
so its coverage is more up-to-date. Second, it
selects references from some 300 periodicals,

including many in related fields. Recent issues list
a number of articles on women and film.

THEATER

Although local feminist performance companies are
well received and have played an important role on the
cultural front of the women's movement, there is a dearth
of literature on this phenomenon. The few published
works will most likely be listed in the catalog under
FEMINIST THEATER.
Unfortunately, specificity is not the rule for
describing works on women and the theater. The subject
heading WOMEN IN LITERATURE covers the portrayal of women
in dramatic literature, and WOMEN AUTHORS subsumes women
playwrights. Before 1970, ACTORS and ACTRESSES were
separate subjects, but since that date the single heading
ACTORS AND ACTRESSES has been employed. However,
unambiguous headings such as WOMEN DANCERS and WOMEN
ENTERTAINERS are also used.

GUIDES TO RESEARCH

Whalon, Marion K. Performing Arts Research: A Guide to
Information Sources. Detroit: Gale, 1976. Z6935.
PN1584. 016.7902.

BIBLIOGRAPHIES ON WOMEN

Coven, Brenda. American Women Dramatists of the
Twentieth Century: A Bibliography. Metuchen, NJ:
Scarecrow, 1982. Z1231.D7. PS351. 016.812.

This easy-to-use bibliography treats 133 of the most
important American women dramatists of this century.
After a brief list of general works, the book is
divided into sections on the individual women,
providing for each a complete list of her plays,
sources for biographical information, and references
to criticism and reviews. There is a title index.

INDEXES AND CONTINUING BIBLIOGRAPHIES

Cumulated Dramatic Index, 1909-1949. 2 vols. Boston:

G. K. Hall, 1965.   Z5781.

Dramatic Index was issued as part two of the Annual Magazine Subject Index; some libraries will hold it in its original, uncumulated form. Articles and illustrations covering theater, musical theater, and motion pictures are included. The subject listing has topical headings, personal names, and titles of dramatic works. Volume 2 offers an author list of 6,500 books on drama, and author and title lists of 24,000 published plays.

Play Index. New York: H. W. Wilson, 1949 to 1977. Z5781.

This index to separately published plays and plays in anthologies is published every five years; the latest volume covers 1978 to 1982. The full set lists some 23,000 plays under their authors, titles, and subjects. Play Index is useful for locating scripts by women playwrights and for identifying plays on topics of particular interest to women.

Guide to the Performing Arts. Metuchen, NJ: Scarecrow, 1957 to present.   ML118.   016.78.

An annual periodical index emphasizing North American writings on the theater. Reviews of performances are included. Citations may be found under author, title, and subject.

New York Public Library. Research Libraries.
Bibliographic Guide to Theatre Arts. Boston: G. K. Hall, 1975 to present.   Z6935.   PN1584.   016.792.

New York Public Library. Research Libraries.
Bibliographic Guide to Dance. Boston: G. K. Hall, 1975 to present.   Z7514.D2.   GV1594.   016.7933.

These annual bibliographies, on the theater and the dance respectively, are based on the cataloging of new books at the New York Public Library and the Library of Congress. Author, title, and subject entries are in one alphabetic sequence.

POPULAR CULTURE

Many sources cited elsewhere in this chapter are relevant to studies of popular culture; see especially the film and music listings. The works cited in this section, by contrast, are not limited to any one field of the arts. To locate such interdisciplinary materials in the catalog, try WOMEN IN POPULAR CULTURE, as well as the broader headings POPULAR CULTURE and POPULAR LITERATURE.

GUIDES TO RESEARCH

Landrum, Larry N. American Popular Culture: A Guide to Information Sources. Detroit: Gale, 1982. Z1361.C6. E169.1. 016.7.

BIBLIOGRAPHIES ON WOMEN

Fishburn, Katherine. Women in Popular Culture: A Reference Guide. Westport, CT: Greenwood, 1982. HQ1426. 305.4.

This is a collection of well crafted bibliographic essays on the following topics: histories of women in popular culture; women in popular literature; women in magazines and magazine fiction; women in film; women in television; women in advertising, fashion, sports, and comics; and theories of women in popular culture. Appendices point to periodicals, bibliographies, biographies, information guides, and important research centers and institutions.

Friedman, Leslie J. Sex Role Stereotyping in the Mass Media: An Annotated Bibliography. New York: Garland, 1977. Z7164.S42. P96.S5. 016.30141.

This bibliography on the portrayal of male and female roles in the mass media covers television, film, advertising, magazines, newspapers, children's media, and popular culture. This last category encompasses music, comic books, pornography, humor, and science fiction. Materials on the employment of women in media occupations are also listed.

INDEXES AND CONTINUING BIBLIOGRAPHIES

Abstracts of Popular Culture. Bowling Green, OH: Bowling Green University Popular Press, 1976 to present.
Z7164.S66.   HN17.5.   016.909.

According to the publishers of this biannual abstracting service, "the term 'popular culture' comprehends all aspects of life which are not academic or creative in the narrowest and most elite sense of the word." Articles from both scholarly journals and popular magazines are cited. References are presented alphabetically by author. The subject index uses such terms as WOMEN, WOMEN'S RIGHTS, and FEMINISM, plus related phrases such as LITERATURE, WOMEN IN.

9.3 BUSINESS, ECONOMICS, AND LABOR STUDIES

This chapter encompasses sources on women's employment, the role of women in the economy, and women in economically underdeveloped areas. The topics for study are almost infinite. Sex discrimination in hiring and advancement, women managers, women as consumers, the economic value of women's unpaid work in the home, sexual harassment on the job, women in non-traditional occupations, women in labor unions, the image of women in advertising -- this is but a sampling of possible research topics.

In the catalog the following headings are pertinent: WOMEN--EMPLOYMENT; SEX DISCRIMINATION IN EMPLOYMENT; WAGES--WOMEN; and WOMEN-OWNED BUSINESS ENTERPRISES. The general heading WOMEN--ECONOMIC CONDITIONS is also widely used. Books on women in various occupational fields are found under "women in ..." headings -- for example, WOMEN IN BUSINESS, WOMEN IN THE PROFESSIONS, WOMEN IN TRADE-UNIONS. For books on women working in particular jobs, see entries like WOMEN FARMERS or WOMEN EXECUTIVES.

The coverage of women and development in a chapter on economic issues is perhaps somewhat misleading. Economic development is a process that forces far-reaching social and cultural changes upon a society. Feminist scholars have demonstrated how development disrupts traditional ways of life and frequently has very different consequences for men and women. The works listed here approach the complex subject of women in the development process from a multidisciplinary perspective. (Other useful bibliographies are described in the chapter devoted to national and area studies, chapter 9.12.)

Works on women and development are entered in the catalog under UNDERDEVELOPED AREAS--WOMEN and UNDERDEVELOPED AREAS--WOMEN'S EMPLOYMENT, and also under the more specific heading WOMEN IN RURAL DEVELOPMENT.

GUIDES TO RESEARCH

Daniells, Lorna. Business Information Sources.
Berkeley: University of California Press, 1976.   Z7164.
HF5030.   016.33.

Melnyk, Peter. Economics: Bibliographic Guide to
Reference Books and Information Sources. Littleton, CO:
Libraries Unlimited, 1971.   Z7164.E2.   016.33.

BIBLIOGRAPHIES ON WOMEN

Astin, Helen S., Nancy Suniewick, and Susan Dweck.
Women: A Bibliography on Their Education and Careers.
New York: Behavioral Publications, 1974.   Z7963.E7.
016.3314.

> Determinants of career choice, marital and family status of working women, the history and economics of women at work, and continuing education are among the topics covered. Primarily cites reports of research done in the 1960s, with an abstract for each entry. Author and subject indexes.

Bickner, Mei Liang. Women at Work: An Annotated
Bibliography. Los Angeles: Manpower Research Center,
University of California, 1974.   Z7963.E7.   HD6095.
016.3314.

Bickner, Mei Liang, and Marlene Shaughnessy. Women at
Work - Volume II: An Annotated Bibliography. Los
Angeles: Institute of Industrial Relations, University of
California, 1977.   Z7963.E7.   HD6095.   016.3314.

> These selective bibliographies list scholarly articles and research reports on working women, mostly published since 1960. The emphasis is on legal developments affecting women workers, women in the labor movement, and non-professional and minority women. Items are grouped in subject categories and indexed by author, title, and keyword.

Feinberg, Renee. Women, Education, and Employment: A
Bibliography of Periodical Citations, Pamphlets,
Newspapers, and Government Documents, 1970-1980.
Z5815.U5.   016.376.

> See chapter 9.4, "Education," for annotation.

Leavitt, Judith A. Women in Management: An Annotated Bibliography and Sourcelist. Phoenix: Oryx Press, 1982. Z7963.E7. HF5500.3.U54. 016.658.

Provides references to over 800 books, papers, newspaper and journal articles, and dissertations, all published between 1970 and 1981. The citations are arranged in 20 subject categories and represent the scholarly, professional, and popular literature. At this writing, the best bibliography available on women managers.

McFeely, Mary Drake. Women's Work in Britain and America from the Nineties to World War I: An Annotated Bibliography. Boston: G.K. Hall, 1982. Z7963.E7. HD6135. 016.3314.

Citing books, articles, and pamphlets written during or concerning the period from 1890 to 1914, this bibliography features informative annotations for 549 entries. There are two sections, one treating Great Britain and a shorter one devoted to the U.S. Author, title, and subject indexes compensate for the lack of more specific categories in the organization of entries.

Nicolas, Suzanne. Bibliography on Women Workers (1861-1965). Geneva: International Labour Office, 1970. Z7963.E7. 016.3314.

Despite its age, this bibliography is recommended for its international scope and its historical focus. Citations are arranged under eleven broad topics, with personal author, corporate author, subject, and geographic indexes.

Phelps, Ann T., Helen S. Farmer, and Thomas E. Backer. New Career Options for Women: A Selected Annotated Bibliography. New York: Human Sciences Press, 1977. Z7963.E7. HD6058. 016.3314.

Other bibliographies provide fuller coverage of books and articles, but this one, aimed at counselors, is an excellent source for research reports and government publications. Topic arrangement. Among the subjects addressed are professional women, craftswomen, women's earnings, working mothers, and sex bias in career counseling.

Soltow, Martha Jane, and Mary K. Wery. American Women and the Labor Movement, 1825-1974: An Annotated Bibliography. Metuchen, NJ: Scarecrow, 1976. Z7963.E7. HD6079.2.U5. 016.3314.

This annotated bibliography concentrates on the historical role of women in American labor unions. Background materials on factory conditions, protective legislation, and similar concerns are also included. Books, journal articles, pamphlets, and government publications are listed. U.S. archives of material on women and labor are mentioned in an appendix. A very useful source.

U.S. Air Force Academy. Library. Women and the American Economy. Colorado Springs: U.S. Air Force Academy Library, 1976. Z7963.E7. HQ1426. 016.3314.

In this easy-to-use bibliography, items are arranged under such categories as history, discrimination, and equal rights, and sub-divided by form: books, periodical articles, and government publications. Not annotated.

U.S. Office of Education. Bureau of Occupational and Adult Education. Women in Non-Traditional Occupations -- A Bibliography. Washington: U.S. Government Printing Office, 1976. HD6058. SuDoc. no. HE19.128:W84.

A "non-traditional occupation" is defined as any field in which women constitute less than 38% of the work force. This bibliography lists books, articles, pamphlets, published papers, and dissertations -- all published between 1970 and June 1976 -- about women in "male" jobs. References are grouped in three sections: overview materials; women in non-traditional skilled/vocational occupations; and women in non-traditional professional occupations.

BIBLIOGRAPHIES ON WOMEN AND DEVELOPMENT

Bibliographic Guide to Studies on the Status of Women: Development and Population Trends. New York: UNIPUB, 1983. Z7961. 016.305.

For annotation, see chapter 7, "General Women's Studies Bibliographies."

Buvinic, Mayra. Women and World Development: An Annotated Bibliography. Washington: Overseas Development Council, 1976. Z7961. HQ1390. 016.30141.

This annotated bibliography focuses on "the effects of socio-economic development and cultural change on women." Books, articles, unpublished reports, government documents, and conference papers are arranged in nine subject categories and sub-divided by geographic area. Topics covered include the role and status of women, female customs, the socio-economic participation of rural and urban women, education, health, politics, law, and women's formal and informal associations.

Rihani, May. Development as if Women Mattered: An Annotated Bibliography With a Third World Focus. Washington: New TransCentury Foundation, Secretariat for Women in Development, 1978. Z7963.E7. HD6223. 016.3314.

A selected bibliography of nearly 300 journal articles, conference papers, research reports, books, and documents, the majority in the English language. The emphasis is on "fugitive" publications and unpublished reports not listed in other bibliographies. Topical arrangement, with sub-groupings by region.

Saulniers, Suzanne Smith, and Cathy A. Rakowski. Women in the Development Process: A Select Bibliography on Women in Sub-Saharan Africa and Latin America. Austin: Institute of Latin American Studies, University of Texas, 1977. Z7961. HQ1870.9. 016.30141.

The compilers of this bibliography set out to "draw together references that can be used to evaluate women's actual and potential roles in institutional settings and in societal development in both sub-Saharan Africa and Latin America." Nearly 3,000 items -- books, articles, conference papers, pamphlets, and unpublished documents -- are listed, all issued between 1900 and 1975. Citations are grouped in ten topical chapters (e.g., "Women and the Family," "Women and the Polity," "Women and Social Change") and then arranged by country or region.

INDEXES AND CONTINUING BIBLIOGRAPHIES

The Business Index. Los Altos, CA: Information Access Corporation, 1979 to present.

This computer-generated microfilm index is updated each month. It fully indexes about 375 business periodicals, The Wall Street Journal, and Barron's, and also provides selected references to business-related articles in some 1,100 other periodicals and The New York Times. Books on business are included too. The A to Z listing includes subjects, titles, persons in the news, and authors. Under each heading, the most recent items are listed first. Short abstracts for journal articles appear at the end of the microfilm and are identified by number in the citations. Subject headings echo those used in the library's catalog; there are many references under WOMEN--EMPLOYMENT.

Business Periodicals Index. New York: H.W. Wilson, 1958 to present.   Z7164.C81.   016.6505.

In addition to general business periodicals and a few scholarly journals in economics, this monthly index covers a host of specialized trade publications. The total number of indexed periodicals is about 270. Articles on women are cited under the subject heading WOMEN and under headings starting with the word "women" -- e.g., WOMEN AS CONSUMERS, WOMEN EXECUTIVES, and WOMEN IN CONSTRUCTION. Other subjects include EQUAL PAY FOR EQUAL WORK, SEX DISCRIMINATION, WIVES, and the awkwardly constructed ADVERTISING, WOMEN, APPEAL TO. Cumulated annually.

Index of Economic Articles in Journals and Collective Volumes, 1886/1924-- . Homewood, IL: Irwin, 1961 to present.   Z7164.E2.   016.33.

This index lists English-language articles in 234 journals and anthologies. The early volumes spanned several years; volumes now appear annually. The first half of the volume arranges the references by subject in a complicated numerical classification. Use the "Topical Guide to Classification System" in the back of the volume to determine which categories contain articles about women. In the second half, references are alphabetical by the author's name.

International Bibliography of Economics. Chicago: Aldine, 1955 to present. Z7164.E2. 016.33.

An annual bibliography of scholarly books, articles, and research reports in economics. Citations are arranged in a classified topical outline. "Women" appears as a sub-section of the section on "Labor Problems," which in turn is one division of the broader category, "Organization of Production." Additional references related to women can be discovered by using the subject index. The bibliography's scope is international; all classification headings, introductory matter, and indexes are in both French and English.

Management Contents. Skokie, IL: G. D. Searle, 1975 to present. Z7164.07.

A biweekly compendium of the tables of contents of some 350 journals in the fields of business, management, accounting, economics, finance, management science, operations research, marketing, and personnel. WOMEN appears in the subject index. The index does not cumulate, so this is useful only a guide to the very latest articles.

Predicasts F & S Index United States. Cleveland: Predicasts, 1960 to present. Z7165.U5. 016.3380973.

A weekly index with monthly, quarterly, and annual cumulations. Citations from financial publications, business-oriented newspapers, trade magazines, and special reports are presented in two sections. The first section, "Industries and Products," is arranged by a coded classification scheme that enables one to zero in on articles about manufactured goods for women (e.g., tampons, women's apparel) or about industries employing women (e.g., textile mills). Section Two, "Companies," is arranged alphabetically by company name and allows one to investigate particular firms. Profiles of women executives, for instance, are listed by their companies. This source is complemented by the F & S Index International and the F & S Index Europe.

9.4 EDUCATION

The education of women has engendered much research and debate over the centuries, some of it objective and some highly polemical. The materials available range from historical studies of the gradual admission of women to higher levels of schooling, to assessments of the needs of today's women for scholarly and vocational training. Along the way, such issues as sexual harassment in the classroom, equity in school athletics, and career paths of female teachers are explored.

EDUCATION OF WOMEN is the basic subject heading used in the library's catalog, but a number of others also apply:

> COEDUCATION
> SEX DISCRIMINATION IN EDUCATION
> SEXISM IN TEXTBOOKS
> VOCATIONAL EDUCATION OF WOMEN
> WOMEN COLLEGE STUDENTS
> WOMEN COLLEGE TEACHERS
> WOMEN TEACHERS
> WOMEN'S COLLEGES
> WOMEN'S STUDIES

The issues of education and employment are closely linked. Background readings on women's educational preparation for particular careers will be found under headings such as WOMEN SCIENTISTS or WOMEN IN THE PROFESSIONS.

GUIDES TO RESEARCH

Berry, Dorothea M. A Bibliographic Guide to Educational Research. 2nd ed. Metuchen, NJ: Scarecrow, 1980. Z5811. LB17. 016.37.

Kennedy, James R., Jr. Library Research Guide to Education: Illustrated Search Strategy and Sources. Ann Arbor: Pierian Press, 1979. LB1028. 025.5.

Woodbury, Marda. A Guide to Sources of Educational Information. Washington: Information Resources Press, 1976. Z5811. LB7. 016.37.

BIBLIOGRAPHIES ON WOMEN

Astin, Helen S., Nancy Suniewick, and Susan Dweck. Women: A Bibliography on Their Education and Careers. New York: Behavioral Publications, 1974. Z7963.E7. 016.3314.

> See chapter 9.3, "Business, Economics, and Labor Studies," for annotation.

Cismaresco, Francoise. "Education and Training of Women." Educational Documentation and Information 196 (1975): 14-46. L10. 370.621.

> One of a series of multilingual bibliographic bulletins published by Unesco's International Bureau of Education. The 233 items are grouped by continent, with a "General Works" section of bibliographies, international documents, and comparative studies. This source updates an earlier bulletin, no. 174, "Access of Women to Education," published in 1970.

Feinberg, Renee. Women, Education, and Employment: A Bibliography of Periodical Citations, Pamphlets, Newspapers, and Government Documents, 1970-1980. Hamden, CT: Library Professional Publications, 1982. Z5815.U5. 016.376.

> The weak aspects of this bibliography are its lack of annotations and its complete exclusion of books and dissertations. Its strengths are an easy-to-use topical index and a well thought-out subject arrangement geared to the research needs of undergraduates. A good place to begin searching for writings on women's work and education from the 'seventies.

Froschl, Merle, and Jane Williamson. Feminist Resources for Schools and Colleges: A Guide to Curricular

Materials. 2nd ed. Old Westbury, NY: The Feminist Press, 1977. Z5817. LB3047. 016.379.

A handy annotated bibliography of nonsexist curricular materials for preschoolers through college students, plus recommended readings for educators and counselors. In addition to textbooks, anthologies, pamphlets, and articles, many nonprint sources -- such as films, recordings, posters, and games -- are listed.

Kelly, David H., and Gail P. Kelly. "Education of Women in Developing Countries." Educational Documentation and Information 222 (1982). L10. 370.621.

A bibliography of books, articles, reports, and conference proceedings on women's education in developing nations, organized by topic rather than country. The subjects covered include access of women and girls to education, aspiration and attitudes of female students, education and the workforce, and education and the family.

Parker, Franklin, and Betty June Parker. Women's Education - A World View. Vol. 2: Annotated Bibliography of Books and Reports. Westport, CT: Greenwood, 1981. Z7963.E2. LC1481. 016.376.

An exhaustive bibliography of nearly 4,000 books, government documents, and reports on every aspect of the education of women and girls. Unfortunately, citations are arranged alphabetically by author, with an inadequate subject index. Volume 1 of the set, published in 1979, covers doctoral disserions.

U.S. Office of Education. Women's Educational Equity Communications Network. Resources in Women's Educational Equity. Washington: U.S. Government Printing Office, 1977 to 1980. Z5815.U5. LC1751. 016.376 SuDoc no. HE19.128:W84.

Sadly, this useful annual bibliography was discontinued. The existing volumes (vols. 1-4, plus two special issues) cover thousands of books, articles, government documents, dissertations, and reports issued since 1971. Citations and abstracts are culled from twelve major data bases. In addition to writings on education, much background material is cited.

Wilkins, Kay S. Women's Education in the United States:
A Guide to Information Sources. Detroit: Gale, 1979.
Z7963.E2.   LC1752.   016.376.

This bibliography emphasizes publications from 1968
to 1978, although older historical materials are also
cited. The arrangement is topical, with author,
title, and subject indexes. A good starting point
for research on any aspect of women's schooling in
the U.S.

INDEXES AND CONTINUING BIBLIOGRAPHIES

Education Index. New York: H. W. Wilson, 1929 to
present.   Z5813.   016.3705.

The standard subject index to English-language
journals on education. In addition to articles on
all aspects and levels of education, this monthly
index covers child development, employment, and the
psychology of learning processes. Examples of
women's studies topics for which Education Index is
an excellent source are: math anxiety; women in
athletics; career counseling; home economics; sexism
in textbooks. Use the following subject headings:
WOMEN; BLACK WOMEN; COLLEGE STUDENTS; GIRLS; MOTHERS;
WOMEN AS EDUCATORS; WOMEN'S STUDIES; SEX ROLE; and
SEX DIFFERENCES.

Current Index to Journals in Education. Phoenix: Oryx
Press, 1969 to present.   Z5813.   016.370.

This monthly index is not quite as simple to use as
Education Index (see above), but it has the advantage
of annotations. Relevant subject headings include:
WOMEN'S EDUCATION; WOMEN'S STUDIES; WOMEN TEACHERS;
WOMEN'S ATHLETICS; FEMALES; FEMINISM. CIJE serves as
a companion source to Resources in Education (see
below).

Resources in Education. Washington: U.S. Department of
Education, National Institute of Education, 1966 to
present.   Z5813.   LB1028.   016.370   SuDoc no.
HE19.210.

Called Research in Education from 1966 to 1974. This
collection of abstracts, issued monthly with
semiannual and annual indexes, is in reality a
catalog of reports gathered by the sixteen

Educational Resources Information Center (ERIC) clearinghouses. Many libraries own the ERIC reports on microfiche; individual reports can be ordered on fiche or in paper copy. About 10,000 items are listed each year, many of them local documents that are not otherwise easily available. Indexing terminology is the same as that used in Current Index to Journals in Education (see above) and is outlined in the Thesaurus of ERIC Descriptors (see below).

Educational Resources Information Center. Thesaurus of ERIC Descriptors. 10th ed. Phoenix: Oryx Press, 1984. Z695.1.E3.   025.3.

A guide to the subject vocabulary used in Current Index to Journals in Education and Resources in Education (see above for both), as well as in their computerized counterpart, the ERIC data base.

9.5 HEALTH AND MEDICINE

Health issues have been a focal point of the women's movement since its beginnings. The first edition of the classic self-help sourcebook, Our Bodies, Ourselves appeared in 1971. Amid a welter of consumer-oriented publications on birth control, pregnancy, psychotherapy, drugs, occupational hazards, nutrition, and other health issues, there is a growing attention to women in the professional literature of the medical, psychiatric, and public health fields. Researchers are also studying the roles of women as providers of health care, in addition to their roles as consumers of health-related services and products.

This chapter is concerned only with general works on women's health and women in the medical professions. No attempt is made to include bibliographies that focus on narrower topics. One deserving of mention, however, is the annual Abortion Bibliography, covering the medical and popular literature since 1970 (Troy, NY: Whitston, 1972 to present). You can find other specialized bibliographies by looking in the catalog under the specific subjects.

Most general works on women's health and medical care are entered in the catalog under the heading WOMEN--HEALTH AND HYGIENE. Other relevant subject headings are:

    WOMEN--DISEASES
    WOMEN--MENTAL HEALTH
    PHYSICAL FITNESS FOR WOMEN
    DRUGS AND WOMEN
    GYNECOLOGY
    WOMEN--PHYSIOLOGY
    WOMEN'S HEALTH SERVICES
    WOMEN IN MEDICINE
    WOMEN PHYSICIANS.

GUIDES TO RESEARCH

Morton, Leslie Thomas. How to Use a Medical Library.
6th ed. London: Heinemann Medical, 1979.   Z675.M4.
026.61.

BIBLIOGRAPHIES ON WOMEN

Cowan, Belita. Women's Health Care: Resources,
Writings, Bibliographies. Ann Arbor, MI: Anshen
Publishing, 1977.   RG121.

   A collection of short articles on many aspects of
   women's health care, each with a bibliography of
   books, journal articles, government documents, and
   reports. Also listed are films, periodicals, and
   organizations.

Women and the Health System: Selected Annotated
References. Hyattsville, MD: U.S. Department of Health,
Education and Welfare, Public Health Service, Health
Resources Administration, 1978.   R692.   362.1.   SuDoc
no. HE20.6112/2:4.

   This selective bibliography treats women as health
   care consumers, as paid health care providers and
   decision makers, and as extra-market health care
   providers. Only publications of the 1970s are
   included. The lengthy annotations are a plus.

Women in Medicine: A Bibliography of the Literature on
Women Physicians. Compiled by Sandra L. Chaff, Ruth
Haimbach, Carol Fenichel, and Nina B. Woodside.
Metuchen, NJ: Scarecrow, 1977.   Z7963.M43.   R692.
016.61069.

   This comprehensive bibliography cites over 4,000
   books, articles, and doctoral theses on women as
   physicians and healers. Literature on nursing is not
   included. Dates of publication range from the mid-
   18th century to 1975. Nearly all the entries are
   annotated. The scope of each topical section is
   explained in the table of contents; within each
   chapter, entries are grouped geographically. Author
   and subject indexes add to the usefulness of this
   bibliography.

INDEXES AND CONTINUING BIBLIOGRAPHIES

Bibliography on the History of Medicine. Washington: U.S. Department of Health and Human Services, Public Health Service, National Institutes of Health, 1964 to present.   Z6660.   016.61.   SuDoc no. HE20.3615.

This annual bibliography, cumulated quinquennially, has three parts: biographies, subjects, and authors. There is a category called "Women in Medicine" in the subject section. Additional works on women's health and women as medical practitioners can be found under "Nursing," "Witchcraft," "Birth control," "Obstetrics," and "Gynecology."

Index Medicus. Washington: National Library of Medicine, 1960 to present.   Z6660.   016.61.   SuDoc no. HE20.3612.

This index has been issued under various titles since 1879. The current monthly series covers some 3,000 journals in medicine and related fields. A thesaurus, Medical Subject Headings, is published annually and should be consulted before attempting to search the index.

International Nursing Index. New York: American Journal of Nursing, 1966 to present.   Z6675.N7.   610.73.

This quarterly index covers over 200 professional nursing journals from around the world and also indexes nursing articles in some 2,200 other periodicals. Citations are entered under both authors and subjects. The annual cumulation contains a thesaurus of subject headings. Besides the term WOMEN, there are topical entries such as MASTECTOMY, CONTRACEPTION, MIDWIFERY, and NURSES, MALE, plus many entries for scientific medical terms.

Nursing and Allied Health Index. Glendale, CA: Glendale Adventist Medical Center, 1961 to present.   Z6675. 016.61.

This bimonthly index covers some 300 English-language nursing and medical periodicals. The final issue of the year is an annual cumulation, titled Cumulative Index to Nursing and Allied Health Literature. Each issue is divided into two sections, for subjects and authors, with listings in the back for audiovisual materials, book reviews, and pamphlets. The annual volume includes a thesaurus of subject headings. In addition to WOMEN, there are numerous topical headings such as RAPE, OBSTETRICS, MIDWIFERY, and SEX BEHAVIOR. Researchers without medical training may feel more comfortable with the subject indexing in this source than with the more technical terms used in <u>International Nursing Index</u> (see above).

9.6 HISTORY

The secondary literature of women's history -- especially American women's history -- is more fully documented than in most other branches of women's studies. You will find, for instance, that many of the bibliographies contained in other chapters include historical studies. Recovering women's lost "herstory" has been a priority not only for historians, but for scholars in every field. Art critics have revived interest in forgotten female painters, sculptors, and quilters. Literary scholars have pored over dusty novels to discern a tradition in the themes and styles of women authors over the centuries. Women entering a predominantly male field -- be it mathematics, mining, or the military -- have recorded the lives of those who preceded them and who serve as inspiring role models. Knowledge of women's history illuminates the present and shapes women's visions of the future. While the full picture of women's past is far from complete, the secondary literature is rich indeed.

Well-trained historians, of course, require more than the writings of other historians. Whenever possible, they must examine original documents from the period they are studying. Researchers who rely heavily on primary sources are blessed with <u>Women's History Sources</u> (see chapter 10), a groundbreaking guide to collections of manuscripts and archives. Some of the bibliographies presented in this chapter cover primary sources as well. You can consult the chapters on newspapers, government documents, and catalogs of special collections for further aid in identifying and locating source materials.

In the library catalog, general works on the history of women are entered under WOMEN--HISTORY. Headings such as WOMEN--EMPLOYMENT--HISTORY, AFRO-AMERICAN WOMEN--HISTORY, and WOMEN--FRANCE--HISTORY are applied to books with a narrower focus. In addition, look for both current historical studies and older writings under such entries as WOMEN--SUFFRAGE and WOMEN--SOCIAL AND MORAL

QUESTIONS.
A number of bibliographies have been published which deal with state or local history. An example is New Jersey Women, 1770-1970, by Elizabeth Steiner-Scott and Elizabeth Pearce Wagle (Rutherford, NJ: Fairleigh Dickenson University Press, 1978). You can find such specialized aids in your library's catalog under the subject entry WOMEN--[PLACE]--BIBLIOGRAPHY.

Older bibliographies on contemporary topics often have historical significance today. Two examples are: Margaret Ladd Franklin, The Case for Woman Suffrage: A Bibliography (New York: National College Equal Suffrage League, 1913); and Marion R. Nims, Women in the War: A Bibliography (Washington: U.S. Government Printing Office, 1918). Finding a bibliography compiled during the period you're studying can save you untold hours of digging through general sources.

Because the history of women is inextricably entwined with their roles in the family, this chapter includes a short section on the relatively new field of family history.

GUIDES TO RESEARCH

Benjamin, Jules R. A Student's Guide to History. 3rd ed. New York: St. Martin's, 1983. D16.3. 907.

Frick, Elizabeth. Library Research Guide to History: Illustrated Search Strategy and Sources. Ann Arbor: Pierian Press, 1980. D16. 907.

McCoy, Florence N. Researching and Writing in History: A Practical Handbook for Students. Berkeley: University of California Press, 1974. D16. 808.

Poulton, Helen J. The Historian's Handbook: A Descriptive Guide to Reference Works. Norman: University of Oklahoma Press, 1972. Z6201. 016.9.

Shafer, Robert Jones. A Guide to Historical Method. 3rd ed. Homewood, IL: Dorsey, 1980. D16. 902.

BIBLIOGRAPHIES ON WOMEN - UNITED STATES

Bass, Dorothy. American Women in Church and Society, 1607-1920: A Bibliography. New York: Union Theological Seminary, 1973. Z7964.U49. 016.30141.

This annotated bibliography is a handy source for

references on the history of women in America before
1920. Items are arranged in subject categories,
covering such areas as women on the frontier, women
and slavery, family life and the cult of domesticity,
sects and utopian communities, women in the church,
and working women. The real strength of this
bibliography is the inclusion of selected nineteenth-
century materials -- books on etiquette, dress, and
sexual hygiene, early essays on women's education,
contemporary accounts of the suffrage and temperance
movements, and so on.

The Common Women Collective. Women in U.S. History: An Annotated Bibliography. Cambridge, MA: The Collective, 1976. Z7964.U49. HQ1410. 016.30141.

This selective bibliography has been praised for its
emphasis on Third World and working women and
criticized for the unevenness of its topical
coverage. Since many valuable references are omitted
and it is now several years old, one should use this
bibliography as a starting point but never rely on it
solely. Citations are arranged by topic, with cross-
references between categories. Evaluative
annotations are provided.

Conway, Jill. The Female Experience in Eighteenth- and Nineteenth-Century America: A Guide to the Study of the History of American Women. New York: Garland, 1982. Z7961. HQ1410. 016.3054.

The compiler describes this work as "a bibliography
and an interpretive guide to sources on the history
of women in America and an extended commentary about
the theories and assumptions which have shaped
secondary writing on that history." The volume
consists of over 50 short essays surveying the
literature on various aspects of American women's
history, followed by bibliographies of both primary
and secondary works.

Harrison, Cynthia, editor. Women in American History: A Bibliography. Santa Barbara: ABC-Clio, 1979. Z7962. HQ1410. 016.30141.

This cumulated bibliography offers an efficient means
of identifying historical writings on all aspects of
the lives of women in the United States and Canada.
Topics range from women's roles in the political and
economic spheres to their self-image and cultural

participation. Most of the abstracts in this volume were culled from the 1964-1977 issues of America: History and Life (see below), and that series should be used when searching for more recent publications. Both sources use a similar chronological and topical pattern of organization.

Krichmar, Albert. The Women's Rights Movement in the United States, 1848-1970: A Bibliography and Sourcebook. Metuchen, NJ: Scarecrow, 1972. Z7964.U49. 016.30141.

This impressive bibliography covers the legal, political, economic, religious, educational, and professional status of American women between 1848 and 1970. 5,170 books, periodical articles, dissertations, pamphlets, and federal and state documents are listed. Biographies, manuscript collections, and women's liberation periodicals are covered in separate sections. Arrangement of citations is by subject, with author, subject, and manuscript indexes. Coverage for the 1970s can be found in Krichmar's later work, The Women's Movement in the Seventies: An International English-Language Bibliography (see chapter 7).

Leonard, Eugenie A., Sophie H. Drinker, and Miriam Y. Holden. The American Woman in Colonial and Revolutionary Times, 1565-1800: A Syllabus with Bibliography. Philadelphia: University of Pennsylvania Press, 1962. Z7964.U49. 016.3960973.

This guide to information on women during the Colonial and Revolutionary periods combines a syllabus (arranged by topic) with a lengthy bibliography (arranged by author). 1,084 books and articles are listed in the bibliography. The syllabus, in outline form, refers the user to specific readings. Material on 104 outstanding colonial women is presented in an appendix. Many aspects of women's lives are covered, including status and rights, religion, schooling, home life, business and industry, and the arts. Because this volume was published in 1962, the rich harvest of recent scholarship is of course not reflected in it.

Lerner, Gerda. Bibliography in the History of American Women. 3rd ed. Bronxville, NY: Sarah Lawrence College, 1978.

The final version of a reading list prepared by one

of the leading scholars in women's history. To date, no trade publication has equaled this bibliography in its interdisciplinary scope and informed selectivity. Over a thousand citations are listed under broad subject categories; older books and articles as well as newer scholarship are included. There are no annotations nor indexes.

Tingley, Elizabeth, and Donald F. Tingley. <u>Women and Feminism in American History: A Guide to Information Sources.</u> Detroit: Gale, 1981.   Z7964.U49.   HQ1410. 016.3054.

A selected bibliography on women's history in the U.S., listing primarily books. All citations are briefly annotated. The thirty-three chapters cover types of publications (bibliographies, biographical directories, and periodicals, for example), periods of American history, areas of women's activities ("Women in the Arts" and "Women in Business and the Professions," for example), and specific issues, including ethnic and minority women, psychology, sexuality and sexual orientation, abortion and birth control, motherhood, and more. Author, title, and subject indexes.

BIBLIOGRAPHIES ON WOMEN - FOREIGN

NOTE: Most bibliographies treating specific countries have been placed in chapter 9.12, "National and Area Studies." The majority of such works contain helpful sections on history. The sources listed below, by contrast, either are purely historical in their focus or treat more than one nation.

Frey, Linda, Marsha Frey, and Joanne Schneider. <u>Women in Western European History: A Select Chronological, Geographical, and Topical Bibliography from Antiquity to the French Revolution.</u> Westport, CT: Greenwood, 1982. Z7961.   016.3054.

This massive bibliography offers citations to 6,894 secondary works on the history of women in Western Europe to 1789. Primary sources, such as memoirs and letters, are not listed, nor are literary works. Citations are presented in a complex outline based first on traditional historical periods and then on geographic/political divisions. Within these sections, entries are categorized in topical hierarchies, making it possible to look up very specific subjects (including individual women) using the introductory outline and topical guide. There is also a subject index, as well as indexes to authors and names. Entries are not annotated. A second volume is promised to continue the survey to the present.

Goodwater, Leanna. Women in Antiquity: An Annotated Bibliography. Metuchen, NJ: Scarecrow, 1975. Z7961. HQ1127. 016.30141.

An annotated bibliography covering the political, social, legal, and cultural position of women in Greece and Rome from the earliest records to 476 A.D. Both original classical sources and modern studies are included. English-language works are covered comprehensively; writings in other languages are listed selectively.

Kelly, Joan. Bibliography in the History of European Women. 4th ed. Bronxville, NY: Sarah Lawrence College, 1976. Z7961.

A reading list compiled by one of the leading scholars of women's history. Both primary and secondary sources on European women from antiquity to World War II are cited. The basic arrangement of the bibliography is by standard chronological periods, with additional topical sections. Under WOMEN IN THE MIDDLE AGES, for instance, there are sub-sections focusing on socio-economic and political conditions, literature and the arts, monasticism and the Church, courtly love, law and the family, and the Mary cult. So far, no trade bibliography has duplicated the scope, selectivity, and wide time frame of this source.

BIBLIOGRAPHIES ON FAMILY HISTORY

History of the Family and Kinship: A Select International Bibliography. Edited by Gerald L. Soliday. Millwood, NY: Kraus, 1980. Z7164.M2. HQ503. 016.3068.

The compilation of this mammoth bibliography was a special project of the Journal of Family History. The scope is international, from pre-history to the present. Over 6,000 citations to books and articles are grouped by geographic area. Since different scholars were responsible for the various areas, the schemes for ordering references within each section vary. For example, works on Central Europe are listed chronologically, those on Southeast Asia by nation, and those on the Middle East and North Africa by topic.

Milden, James Wallace. The Family in Past Time: A Guide to the Literature. New York: Garland, 1977. Z5118.F2. HQ503. 016.907.

The subject scope of this annotated bibliography is international, but all of the writings cited are in English. Section I treats methodology and theory. Sections II, III, and IV focus on the family in European history, American history, and non-Western history, respectively. Section V, titled "Family History Projects," includes some materials on genealogy. Birth control, children, demography, domestic architecture, domestic life and customs, family composition and structure, family law and inheritance, kinship, sexuality, and women are the categories employed within each section.

INDEXES AND CONTINUING BIBLIOGRAPHIES

America: History and Life. Santa Barbara: ABC-Clio, 1964 to present. Z1236. 016.917.

A classified abstracting service on American and Canadian history. As of 1975, it is issued in four parts. Part A, published three times a year, contains abstracts of articles, arranged by period before 1945 and by topic post-1945. Women's studies topics are best approached through the detailed subject index in each issue. Part B, published twice a year, is an index to book reviews. Part C, issued annually, is an unannotated bibliography of books, articles, and dissertations. Part D is a cumulative index for the year. Abstracts of articles on women's history are reproduced in Women in American History: A Bibliography (see above), so only the post-1977 issues need to be consulted.

Historical Abstracts. Santa Barbara: ABC-Clio, 1955 to present. D229. 909.8082.

World history from 1775 to 1945 is covered in this

quarterly abstracting journal. American history is included only in issues before 1963, when <u>America: History and Life</u> began publication (see above). Each issue consists of two parts. Part A is titled "Modern History Abstracts." Part B is "Twentieth Century Abstracts." Each section is arranged by topic and area or country. Women's history is generally subsumed under "Social and Cultural History." The subject index is the key to relevant abstracts in other categories. Full abstracts are provided for periodical articles; books and dissertations are merely cited. Cumulative author and subject indexes are compiled every five years.

<u>Recently Published Articles</u>. Washington: American Historical Association, 1976 to present. Z6205. D1. 016.905.

An up-to-date bibliography of periodical articles in world history, classified by area and period, issued three times a year. Unfortunately, there is no topical index.

<u>Writings on American History</u>. Washington: American Historical Association, 1908 to present. Z1236. 016.97.

A classified annual bibliography of books, articles, and reviews in both English and foreign languages. Since 1936, coverage is limited to the U.S.; earlier volumes treat Canada and Latin America as well. In 1948 reviews were dropped, and as of 1973 coverage was limited to periodical articles. Entries are not annotated. Recent volumes include a separate section on women's history under the larger category of social history. Author, title, and subject indexes are provided.

9.7 LAW AND CRIMINOLOGY

Women's legal rights vary from country to country and from state to state. New laws and court rulings -- decriminalizing abortion, for example, and mandating affirmative action -- have materially affected the lives of contemporary men and women. The sudden rise in the number of female lawyers has also altered women's relationship to the legal process.
This chapter contains general bibliographic works on law and crime, plus bibliographies on legal issues and crimes that particularly affect women -- the Equal Rights Amendment, sexual discrimination, rape, and prostitution. Legal information is codified in ways that can bewilder non-specialists, so if you are using a law library for the first time, be bold in seeking the advice of a librarian.
Probably the most common headings in the catalog for works on laws relating to women are SEX DISCRIMINATION AGAINST WOMEN--LAW AND LEGISLATION and WOMEN--LEGAL STATUS, LAWS, ETC. The phrase LAW AND LEGISLATION is also appended to more specific subject entries such as SEX DISCRIMINATION IN EDUCATION and SEX DISCRIMINATION IN CONSUMER CREDIT. Headings such as WOMEN LAWYERS and WOMEN JUDGES identify books about women in the legal professions, while FEMALE OFFENDERS is the broad term for women criminals. Specific topics such as RAPE or PROSTITUTION are accorded their own headings.

GUIDES TO RESEARCH

Cohen, Morris L. Legal Research in a Nutshell. 3rd ed. St. Paul: West, 1978. KF240. 340.

Jacobstein, J. Myron, and Roy M. Mersky. Fundamentals of Legal Research. 2nd ed. Mineola, NY: Foundation Press, 1981. KF240. 340.

Price, Miles O., Harry Bitner, and Shirley R. Bysiewicz.
Effective Legal Research. 4th ed. Boston: Little,
Brown, 1979. KF240. 340.

Wren, Christopher G., and Jill Robinson Wren. The Legal
Research Manual: A Game Plan for Legal Research and
Analysis. Madison, WI: A-R Editions, 1983. KF240.
340.

BIBLIOGRAPHIES ON WOMEN

Kemmer, Elizabeth Jane. Rape and Rape-Related Issues:
An Annotated Bibliography. New York: Garland, 1977.
Z7164.S44. HV6561. 016.3641.

The books and periodical articles listed in this
bibliography are described in long, well phrased
annotations. Entries are arranged alphabetically by
author, with a subject index.

A Bibliography of Prostitution. By Vern Bullough and
others. New York: Garland, 1977. Z7164.P9. HQ111.
016.30141.

An exhaustive interdisciplinary listing of 6,494
books, periodical articles, documents, and reports on
prostitution, from the 19th and 20th centuries.
Arranged in subject categories, with an author index.

Equal Rights Amendment Project. The Equal Rights
Amendment: A Bibliographic Study. Westport, CT:
Greenwood, 1976. KF4758.A1. 016.342.

Compiled when passage of the ERA seemed within reach,
this comprehensive bibliography lists items published
between 1914 and January 1976. Arranged by type of
material: 1) Congressional publications; 2) other
federal and state publications; 3) books, portions of
books, and dissertations; 4) pamphlets, brochures,
reports, papers, etc.; 5) periodical materials,
encompassing newspapers, newsletters, legal and
scholarly journals, and popular magazines. An author
index and an organization index are appended.

Hughes, Marija Matich. The Sexual Barrier: Legal,
Medical, Economic, and Social Aspects of Sex
Discrimination. Washington: Hughes Press, 1977.
KF4758.A1. 016.30141.

Not limited to legal issues, this bibliography lists
over 8,000 books, journal articles, pamphlets, and
government documents published between 1960 and 1975,
on every aspect and type of sex discrimination. The
chapter on employment, for instance, includes
sections on affirmative action, career counseling,
labor unions, parttime work, equal wages, and want
ads. Many of the entries are annotated. The
compiler of this monumental guide is chief librarian
of the U.S. Commission on Civil Rights.

INDEXES AND CONTINUING BIBLIOGRAPHIES

Index to Legal Periodicals. New York: H.W. Wilson, 1908
to present.   K9.N32.   016.34705.

This is the index to law journals most likely to be
in general libraries. It is issued monthly, with
cumulated issues every quarter and cumulated bound
volumes annually and triennially. Articles in over
370 periodicals and annual reviews are indexed by
subject and author. Among the useful headings are:
DISCRIMINATION:SEX; WOMEN; MARRIED WOMEN; HUSBAND AND
WIFE; ABORTION; RAPE; and for articles on
pornography, OBSCENITY. Each issue includes a
separate "Table of Cases Commented Upon," a "Table of
Statutes Commented Upon," and an index to book
reviews.

Index to Periodical Articles Related to Law. Dobbs
Ferry, NY: Glanville, 1958 to present.   KF8.   016.34.

This quarterly index is designed to complement the
Index to Legal Periodicals (see above). Unlike its
companion, however, Index to Periodical Articles
Related to Law does not fully index a select number
of journals, but instead culls relevant articles in
the social and behavioral sciences from a wide range
of scholarly and popular publications. Arrangement
is by subject. WOMEN is used as a term, as are
specific issues such as ABORTION and RAPE. Writings
on sex discrimination, however, are not separately
identified.

Legal Resources Index. Los Altos, CA: Information Access
Corporation, 1980 to present.

This index on microfilm, which is cumulated and
reissed monthly, offers an alternative to the

standard printed indexes. Its advantages are several. First, full bibliographic information is given at every indexing point. Second, subject headings are based on the <u>Library of Congress Subject Headings</u>, making it easy to move between the library catalog and this index to identify both books and articles on a chosen topic. Third, a number of non-law publications are also indexed, including newspapers, government documents, and journals in fields such as labor relations and politics. Instructions in the use of the index are printed at the start of the film.

9.8 LESBIAN STUDIES

The lesbian perspective has been important in the evolution of women's studies, particularly in theoretical areas. In addition, lesbian feminists have nourished an alternative "womyn's culture" that sustains and supports unconventional women both within and outside of academia.

A small number of reference works focus exclusively on lesbian materials, but works by and about lesbians can often be located in more general women's studies sources. Lesbian feminists have established several publishing houses and periodicals; their publications are a good source of information and opinion not often found in more scholarly sources.

In the catalog, materials are listed under LESBIANS, LESBIANISM, and LESBIAN COUPLES. Works treating both lesbians and gay men will be found under the broader headings HOMOSEXUALS and HOMOSEXUALITY.

Lesbian Studies: Present and Future. Edited by Margaret Cruikshank. Old Westbury, NY: The Feminist Press, 1982. HQ75.3.   306.7.

This pathbreaking collection of essays on studying and teaching about lesbians includes a long bibliographic appendix (pp. 237-274). The "Books" section of the appendix covers both fiction and nonfiction and is usefully organized by subject and genre. "Articles," on the other hand, is an uncategorized listing by author. To date, this is the most comprehensive general bibliography in lesbian studies. Additional reference information is included elsewhere in the volume -- e.g., an extensive list of current and ceased lesbian periodicals in an article about the Lesbian Periodicals Index (which is yet to be published). An appendix titled "Resources" covers archives, special projects, slide shows and other audiovisual materials, groups, publishers, dissertations, works-in-progress, and more.

Grier, Barbara. <u>The Lesbian in Literature: A Bibliography</u>. 3rd ed. Tallahassee: Naiad Press, 1981. Z5866.L4. PN56.L45. 016.8088.

Novels, short stories, poetry, drama, and biography (both factual and fictionalized) are included in this bibliography. The compiler uses a letter code to indicate the degree of emphasis on lesbian characters and action in each work cited, and asterisks to convey her judgment of the quality.

Roberts, J.R. <u>Black Lesbians: An Annotated Bibliography</u>. Tallahassee: Naiad Press, 1981. HQ75.6.U5. 306.7.

A comprehensive, thematically organized, annotated bibliography of writings by and about Black lesbians. Fiction and musical recordings are included, in addition to nonfiction books, articles, and periodicals.

9.9 LINGUISTICS

Feminist language reform has often been ridiculed. Its detractors object to neologisms such as "Ms.," "chairperson," and "herstory," and view attempts to create gender-neutral texts as assaults on the English tongue. Nonetheless, recent scholarship has shown that the language we use and receive, both in formal and informal communication, significantly affects the ways in which we perceive our world and the people who populate it. Linguists study how women and men communicate with different vocabularies, inflections, and gestures; how adults speak differently to boys and girls; and how conversation patterns are established in mixed-sex groups. The notion of a "female language" has become one of the central concerns of feminist literary criticism, and the belief that language directly influences learning has led to widespread revision of the prose, as well as the subject content, of elementary readers.

In the card catalog, you will find the headings WOMEN--LANGUAGE, LANGUAGE AND LANGUAGES--SEX DIFFERENCES, and SEXISM IN LANGUAGE. Additional materials may be listed under the more general subject SOCIOLINGUISTICS and under phrases such as ENGLISH LANGUAGE--SEX DIFFERENCES or GERMAN LANGUAGE--SOCIAL ASPECTS.

GUIDES TO RESEARCH

There is no recent basic guide to recommend.

BIBLIOGRAPHIES ON WOMEN

Jarrard, Mary E. W., and Phyllis R. Randall. <u>Women Speaking: An Annotated Bibliography of Verbal and</u>

Nonverbal Communication, 1970-1980. New York: Garland, 1982.   HQ1426.   016.3054.

Although it only covers a decade of publications, this is the most comprehensive bibliography in print on women and language. The compilers cite over 1,300 studies, primarily reported in journals, from a multitude of disciplines. Women's literary expression and studies of the mass media are not covered.

Language, Gender, and Society. Edited by Barrie Thorne, Cheris Kramarae, and Nancy Henley. Rowley, MA: Newbury House, 1983.   P120.S48.   401.

The first half of this volume is a collection of ten essays. The second half (pp. 153-342) is titled "Sex Similarities and Differences in Language, Speech, and Nonverbal Communication: An Annotated Bibliography." The bibliography has several major divisions, covering such topics as stereotypes and perceptions of language use, conversational interaction, children and language, and gender marking and sex bias in language structure and content. It updates an earlier reading list in Language and Sex: Difference and Dominance, edited by Thorne and Henley (Rowley, MA: Newbury House, 1975).

INDEXES AND CONTINUING BIBLIOGRAPHIES

LLBA: Language and Language Behavior Abstracts. La Jolla, CA: Sociological Abstracts, 1967 to present. Z7001.   016.4.

This quarterly abstracting service uses a classified arrangement. Citations on women and language fall into the category "Sociolinguistics." Unfortunately, the subject index is of no help in identifying specific entries relevant to women's studies.

Modern Language Association of America. MLA International Bibliography of Books and Articles on the Modern Languages and Literatures. New York: Modern Language Association of America, 1963 to present. Z7006.   016.4.

Volume III of this essential series covers linguistics. Entries are classified by topic and language group. Citations on women and language

generally fall into "Sociolinguistics," and
especially into the sub-category "Social dialects."
In the subject index, WOMEN'S SPEECH and WOMEN--
LANGUAGE reveal additional references. (For a fuller
description of the MLA International Bibliography and
its publishing history, see chapter 9.10,
"Literature.")

9.10 LITERATURE

Literary history and criticism were early outposts of women's studies, perhaps because novels, stories, poems, and plays that pictured women's lives were more readily accessible than other documentary sources, or perhaps simply because English departments employ more female professors than most departments. Two major streams of scholarship swell and intermingle in the field of literature. One current focuses on re-examining the work of well-known writers from a feminist perspective, with particular attention to their treatment of female characters. The other attempts to learn about women from their own creative output. Many "lost" women writers have been rediscovered, and the works of the famous few -- Jane Austen, Emily Dickinson, Virginia Woolf, for example -- have been reappraised.
Feminist critics cast a wide net, analyzing not only writing deliberately addressed to an audience of educated readers, but also popular "sentimental" fiction and letters and diaries never intended for publication. In this they are like the art historians who point to the skill and inspiration in quilts, woven coverlets, and embroidered bodices. The scholarship on women and literature is rich and varied, and a number of bibliographies and reference works have been compiled to chronicle its progress.
Books about the representation of women in literary works are entered in the library catalog under WOMEN IN LITERATURE. Works about women writers may be found under WOMEN AUTHORS, WOMEN POETS, and so forth, or under such headings as AMERICAN LITERATURE--WOMEN AUTHORS. For books about particular themes, try entries like FEMINISM IN LITERATURE or MOTHERS IN LITERATURE. These headings apply to critical studies; novels are not listed in the catalog under subject. The newer heading FEMINISM AND LITERATURE is applied to many recent works of criticism.
Anthologies of literature by women may be categorized as WOMEN'S WRITINGS or WOMEN--LITERARY COLLECTIONS. When

appropriate, the genre is highlighted (e.g., WOMEN--
POETRY). Books by or about an individual author will be
found under her name, as will bibliographies of an
author's works and/or critical studies of her writings
and life.

GUIDES TO RESEARCH

Fenster, Valmai Kirkham. <u>Guide to American Literature</u>.
Littleton, CO: Libraries Unlimited, 1983.   Z1225.
PS88.   016.81.

Gohdes, Clarence, and Sanford E. Marovitz.
<u>Bibliographical Guide to the Study of the Literature of
the U.S.A.</u> 5th ed. Durham, NC: Duke University Press,
1984.   Z1225.   PS88.   016.81.

Patterson, Margaret C. <u>Literary Research Guide</u>. 2nd ed.
New York: Modern Language Association, 1983.   Z6511.
PN43.   016.8.

Schweik, Robert C., and Dieter Riesner. <u>Reference
Sources in English and American Literature: An Annotated
Bibliography</u>. New York: Norton, 1977.   Z2011.   PR83.
016.82.

NOTE: Research guides are also available for literature
in foreign languages. You can locate such guides by
looking in the library catalog under such headings as
GERMAN LITERATURE--BIBLIOGRAPHY or REFERENCE BOOKS--
SPANISH LITERATURE--BIBLIOGRAPHY.

BIBLIOGRAPHIES OF LITERARY WORKS BY WOMEN

<u>American Women Writers: A Critical Reference Guide from
Colonial Times to the Present</u>. Edited by Lina Mainiero.
New York: Ungar, 1979-82. 4 vols.   PS147.   016.30141.

This set provides biographical and critical
background on over a thousand American women authors.
Each entry includes a checklist of the author's works
and a selected bibliography of secondary literature.
In addition to women of established literary
reputation, these volumes cover authors of popular
fiction, non-literary works, letters, diaries,
autobiographies, and children's books. A good
beginning point for research, especially on minor
writers. Also available in a two-volume paperback
abridged edition.

Daims, Diva, and Janet Grimes. Toward a Feminist Tradition: An Annotated Bibliography of Novels in English by Women, 1891-1920. New York: Garland, 1982. Z2013.5.W6. PR830.W6. 016.823.

Although concentrating on only a thirty-year span, this bibliography includes 3,407 books by 1,723 authors. The compilers selected works that illustrate a "feminist tradition" in writing by women, particularly as evidenced by unconventional female characters. The annotations are derived from contemporary reviews, and therefore they vary greatly in length, style, and relevance to literary research. The arrangement of the entries is alphabetic by author, with a title index; one cannot sift out works with thematic similarities.

Reardon, Joan, and Kristine A. Thorsen. Poetry by American Women, 1900-1975: A Bibliography. Metuchen, NJ: Scarecrow, 1979. Z1229.W8. PS151. 016.811.

A guide to the published works of more than 5,500 women poets in the United States, arranged alphabetically by name with a title index. Particularly useful for its inclusion of elusive small press and feminist press books.

Resnick, Margery, and Isabelle de Courtivron. Women Writers in Translation: An Annotated Bibliography, 1945-1982. New York: Garland, 1984. Z7963.A8. PN471. 016.8088.

A handy guide to English translations of literary writings. Over one-third of the volume cites translations of works by French, French-Canadian, and other Francophone authors. Other chapters treat materials originally published in Portuguese, German, Italian, Japanese, Russian, and Spanish. Chapter introductions outline scope and methodology and highlight important works that remain untranslated. There is a short note on each author, followed by an annotated list of her works. Except for the chapter on German literature, which includes some works published in journals and anthologies, only books are listed.

Women and Literature: An Annotated Bibliography of Women Writers. 3rd ed. Cambridge, MA: Women and Literature Collective, 1976. Z5917.W6. PN3401. 016.80883.

This pioneering bibliography, first issued in 1973, remains an excellent introduction to works of fiction by women. Although many nationalities and time periods are represented, most of the 800-plus entries are for twentieth-century American and British novels. The evaluative annotations and the thematic index make this a handy guide for personal reading. Brief biographies are provided for major authors. Anthologies and book-length critical studies are also listed.

BIBLIOGRAPHIES OF LITERARY WORKS ABOUT WOMEN

Bakerman, Jane S., and Mary Jean DeMarr. Adolescent Female Portraits in the American Novel, 1961-1981. New York: Garland, 1983.   Z1231.F4.   PS374.A3.   813.

579 novels published over a twenty-year period are cited in this guide, including a few aimed at young readers. The introduction delineates common images of adolescent women and provides a checklist that keys the entries to these images. The bibliography is arranged alphabetically by author, with long annotations that summarize the plots and themes of the novels.

Daims, Diva, and Janet Grimes. Toward a Feminist Tradition: An Annotated Bibliography of Novels in English by Women, 1891-1920. New York: Garland, 1982. Z2013.5.W6.   PR830.W6.   016.823.

See above for annotation.

King, Betty. Women of the Future: The Female Main Character in Science Fiction. Metuchen, NJ: Scarecrow, 1984.   PS374.S35.   813.

A guide to women characters in book-length science fiction. The first chapter covers 1818 to 1929; subsequent chapters examine every decade through the 1980s. Selected stories are singled out for in-depth descriptions of their characters and summaries of their plots. Indexes point the researcher to such subjects as the "physical and mental/emotional qualities" of the characters.

Newman, Joan E. Girls Are People Too! A Bibliography of Nontraditional Female Roles in Children's Books.

Metuchen, NJ: Scarecrow, 1982.   Z1037.N66.   PN1009.A1.
011.

An annotated guide to 540 books for children that "exhibit active, adventurous, persistent, self-confident, independent, creative, proud, courageous, and individualistic females." Both fiction and nonfiction are included; books on Blacks, Native Americans, the handicapped, and other minorities are highlighted.

NOTE: Because the above bibliographies are limited in their coverage of time periods and genres, you may need to consult the following general works.

Fiction Catalog. 10th ed. New York: H. W. Wilson, 1980.
Z5916.   PN3451.   016.823.

Cumulated Fiction Index. London: Association of Assistant Librarians, 1945 to present.   Z5916.
016.80883.

Both of these sources index novels in the English language. Fiction Catalog is notable for providing plot summaries and occasional critical remarks. Novels are listed by author, subject, and form; the latest edition includes many titles under WOMEN and related headings. Cumulated Fiction Index uses quite specific subject entries, and this is its real strength. Although you may find nothing under WOMEN, you'll be rewarded if you look under GOVERNESSES, GRANDDAUGHTERS, PREGNANCY, NUNS, and similarly narrow topics. The cumulative volumes are supplemented by the annual Fiction Index.

Granger, Edith. Granger's Index to Poetry. 7th ed. Edited by William James Smith and William F. Bernhardt. New York: Columbia University Press, 1982.   PN1022.
016.80881.

This volume, along with the sixth edition, indexes poems published in collections through 1981. The listing is by title and first line, with an author and subject index. The latter has many entries under WOMEN and WOMEN'S LIBERATION, as well as topics such as WIVES, BIRTH, WIDOWS AND WIDOWERS, etc.

Short Story Index. New York: H. W. Wilson, 1953 to present.   Z5917.S5.   016.80883.

This annual publication indexes short stories published in anthologies; stories from periodicals are also included since 1974. Access is by author, title, or subject. Cumulations appear every five years.

BIBLIOGRAPHIES OF LITERARY CRITICISM

American Women Writers: Bibliographical Essays. Edited by Maurice Duke, Jackson R. Bryer, and M. Thomas Inge. Westport, CT: Greenwood, 1983.   Z1229.W8.   PS147. 016.81.

The essays in this volume review writings by and about twenty-four major authors, ranging from Anne Bradstreet to Sylvia Plath. Each chapter surveys an author's works, assesses critical response, notes the existence of bibliographies and biographies, describes collections of manuscripts and letters, and points to avenues for further research. A welcome shortcut for research on the best-known women writers.

Backscheider, Paula, Felicity Nussbaum, and Philip B. Anderson. An Annotated Bibliography of Twentieth-Century Critical Studies on Women and Literature, 1660-1800. New York: Garland, 1977.   Z2012.   PR449.W65.   016.809.

An exhaustive listing of over 1,500 books and articles published between 1900 and 1975 on women and English literature in the 17th and 18th centuries. This briefly annotated bibliography is "intended for scholars and students of the Restoration and 18th century, of social history, and of women's studies," and therefore it is not limited to purely literary authors. A good portion of the volume is devoted to works on individual women; there are also sections on general background studies, genre studies, and the treatment of women in the fiction of major male writers.

Fairbanks, Carol. Women in Literature: Criticism of the Seventies. Metuchen, NJ: Scarecrow, 1976.   Z6514.C5. PN56.W6.   809.

Fairbanks, Carol. More Women in Literature: Criticism of the Seventies. Metuchen, NJ: Scarecrow, 1979. Z6514.C5.   PN565.W64.   809.

These bibliographies list critical works published
between 1970 and 1977. Included are English-language
books, articles, and dissertations on female
characters in literature, feminist criticism, and
women writers. Book reviews are listed selectively.
The entries are arranged alphabetically by the name
of the writer; both male and female authors are
included. Items not devoted to the lives or works of
individual writers are listed in general
bibliographies at the ends of the volumes. Not
annotated.

White, Barbara Anne. American Women Writers: An
Annotated Bibliography of Criticism. New York: Garland,
1977. Z1229.W8. PS147. 016.81.

This bibliography covers general works on American
women writers. Books and articles devoted to single
authors are not listed, but those treating three or
more authors are. Annotated and arranged by subject,
the entries cover such areas as feminine sensibility
and style, feminist and "phallic" criticism, and
problems faced by women writers. A useful companion
to other sources which are primarily concerned with
individual authors.

NOTE: Bibliographies on narrower aspects of women and
literature can be identified by using the library
catalog. Look under subject headings such as LESBIANISM
IN LITERATURE--BIBLIOGRAPHY, SPANISH LITERATURE--WOMEN
AUTHORS--BIBLIOGRAPHY, and WOMEN POETS--BIBLIOGRAPHY.
Bibliographies of works by and/or about an individual
author will be found under her name.

INDEXES AND CONTINUING BIBLIOGRAPHIES

Abstracts of English Studies. Boulder, CO: National
Council of Teachers of English, 1958 to present. PE25.
820.

The only bibliographic source in literature that
appears more often than annually, this provides
abstracts for a limited number of articles. Ten slim
issues are published each year, for an annual total
of some 1,800 entries. Selected numbers of twelve to
fifteen journals, on the average, are covered in each
issue; older as well as current items are included.
The subject indexes point to very few women's studies
articles. Like other, more comprehensive sources,

this is most useful for research on individual
authors.

American Literary Scholarship. Durham, NC: Duke
University Press, 1965 to present.   PS3.   016.81.

A yearly anthology of signed bibliographic surveys of
recent books and articles on literature in the U.S.
Part One is devoted to major authors (mostly men),
while Part Two focuses on periods, genres, and
special topics. In recent years, "Women in
Literature and Feminist Concerns" has been included
in the "Themes, Topics, Criticism" section.

English Association. The Year's Work in English Studies.
London: English Association, 1919 to present.   PE58.

A survey of scholarship in English and American
literature and language. Each chapter covers a
period of literary history and is written by a
specialist. The works cited in the essays are
indexed by author (i.e. critic) and by author and
subject treated. See WOMEN, WOMEN'S FICTION, WOMEN'S
MAGAZINES, and WOMEN'S POETRY in the index.

Modern Humanities Research Association. Annual
Bibliography of English Language and Literature. London:
Modern Humanities Research Association, 1920 to present.
Z2011.   016.82.

The British equivalent of the MLA International
Bibliography (see below). There is only about a 20%
overlap in coverage, despite the similarity in their
focus and arrangement.

Modern Language Association of America. MLA
International Bibliography of Books and Articles on the
Modern Languages and Literatures. New York: Modern
Language Association of America, 1963 to present.
Z7006.   016.4.

Published since 1921 under various titles as a
supplement to the MLA's journal Publications, this is
the most comprehensive bibliography in the field of
literature. It covers periodical articles, books,
dissertations, and essays in published collections.
Through 1980, each annual set had three volumes.
Volume I treated English, American, Medieval and Neo-
Latin, and Celtic literatures, plus folklore; volume

II, European, Asian, African, and Latin American literatures; and volume III, linguistics. Within volumes I and II, citations were generally organized by period, then by individual writer. There were author indexes but no subject approach. Hence, the volumes of the MLA International Bibliography prior to 1981 are most useful for locating criticism of particular writers. Broader works on women and literature or on feminist critical theory are hard to dig out. In 1981 the organization of the bibliography was modified. It is now issued in five parts: volume I, British, American, and other English-language literatures; volume II, European, Asian, African, and South American literatures; volume III, linguistics; volume IV, general literature and related topics; and volume V, folklore. Volume IV includes sections on "Feminist Criticism" and "Feminist Literary Theory." There are author and subject indexes to the set. The subject index has many entries under WOMEN, WOMEN WRITERS, FEMINIST APPROACH, and other key terms. To find all relevant citations on a topic, take a dual approach to this set through both the classified arrangement and the index.

The Year's Work in Modern Language Studies. London: Modern Humanities Research Association, 1929 to present. PB1. 405.8.

This annual collection of bibliographic essays covers Romance, Celtic, Germanic, and Slavonic languages and literatures. Use the subject index to find general works about women in literature and women writers in particular centuries and countries. Use the name index to find writings about individual women authors.

9.11 MINORITY STUDIES

In recent years, women of color -- Black women, Latinas, American Indians, Asian Americans, and others -- have raised their voices to simultaneously support and critique the women's movement and women's studies. Jewish women and women of other ethnic and cultural backgrounds have likewise questioned the Anglo-Saxon, middle-class, Christian premises of feminist scholarship. The widening attention to minority women on campus and in the community is evidenced by new courses with titles like "The Jewish Woman in American History" and "The Literature of Black Women Writers in the U.S. and Africa," and by the determined sensitivity to racism within the National Women's Studies Association and other professional groups.

The reference literature on minority women is uneven, as must be expected in any relatively new field. Both commercial publishers and feminist presses have printed some excellent bibliographies on Black women. These include such specialized sources as Marilyn Richardson's Black Women and Religion: A Bibliography (see chapter 9.15) and J.R. Roberts' Black Lesbians: An Annotated Bibliography (see chapter 9.8).

At this writing, other minorities fare less well. A single book-length bibliography on American Indian women has at last appeared. Spanish-speaking women are receiving increasing attention from bibliographers, although the definitive sourcelist has yet to be published. No survey of writings on Asian American women is readily available. The best separately published bibliographies on Jewish women are from a small press.

General works are listed in the library catalog under MINORITY WOMEN. AFRO-AMERICAN WOMEN is the heading for books about Black women in the United States, while WOMEN, BLACK covers Black women in other parts of the world. Some catalogs may still have entries for older materials under NEGRO WOMEN.

Writings on Hispanic women in the U.S. are

categorized as MEXICAN AMERICAN WOMEN, PUERTO RICAN WOMEN, and so on. The heading WOMEN, JEWISH may be modified by place, for example WOMEN, JEWISH--U.S. The Library of Congress has recently added a new heading, ASIAN AMERICAN WOMEN. Books on American Indians will be found under INDIANS OF NORTH AMERICA--WOMEN.

GUIDES TO RESEARCH

Hirschfelder, Arlene B., Mary Gloyne Byler, and Michael A. Dorris. Guide to Research on North American Indians. Chicago: American Library Association, 1983. Z1209.2.N67.   E77.   016.970004.

Miller, Wayne Charles. Comprehensive Bibliography for the Study of American Minorities. New York: New York University Press, 1976.   Z1361.E4.   E184.A1. 016.973.

Schlachter, Gail A. Minorities and Women: A Guide to Reference Literature in the Social Sciences. Los Angeles: Reference Service Press, 1977.   Z7964.U49. HQ1410.   016.30145.

Westmoreland, Guy T. An Annotated Guide to Reference Books on the Black American Experience. Wilmington, DE: Scholarly Resources, 1974.   Z1039.N4.

BIBLIOGRAPHIES ON WOMEN

Cabello-Argandona, Roberto. The Chicana: A Comprehensive Bibliographic Study. Los Angeles: Chicano Studies Center, University of California, 1975. Z1361.M4.   E184.M5.

    Nearly 500 books, articles, conference papers, and government publications are listed in this bibliography. About half the items are annotated. Among the many topics covered are the Chicana and the women's liberation movement, health and nutrition, cultural processes and folk culture, and education.

Cantor, Aviva. The Jewish Woman, 1900-1980: Bibliography. Revised ed. Fresh Meadows, NY: Biblio Press, 1981.   Z7964.J4.   HQ1172.   016.30141.

    This is the most extensive bibliography available on Jewish women, but it is still limited to English-

language books and articles that are currently in
print or obtainable in libraries. The annotations
are short, evaluative, and strongly flavored by the
feminist viewpoint of the compiler. Large sections
are devoted to history, religious life and laws, the
Holocaust, and Jewish women in the U.S. and Canada,
in Israel, and in other countries. Fiction,
biography and poetry are also covered.

Davis, Lenwood G. The Black Woman in American Society:
A Selected Annotated Bibliography. Boston: G. K. Hall,
1975.   Z1361.N39.   E185.86.   016.973.

A reference book on Black women in the United States
throughout the nation's history. Books, articles,
reports, current Black periodicals, pamphlets,
speeches, and government documents are cited. Also
provided is information on Black history collections
in American libraries, national organizations of
Black women, Black women publishers, editors, and
elected officials, and statistics on Black women in
rural and urban areas.

Green, Rayna. Native American Women: A Contextual
Bibliography. Bloomington, IN: Indiana University Press,
1983.   Z1209.2.N67.   E98.W8.   016.3054.

This guide to publications on North American Indian
women lists 672 books, journal articles, films,
recordings, government documents, and dissertations.
Entries are arranged alphabetically by author, with
date and subject indexes. The annotations make this
bibliography especially appealing, for the compiler
is sharp in her criticism of poorly written or racist
studies and forthright in her praise of better
efforts. The introduction is a highly readable and
provocative review of the literature on Native
American women from a historical perspective.

The Jewish Women's Studies Guide. Edited by Ellen Sue
Levi Elwell and Edward R. Levenson. Fresh Meadows, NY:
Biblio Press, 1982.   HQ1172.   016.3054.

An inspiring collection of fifteen syllabi and
reading lists. Several of the courses explore
aspects of Jewish women's experiences from the
perspectives of literature, theology, history, and
psychology. Two (one on the American Jewish
experience and one on women in religious traditions)
attempt to integrate Jewish women into the broader

curriculum.

Klotman, Phyllis Rauch, and Wilmer H. Batz. The Black Family and the Black Woman: A Bibliography. New York: Arno, 1978. Z1361.N39. E185.86. 016.9173.

Besides books and articles, this bibliography includes government documents, sound recordings, and children's literature. It is organized by subject and is not annotated. The call numbers given with the entries are those used at the Indiana University Library; another library's call numbers may be different.

Loeb, Catherine. "La Chicana: A Bibliographic Survey." Frontiers 5 (Summer 1980): 59-74. HQ1101. 301.41.

A useful listing and discussion of resources for the study of Chicanas, but limited to materials in English.

Sims, Janet. The Progress of Afro-American Women: A Selected Bibliography and Resource Guide. Westport, CT: Greenwood Press, 1980. Z1361.N39. E185.86. 016.973.

This is the most comprehensive bibliography in print on Black women in the United States. Over 4,000 sources of information from the nineteenth and twentieth centuries are listed by subject (e.g., "Education," "Family Life," "Suffrage") or by type of material (e.g., "Biographies and Autobiographies," "Slave Narratives"). In addition to books and scholarly articles, a large number of doctoral dissertations, masters' theses, and articles from the popular press are included. Unfortunately, not annotated.

Williams, Ora. American Black Women in the Arts and Social Sciences: A Bibliographic Survey. Revised ed. Metuchen, NJ: Scarecrow, 1978. Z1361.N39. E185.86. 016.3014.

Lists printed works and audiovisual materials on Black women in the United States. In addition to the general chapters on reference books, biographies, and anthologies, there are sections devoted to various fields in the arts, books for young readers, criticism by Black women, and feminist issues. A separate section presents bibliographies of works by and about seventeen prominent Black women. This edition also contains a chronology, a list of Black periodicals, and a list of Black publishing houses.

INDEXES AND CONTINUING BIBLIOGRAPHIES

Chicano Periodical Index: A Cumulative Index to Selected Chicano Periodicals Between 1967 and 1978. Boston: G. K. Hall, 1981.   Z1361.M4.   E184.M5.   016.973.

Chicano Periodical Index: A Cumulative Index to Selected Periodicals, 1979-1981, With Selected Serials Indexed Retrospectively. Boston: G. K. Hall, 1983.   Z1361.M4. E184.M5.   016.973.

These volumes index the most important Chicano periodicals, both academic and popular. There are several pages of references under CHICANAS, and also a number under WOMEN MEN RELATIONS, WOMEN'S RIGHTS, and WORKING WOMEN. The subject index is preceded by a thesaurus of terms and instructions for searching.

HAPI, Hispanic American Periodicals Index. Los Angeles: UCLA Latin American Center Publications, 1975 to present. Z1605.   F1408.   016.98.

This annual index covers Hispanics in the United States as well as in Latin America. For a fuller annotation, see chapter 9.12, "National and Area Studies."

Index to Periodical Articles By and About Blacks. Boston: G. K. Hall, 1950 to present.   AI3.   E185.5. 974.

This annual index was previously titled Index to Periodical Articles By and About Negroes. It currently indexes twenty-three Afro-American periodicals, both popular and academic. Articles are cited under their authors and subjects; Library of Congress-style subject terms are used.

Sage Race Relations Abstracts. London: Sage Publications, 1975 to present.   HT1501.   305.8.

This interdisciplinary index to writings on race includes the category "Women" in its classification scheme. Articles classed under other headings are cross-referenced. Some issues contain bibliographic essays on particular topics.

9.12 NATIONAL AND AREA STUDIES

The United Nations Decade for Women (1975 to 1985) strengthened the concept of global feminism and nurtured the struggle of women throughout the world for peace and equality. In the wake of international conferences and scholarly exchanges, the designers of women's studies courses in the United States have begun to direct ever more attention to their sisters in other countries. From the theoretical debates raging in Western Europe to the tactics of peasant women's organizations in the Third World, women's studies has been immeasurably enriched by a widening international and comparative focus.

This chapter lists bibliographies about women in particular countries or parts of the world. Many of the sources listed in other chapters are international in scope and should also be consulted. For example, if you are interested in the role of women in the economy of West Africa, you should use reference publications in economics as well as those focusing on African women.

Books on women's situations in specific countries can easily be found by looking in the catalog under the subject heading WOMEN followed by the name of the country -- e.g., WOMEN--FRANCE. Books with special themes will be described more specifically: WOMEN--EMPLOYMENT--AUSTRALIA, for instance, or WOMEN--CIVIL RIGHTS--ARGENTINA.

In this chapter, you will also be introduced to some general indexes to foreign periodicals. However, it is not feasible to list here all the bibliographies and retrospective indexes available for each region.

Further resources on women in developing countries are noted in the chapter on business and economics.

AFRICA

There was a flurry of bibliographic activity relating to African women between the mid-1960s and the mid-1970s, resulting in a number of short, non-commercial reference lists that are now largely out-of-date. Kratochvil's and Shaw's remains useful.

AFRICA - BIBLIOGRAPHIES ON WOMEN

Kratochvil, Laura, and Shauna Shaw. African Women: A Select Bibliography. Cambridge, England: African Studies Center, 1974.   Z7964.A3.   016.30141.

This selective bibliography lists 1,210 works on women in Africa. The arrangement is topical, with regional and author indexes. Economic development and the family are both emphasized. Other areas treated include the arts, elite women in African societies, ornamentation, politics, religion and ritual, women's organizations, and youth.

Saulniers, Suzanne Smith, and Cathy A. Rakowski. Women in the Development Process: A Select Bibliography on Women in sub-Saharan Africa and Latin America. Austin: University of Texas, Institute of Latin American Studies, 1977.   Z7961.   HQ1870.9.   016.30141.

For annotation, see chapter 9.3, "Business, Economics, and Labor Studies."

AFRICA - CONTINUING BIBLIOGRAPHIES AND INDEXES

African Bibliographic Center. A Current Bibliography on African Affairs. Farmingdale, NY: Baywood Publishing Co., 1962 to present.   Z3501.

Each quarterly issue contains one or more review articles, several book reviews, and a bibliographical section split into "general subjects" and "regional studies." The topical headings vary slightly from issue to issue, but WOMEN is usually present. Scholarly books, periodical articles, government documents, and publications of international organizations are included. Most entries are briefly annotated.

International African Bibliography. London: Mansell,
1971 to present.   Z3501.

This quarterly bibliography covers "the whole of the
African continent and the adjacent islands, with the
exclusion of Egypt." Books, articles, pamphlets, and
conference proceedings and symposia are included;
fiction, textbooks, theses, government publications,
microforms, and audiovisual materials are not.
Entries are arranged geographically. There is no
subject index, but subject tracings are printed in
capital letters at the end of each entry to
facilitate scanning. For bibliographic coverage from
1929 to 1970, see Africa, the journal of the
International African Institute.

ASIA

Recent comprehensive bibliographies treat women in
the Indian subcontinent, southeast Asia, Japan and Korea,
and China. No separate bibliographies are available for
American readers on women in Vietnam or Cambodia.

ASIA - BIBLIOGRAPHIES ON WOMEN

Fan, Kok Sim. Women in Southeast Asia: A Bibliography.
Boston: G. K. Hall, 1982.   Z7961.   HQ1745.8.
016.3054.

Presents an impressive 3,865 citations to published
and unpublished sources, arranged by topic. Major
categories include: economic conditions and status;
education; family planning and fertility; history;
health and welfare; legal status; marriage and
divorce; social conditions and status. The countries
covered are Brunei, Burma, Indonesia, Malaysia, the
Phillipines, Singapore, and Thailand.

Koh, Hesung Chun. Korean and Japanese Women: An
Analytic Bibliographic Guide. Westport, CT: Greenwood,
1982.   Z7964.K6.   HQ1765.5.   016.3054.

This bibliography covers some 580 items in
unprecedented depth. Indeed, its complexity may
bewilder the reader at first. There are both keyword
and classified subject approaches to the materials.
An additional index profiles the authors of the items

cited and outlines their research designs and
methods, to help the reader assess the
trustiworthiness of their data. Items cited are in
English, Korean, or Japanese. Despite its
complicated organization, this is the only
bibliography for English speakers on women in Korea
and Japan and must therefore be consulted for any
investigation of those countries.

Sakala, Carol. Women of South Asia: A Guide to
Resources. Millwood, NY: Kraus International
Publications, 1980.   Z7964.S65.   HQ1735.3.   016.3054.

This comprehensive annotated bibliography covers the
historical and contemporary role of women in India,
Pakistan, Bangladesh, Sri Lanka, and Nepal. Over
4,600 Western-language materials from the late 18th
century through mid-1979 are cited, including works
which focus directly on women and related writings on
such subjects as kinship, law, and cosmology.
Entries are organized in an extremely complex
chronological and topical outline which emphasizes
such features as major social movements, traditional
literary forms, prominent personalities, and cultural
regions.

Wei, Karen T. Women in China: A Selected and Annotated
Bibliography. Westport, CT: Greenwood, 1984.   Z7964.C5.
HQ1767.   016.3054.

The first book-length bibliography on Chinese women
to be published for readers of English, this volume
contains over 1,100 entries with descriptive
annotations. Nineteenth- and twentieth-century
publications that explore the economic conditions,
status, and liberation of Chinese women are
emphasized in fourteen topical chapters.

ASIA - CONTINUING BIBLIOGRAPHIES AND INDEXES

Bibliography of Asian Studies. Ann Arbor: Association
for Asian Studies, 1969 to present.   Z3001.   016.915.

Citations to Western-language books, articles, and
documents are grouped by area or country, and then
sub-arranged by topic. Under "Anthropology and
Sociology," see the section "Women." This
bibliography covers East, South, and Southeast Asia
in the fields of history, the humanities, and the

social sciences. Annual compilations run about three
years late. (From 1941 through 1969, issued as part
of the Journal of Asian Studies and its predecessor,
Far Eastern Quarterly.)

EUROPE

The bibliographic coverage of Western European
publications in women's studies is spotty but improving.
Sources on Great Britain are readily accessible to
English-speaking American researchers. But despite the
flourishing feminist debates elsewhere in Europe, there
are few sources to aid the researcher from abroad.
Therefore, this section lists, very selectively,
publications in foreign languages most likely to be
familiar to undergraduates.
   At this writing, there are no readily available
bibliographies on women's situations in Spain, Italy,
Portugal, Greece, the Netherlands, Scandinavia, or many
of the smaller nations. Moreover, no single bibliography
on women in the USSR has been published, nor are English-
language guides available on women in other Eastern bloc
countries. Researchers must rely on footnotes and
bibliographies in studies such as Gail Lapidus' Women in
Soviet Society (Berkeley: University of California Press,
1978).

EUROPE - BIBLIOGRAPHIES ON WOMEN

Barrow, Margaret. Women, 1870-1928: A Select Guide to
Printed and Archival Sources in the United Kingdom. New
York: Mansell, Garland, 1981.   HQ1593.   301.41.i

   This guide focuses on the years between 1870, when
   the Married Women's Property Acts were passed, and
   1928, when women were fully enfranchised in the
   United Kingdom. Part I, "Archives," lists documents
   from individuals and institutions. Part II, "Printed
   Works," covers books, pamphlets, and periodicals.
   Pat III, "Non-Book Materials," identifies films,
   photographs, oral history recordings, newspaper
   cuttings, and artifacts. Finally, repositories for
   all these items are listed and described in Part IV,
   "Libraries and Record Offices." Throughout the
   volume, the social and economic position of women is
   the central concern; works of literature are
   excluded. There is a subject index and an author-
   title index.

Bock, Ulla, and Barbara Witych. Thema Frau:
Bibliographie der deutschsprachigen Literatur zur
Frauenfrage 1949-1979. Bielefeld: AJZ-Druck und Verlag,
1980. Z7961. HQ1210. 016.3054.

A bibliography of over 4,000 German-language books
and articles about women published since 1949.
German translations of foreign works are included.
Citations are arranged according to a detailed
subject outline, with an author index. The topical
range is broad. Except for the biography section,
not annotated.

France. Direction de la Documentation. Bibliotheque.
Les Femmes: Guide Bibliographique. Paris: Documentation
Francaise, 1974. Z7961. HQ1121. 016.30141.

Although prepared by a French library, this is an
international bibliography listing works published in
other countries as well. Items are arranged by
subject or country; some entries are annotated. The
original volume includes 1,466 entries; a supplement
published in 1975 adds another 400 entries and
provides a name index to both volumes.

Die Frauenfrage in Deutschland: Bibliographie; Band 10,
1931-1980. Munich: K. G. Saur, 1982. Z7961.

Cumulating earlier volumes, this unannotated
bibliography offers over 12,000 entries organized by
subject. The scope is interdisciplinary, touching on
such fields as history, psychology, and art. For
materials published prior to 1930, see Sveistrup's
and Zahn-Harnack's Die Frauenfrage in Deutschland,
below.

Frey, Linda, Marsha Frey, and Joanne Schneider. Women in
Western European History: A Select Chronological,
Geographical, and Topical Bibliography from Antiquity to
the French Revolution. Westport, CT: Greenwood, 1982.
Z7961. 016.3054.

For annotation, see chapter 9.6, "History."

Kanner, Barbara. "The Women of England in a Century of
Social Change, 1815-1914: A Select Bibliography." In
Suffer and Be Still: Women in the Victorian Age, pp.
173-206. Edited by Martha Vicinus. Bloomington: Indiana
University Press, 1972. HQ1596. 301.41.

Kanner, Barbara. "The Women of England in a Century of Social Change, 1815-1917: A Select Bibliography, Part II." In A Widening Sphere: Changing Roles of Victorian Women, pp. 199-270. Edited by Martha Vicinus. Bloomington: Indiana University Press, 1977. HQ1596. 301.41.

This two-part bibliography covers both contemporary and secondary sources on Victorian women. Topical overviews and commentary on the literature are frequently interjected. Among the subjects included in Part I are the climate of opinion on social roles, women and crime, the expansion of employment, education, political activity, and public service. Part II covers, among other topics, autobiographies and diaries, contemporary writings on marriage and the family, sickness and health care, and organizations (including trade unions, girls' clubs, temperance societies, and the suffrage movement.)

Kelly, Joan. Bibliography in the History of European Women. 4th revised ed. Bronxville, NY: Sarah Lawrence College, 1976. Z7961.

For annotation, see chapter 9.6, "History." This bibliography does not cover women after World War II.

Sveistrup, Hans, and Agnes Zahn-Harnack. Die Frauenfrage in Deutschland: Stroemungen und Gegenstroemungen, 1790-1930. Burg b. M.: A. Hopfer, 1934. Z7961. 016.396.

An exhaustive bibliography on the "woman question" in Germany between 1790 and 1930. Most entries are briefly annotated. For recent coverage, see Die Frauenfrage in Deutschland, 1931-1980 (above).

The Women of England: From Anglo-Saxon Times to the Present; Interpretive Bibliographic Essays. Edited by Barbara Kanner. Hamden, CT: Archon Books, 1979. HQ1599.E5. 301.41.

This anthology of bibliographic essays serves as an introduction to the study of English women. A dozen scholars have contributed surveys of the literature on specific historical periods or particular aspects of women's experience -- for example, "Women Under the Law in Medieval England" and "Women in the Mirror: Using Novels to Study Victorian Women." The essays cover both primary sources and secondary works. Each chapter concludes with a bibliography of works mentioned in the text.

EUROPE - CONTINUING BIBLIOGRAPHIES AND INDEXES

American Bibliography of Slavic and East European Studies. Stanford, CA: American Association for the Advancement of Slavic Studies, 1967 to present. Z2483.016.9147.

Continues the American Bibliography of Russian and East European Studies published by Indiana University from 1956 to 1966. The scope of this annual bibliography has varied over the years. It presently lists books, journal articles, reports, book reviews, and dissertations by U.S. or Canadian authors on Slavic and East European matters in the social sciences and humanities. Over 95% of the works cited are in English. The bibliography is arranged in broad subject categories, sub-divided geographically. Look for WOMEN, MARRIAGE AND THE FAMILY under the heading SOCIOLOGY. No annotations; published about three years late.

British Humanities Index. London: Library Association, 1962 to present. AI3. 011.

Despite its title, this is a general index to popular and scholarly periodicals published in England on a wide range of topics in the humanities and social sciences. Its predecessor, Subject Index to Periodicals, covers the years 1915 to 1961. The subject headings are quite specific -- e.g., WOMEN AND HUSBANDS' CAREERS; WOMEN, ENGLISH, IN PERSIA, HISTORY; and WOMEN IN BRASS BANDS. More general headings are also used. For example, you might find listings under WOMEN ATHLETES as well as WOMEN RUGBY FOOTBALL PLAYERS. Issued quarterly, with an annual bound cumulation.

Internationale Bibliographie der Zeitschriftenliteratur aus allen Gebieten des Wissens/International Bibliography of Periodical Literature Covering All Fields of Knowledge. Osnabrueck: Felix Dietrich, 1965 to present. AI9.

This semiannual index is international in scope, with especially good coverage of European journals. Each issue is comprised of several bound volumes, split into an "Index Rerum" (subjects) and an "Index

Autorus" (authors). In the "Index Rerum," subject
headings are in German, with cross-references from
the English and French forms. For example, under
both WOMAN and FEMME the reader is referred to FRAU.
This index combines an index to German periodicals,
<u>Bibliographie der deutschen Zeitschriftenliteratur</u>,
with an index to non-German journals, <u>Bibliographie
der fremsprachigen Zeitschriftenliteratur</u>, which both
began publication in the early twentieth century.

LATIN AMERICA

As general interest in political and economic
development in Latin America has swelled, so has
scholarly concern for women's place in South American and
Central American societies. Moreover, Latinas in the
United States have contributed unique perspectives on
women's liberation both north and south of the border.

LATIN AMERICA - BIBLIOGRAPHIES ON WOMEN

Cohen-Stuart, Bertie A. <u>Women in the Caribbean: A
Bibliography</u>. The Hague: Smits; Leiden: Department of
Caribbean Studies, Royal Institute of Linguistics and
Anthropology, 1979.   Z7964.C38.   HQ1501.   016.30141.

Over six hundred entries are arranged in a topical
outline, under the following headings: family and
household; cultural factors; education; economic
factors; politics and law. Books and articles in
English, French, Dutch, German, Spanish, Papiamento
and Portuguese are included. Each entry is annotated
in English and coded for the geographic area(s) it
treats.

Knaster, Meri. <u>Women in Spanish America: An Annotated
Bibliography from Pre-Conquest to Contemporary Times</u>.
Boston: G. K. Hall, 1977.   Z7964.L3.   HQ1610.5.
016.30141.

An excellent annotated bibliography on women in the
Spanish-speaking countries of the Western hemisphere.
Books, chapters of books, articles, pamphlets,
memoirs, reports, dissertations, and selected
government documents in English and Spanish are
included. Coverage extends to 1974. Citations are
grouped in broad subject categories and sub-arranged

geographically. Author and subject indexes.

Saulniers, Suzanne Smith and Cathy A Rakowski. <u>Women in the Development Process: A Select Bibliography on Women in Sub-Saharan Africa and Latin America.</u> Austin: University of Texas, Institute of Latin American Studies, 1977.   Z7961.   HQ1870.9.   016.30141.

For annotation, see chapter 9.3, "Business, Economics, and Labor Studies."

LATIN AMERICA - CONTINUING BIBLIOGRAPHIES AND INDEXES

<u>HAPI: Hispanic-American Periodicals Index.</u> Los Angeles: UCLA Latin American Center Publications, University of California, 1975 to present.   Z1605.   F1408.   016.98.

This annual index covers nearly 250 journals published throughout the world "which regularly treat Latin America or people of Latin American heritage living in the United States." All fields of the humanities and social sciences are represented. Articles are listed under their authors and their subjects, in separate sections. Entries under the subject heading WOMEN are sub-divided by country or, less frequently, by topic (education, social conditions, etc.). For additional entries, look under such subjects as SEX ROLES and MEXICAN AMERICAN WOMEN. About three years behind in publication, this is nevertheless a very valuabe and easy-to-consult source.

<u>Handbook of Latin American Studies.</u> Austin: University of Texas Press, 1935 to present.   Z1605.

This respected bibliographic series provides a useful overview of scholarship on Latin America. Since volume 26 (1964), annual volumes have alternated coverage of the social sciences and the humanities. The social science volumes include works in anthropology, economics, education, geography, government and politics, international relations, and sociology. The humanities volumes take up the fields of art, film, folklore, history, language, literature, music, and philosophy. The bibliography of books and articles is arranged largely by discipline. Each section is annotated and introduced by a specialist in the field. The subject index is helpful in identifying references about women.

MIDDLE EAST

Writings from the 1970s and earlier on women in the Middle East are easy to unearth, thanks to three specialized bibliographies. See also sources on Jewish women, listed in the chapters on minority studies and religion, for additional leads on women in Israel.

MIDDLE EAST - BIBLIOGRAPHIES ON WOMEN

Al-Qazzaz, Ayad. Women in the Middle East and North Africa: An Annotated Bibliography. Austin: Center for Middle Eastern Studies, University of Texas, 1977. Z7964.N42.   HQ1726.5.   016.30141.

Meghdessian, Samira Rafidi. The Status of the Arab Woman: A Select Bibliography. Westport, CT: Greenwood, 1980.   Z7964.A7.   HQ1784.   016.3054.

Raccagni, Michelle. The Modern Arab Woman: A Bibliography. Metuchen, NJ: Scarecrow, 1978. Z7964.A7.   016.30141.

None of these bibliographies is exhaustive, but taken together they can be useful for locating scholarship on Middle Eastern women. Meghdessian's work lists materials in Western languages (primarily English and French), while Raccagni's includes transliterated Arabic citations as well. Raccagni's subject arrangement is more detailed than Meghdessian's, and she provides almost twice as many citations. Both volumes have author indexes and equally inadequate subject indexes. By contrast, the alphabetically arranged bibliography by Al-Qazzaz is far more selective; only English-language sources are included. Long, well written annotations are its most valuable feature.

MIDDLE EAST - CONTINUING BIBLIOGRAPHIES AND INDEXES

The Middle East: Abstracts and Index. Pittsburgh: Library Information and Research Service, 1978 to present.   DS41.   016.956.

A quarterly interdisciplinary index to English-language writings on the Middle East. The basic arrangement is by country, with additional categories for materials on general topics, the Arab-Israeli

conflict, and "the Arab world." Within each
division, citations are grouped by type of
publication: journal articles; dissertations;
editorials; government documents; interviews;
research reports; news conferences; speeches and
statements; statistics; and books and book reviews.
Not every category offers abstracts. To find
references on women, check the subject index under
WOMEN and under the names of countries, where WOMEN
appears as a sub-topic.

Mideast File. Oxford, England: Learned Information, 1982 to present. DS42.4. 956.

Compiled four times a year at Tel-Aviv University, this index offers abstracts of documents, articles, and reports. Books and book reviews are also cited but not abstracted. Coverage emphasizes history, demography, politics, government, regional and international relations, economics, finance, oil, law, science and technology, arms and armaments, education, and religion. Entries are classified by country, with additional categories for general and inter-regional issues. The best approach to information about women is through the subject index, under WOMEN.

NORTH AMERICA

This section has a dual focus -- works on women in Canada and works on specific regions of the United States. Many more works about the United States as a whole -- which may of course contain extensive references to information about particular regions, states, and localities -- are listed in other chapters.

NORTH AMERICA - BIBLIOGRAPHIES ON WOMEN

Fairbanks, Carol, and Sara Brooks Sundberg. **Farm Women on the Prairie Frontier: A Sourcebook for Canada and the United States.** Metuchen, NY: Scarecrow, 1983. HQ1438.A17. 305.4.

Four introductory essays provide historical background on topics ranging from grasslands ecology to images of "prairie matriarchs" in women's fiction. The remainder of the volume is an annotated

bibliograpy of secondary and primary sources on the
experiences of pioneer women, including many first-
person accounts. The interdisciplinary scope of the
bibliography is noteworthy; it embraces social
history, works of fiction, literary criticism, and
natural history.

Farr, Sidney Saylor. Appalachian Women: An Annotated
Bibliography. Lexington: University Press of Kentucky,
1981.   Z7964.A127.   HQ1438.A127.   016.3054.

An interdisciplinary bibliography on the women of
Appalachia. Included are 1,328 books, magazine
articles, short stories, oral history tapes, and
other materials from 1825 to 1979. Annotated entries
are arranged under the following headings:
autobiography and biography; coal mining; education;
fiction and drama; health conditions and health care;
industry; life styles; migrants; music; oral history;
poetry; religion and folklore; studies and surveys.

Light, Beth, and Veronica Strong-Boag. True Daughters of
the North: Canadian Women's History: An Annotated
Bibliography. Toronto: Ontario Institute for Studies in
Education, 1980.   Z7964.C36.   HQ1453.   016.3054.

This is the latest and best guide to the growing
literature on women in Canada. The bibliography is
annotated and covers both primary and secondary
sources. The five chapters -- General References;
New France; British North America; Canada 1867-1917;
and Post-World War I Canada -- are further divided by
subject. The topics treated include: demographic and
community studies; education; law; literature and the
arts; marriage and the family; material history
(cookbooks, fashion, etc.); medicine; organizational
involvement; political involvement; religion;
sexuality, morality and sex role images; sport,
recreation, and leisure; and work.

Patterson-Black, Sheryll, and Gene Patterson-Black.
Western Women in History and Literature. Crawford, NE:
Cottonwood Press, 1978.   Z7964.U5.   HQ1438.A17.

A bibliography on women in the American West from
pre-Anglo settlement through World War II. Over
2,000 references to letters, diaries, memoirs,
autobiographies, oral histories, and literary works
by and about Western women are included. Background
sources on women's history and regional and local

history are also noted.

Strong-Boag, Veronica. "Cousin Cinderella: A Guide to
Historical Literature Pertaining to Canadian Women."

Eichler, Margit. "A Bibliography of Materials on
Canadian Women Pertinent to the Social Sciences and
Published Between 1950 and 1975."

Both in Women in Canada, pp. 245-360. Ed. by Marylee
Stephenson. Revised ed. Don Mills, Ontario: General
Publishing, 1977. HQ1453. 301.41.

Strong-Boag's bibliographic essay emphasizes primary
sources on the history of women in Canada, although
secondary works are also noted. The section covering
biographies, autobiographies, and diaries is
especially valuable. Eichler's bibliography is
arranged by subject and includes over 1,100 books,
journal articles, theses, and federal and provincial
documents.

NORTH AMERICA - CONTINUING BIBLIOGRAPHIES AND INDEXES

Canadian Periodical Index/Index de periodique canadiens.
Ottawa, Ontario: Canadian Library Association, 1928 to
present.   AI3.

An author and subject index to over 130 specialized
journals and general interest magazines published in
Canada. English subject headings are used, with
cross-references from French headings for articles
written in French. See the subject WOMEN (with its
numerous sub-headings) and subject phrases that begin
with the word WOMEN, such as WOMEN AND MEN and WOMEN
AUTHORS. Published monthly, with annual cumulations.

Resources for Feminist Research/Documentation sur la
recherche feministe. Toronto: Ontario Institute for
Studies in Education, 1972 to present.   HQ1101.
305.41.

For annotation, see chapter 7, "General Women's
Studies Bibliographies."

OCEANIA

The women's movement is strong in New Zealand and Australia, as evidenced in such vital periodicals as Broadsheet and Hecate, but Western women rarely learn of their sisters "down under." Feminism and women's history in Oceania is complex, fascinating, and sorely neglected in the United States.

OCEANIA - BIBLIOGRAPHIES ON WOMEN

Bettison, Margaret, and Anne Summers. Her Story: Australian Women in Print, 1788-1975. Sydney: Hale and Tremonger, 1980.   Z7964.A8.   HQ1822.   016.3054.

A bibliography of over 3,000 publications about Australian women. Books are emphasized, although there are also some entries for individual chapters, journal articles, parliamentary papers, theses, and manuscripts. Citations are arranged by topic, with an author index.

9.13 POLITICAL SCIENCE

Feminism has redefined the sphere of political action. The slogan "the personal is political" and the catch phrase "sexual politics" sum up the conceptual shift. Yet even within the traditional boundaries of the field of political science -- the analysis of political and governmental institutions and processes -- there is a burgeoning interest in women. The "gender gap" in voting behavior has lent impetus to research on women's political attitudes and activities.
   WOMEN IN POLITICS is the subject heading used in the library's catalog to identify books on the roles of women in political life. Other books may be found under headings describing the women themselves: WOMEN LEGISLATORS, WOMEN REVOLUTIONISTS, POLITICIANS' WIVES, and so forth. WOMEN IN PUBLIC LIFE, WOMEN'S RIGHTS, and WOMEN AND SOCIALISM are typical of yet other terms applied to writings in political science.

GUIDES TO RESEARCH

Brock, Clifton. The Literature of Political Science: A Guide for Students, Librarians, and Teachers. New York: Bowker, 1969.   Z7161.   016.32.

Holler, Frederick. The Information Sources of Political Science. 3rd ed. Santa Barbara: ABC-Clio, 1981. Z7161.   JA71.   016.32.

Merritt, Richard L., and Gloria J. Pyszka. The Student Political Scientist's Handbook. Cambridge, MA: Schenkman, 1969.   JA86.   320.

Vose, Clement E. A Guide to Library Sources in Political Science: American Government. Washington: American

161

Political Science Association, 1975.   Z7165.U5.   JK31.
016.3209.

BIBLIOGRAPHIES ON WOMEN

Buhle, Mari Jo. Women and the American Left: A Guide to Sources. Boston: G. K. Hall, 1983.   Z7964.U49. HQ1420.   016.3054.

This exemplary annotated guide has four major sections, treating the years 1871-1900, 1901-1919, 1920-1964, and 1965-1981. The chronological divisions are further broken down by types of sources: histories and general works; autobiographies and biographies; books and pamphlets on the woman question; periodicals; and fiction and poetry. Helpful notes head each section. Historians and present-day activists, as well as political scientists, can use this bibliography profitably.

Fitch, Nancy Elizabeth. Women in Politics: The United States and Abroad; A Select Annotated Bibliography, 1970-Oct. 1980. (Public administration series: Bibliography no. P-880) Monticello, IL: Vance Bibliographies, 1982.   Z7164.A2.   016.71.

This short bibliography is not comprehensive, but it is relatively up-to-date. Entries are grouped in two broad categories, "U.S." and "Abroad," and then by type of publication -- books, articles, and entries in the series, Current Biography. Coverage of newspapers, leading academic journals, and newsstand magazines is strongest.

Levenson, Rosaline. Women in Government and Politics: A Bibliography of American and Foreign Sources. (Exchange bibliography no. 491) Monticello, IL: Council of Planning Librarians, 1973.   Z7164.A2.   016.71.

Sapiro, Virginia. Guide to Published Works on Women and Politics II. Ann Arbor: Center for Political Studies, Institute for Social Research, University of Michigan, 1975.   Z7963.S9.   HQ1236.   016.30141.

These two non-commercial bibliographies are similar in size and format. Both list works by subject, emphasizing twentieth-century English-language publications. Levenson focuses on the practical side of politics, covering such topics as women in municipal and state management, Congresswomen, the suffrage movement, etc. Sapiro takes a broader view, including background material on historical, sociological, psychological, and economic factors which affect women's political participation. Both bibliographies include selected materials on foreign countries; neither is annotated. Both are now somewhat dated.

Manning, Beverley. Index to American Women Speakers, 1828-1978. Metuchen, NJ: Scarecrow, 1980.   Z1231.07. PS400.   016.815.

An impressive index to over 3,000 speeches made by women in the past 150 years and printed in 125 sources. Congressional hearing are included. Access is provided by speaker, title of speech, and subject. Useful for historical research as well as for locating present-day opinion.

Nelson, Barbara A. American Women and Politics: A Bibliography and Guide to the Sources. New York: Garland, 1983.   Z7964.U49.   HQ1236.   016.3054.

A broadly conceived bibliography that cites materials on women's history, feminist theory, the nature-vs-nurture controversy, and women in the paid labor force, in addition to writings on electoral politics, social movements, adult political socialization, and women's role in the welfare state. References to over 1,600 publications, most from 1970 to 1982, are topically arranged; there are no annotations. A good gateway to the literature of women in poliical science and related fields.

Rowbotham, Sheila. Women's Liberation and Revolution: A Bibliography. 2nd ed. Bristol, England: Falling Wall Press, 1973.   Z7961.   HQ1154.   016.30141.

This bibliography places radical feminism in historical perspective. Books, pamphlets, and articles which explore the relationship between feminism and revolutionary politics are arranged under such headings as "Marx and Engels on Women's Liberation," "Feminism and Socialist and Anarchist Movements," and "Women and the Puritan Revolution." Brief annotations.

Stanwick, Kathy, and Christine Li. The Political
Participation of Women in the United States: A Selected
Bibliography 1950-1976. Metuchen, NJ: Scarecrow, 1977.
Z7961. HQ1236. 016.3015.

A selective bibliography of works from the last
quarter century on women in American politics. The
emphasis is on scholarly works -- published,
unpublished, and in-progress. Citations are grouped
by format (e.g., articles, books, dissertations,
conference papers) with an author index.
Unfortunately, there is no subject approach and the
entries are not annotated.

Stineman, Esther. American Political Women:
Contemporary and Historical Profiles. Littleton, CO:
Libraries Unlimited, 1980. HQ1236. 320.973.

This bio-bibliographical work profiles sixty women
who served in the late 1970s or early 1980s as
members of Congress, ambassadors, special presidental
assistants, governors, lieutenant governors, and
mayors. Each entry includes a selected bibliography
of the woman's speeches and writings and a list of
works about her. General studies of women in
politics and women's issues are noted in a separate
bibliography (pp. 161-188); other sources of
information are also listed. Five appendices
identify other women who now hold or once held
important political posts.

INDEXES AND CONTINUING BIBLIOGRAPHIES

ABC Pol Sci. Santa Barbara: ABC-Clio, 1969 to present.
Z716.   016.32.

Published five times a year, this source lists and
indexes the contents of about 300 journals in
political science, government, and related
disciplines. Although no women's studies journals
are covered, relevant items are listed under the
heading WOMEN. Useful for keeping abreast of the
latest scholarship.

International Bibliography of Political Science.
Chicago: Aldine, 1953 to present. Z7163.

An annual bibliography published under the auspices
of UNESCO. The scope is international, and

publications in many languages are indexed. Entries
are not annotated. The introduction, outline
headings, and indexes are all in both English and
French. Entries are classified by topic and nation.
Subjects relevant to women's studies are best
approached through the subject index in the back of
each volume.

<u>International Political Science Abstracts</u>. Paris:
International Political Science Association, 1951 to
present.   JA36.   320.82.

This bimonthly index covers approximately 700
periodicals in many languages. Abstracts are written
in either English or French. Entries are grouped in
six broad categories: methods and theory; political
thinkers and ideas; government and administrative
institutions; political processes; international
relations; national and area studies. A subject
index, cumulated annually, makes it possible to find
references about women.

<u>United States Political Science Documents</u>. Pittsburgh:
University Center for International Studies, with the
American Political Science Association, 1976 to present.
Z7163.   H9.   016.3.

This annual abstracting service is noted for its
depth of coverage. Part I consists of a series of
indexes which permit access to citations by topical,
geographic, and personal name subjects, as well as by
names of authors and contributors. The numbered
abstracts (termed "Document Descriptions") are
randomly arranged in Part 2. In addition to an
abstract of the article's text, each description
contains a list of special features such as tables
and figures and a list of "cited people." Searching
through the subject index is the most profitable
approach for women's studies. The phrases used
include WOMEN'S RIGHTS, WOMEN'S STUDIES, SEX
INEQUALITY, SEX DISCRIMINATION, SEX ROLE, WOMEN'S
LIBERATION MOVEMENT, and FEMINISM. These and all
headings are selected from the <u>Political Science
Thesaurus II</u>, by Carl Beck, Thomas McKechnie, and
Paul Evan Peters (Pittsburgh: University Center for
International Studies, University of Pittsburgh,
1979).

9.14 PSYCHOLOGY

"The Psychology of Women" is a popular course on many college campuses. Considerable research, both theoretical and applied, is carried out and reported in this field each year. Women have been the objects of psychologists' and psychiatrists' investigations for some time. Only in recent years, however, has the psychology of women become established as a legitimate sub-field, as feminists examine and reformulate the basic theories of sex role development and expression.

The general subject heading WOMEN--PSYCHOLOGY will point you to the new scholarship and also to less scientific self-help books on mental health, assertiveness, and coping mechanisms for women. The following more specific headings will also prove useful:

       SEX ROLE
       SEX DIFFERENCES (PSYCHOLOGY)
       MASCULINITY (PSYCHOLOGY)
       FEMININITY (PSYCHOLOGY)
       ASSERTIVENESS (PSYCHOLOGY)
       WOMEN--ATTITUDES
       WOMEN--MENTAL HEALTH
       FEMINIST THERAPY
       MEN (PSYCHOLOGY)

GUIDES TO RESEARCH

McInnis, Raymond G. Research Guide for Psychology. Westport, CT: Greenwood, 1982.   Z7201.   BF76.5. 016.15.

Reed, Jeffrey G. and Pam M. Baxter. Library Use: A Handbook for Psychology. Washington: American Psychological Association, 1983.   BF76.8.   025.5.

Sternberg, Robert J. Writing the Psychology Paper.
Woodbury, NY: Barron's Educational Series, 1977.
BF76.8.   808.

BIBLIOGRAPHIES ON WOMEN

Astin, Helen S., Allison Parelman, and Anne Fisher. Sex Roles: A Research Bibliography. Rockville, MD: National Institute of Mental Health, 1975.   BF692.   301.41. Sudoc no. HE20.8113:Se9.

    A bibliography of research on sex roles, covering 1960 to 1972. Arranged by broad subject categories, with detailed subject and author indexes. Because empirical studies are emphasized, few feminist commentaries or essays are included.

Baer, Helen, and Carolyn Sherif. Topical Bibliography (Selectively Annotated) on the Psychology of Women. Washington: American Psychological Association, 1974. Z7961.

    An early attempt to gather citations relevant to the study of women, particularly from the viewpoint of social psychology. Over a thousand works are listed, culled from both scholarly and popular sources.

Beere, Carole A. Women and Women's Issues: A Handbook of Tests and Measures. San Francisco: Jossey-Bass, 1979. HQ1180.   301.41.

    This guide offers detailed descriptions of 235 instruments for psychological and sociological measurement, ranging from rating scales and true-false quizzes to toy preference tests and projective storytelling. The areas covered are sex roles, sex stereotypes, sex role prescriptions, children's sex roles, gender knowledge, marital and parental roles, employee roles, multiple roles, attitudes toward women's issues, and somatic and sexual issues. Each entry includes a bibliography of reported research in which the instrument was utilized.

Chalfant, H. Paul, and Brent S. Roper. Social and Behavioral Aspects of Female Alcoholism: An Annotated Bibliography. Westport, CT: Greenwood, 1980. HV5824.W6.   362.2.

Nearly 500 publications are listed and described under eight topical categories. In addition to materials on women alcoholics, there are references to works about their families, and even some works on wives of male alcoholics.

Cromwell, Phyllis E. Women and Mental Health: A Bibliography. Rockville, MD: National Institute of Mental Health, 1975.   Z7961.   HQ1206.   016.1556. Sudoc no. HE20.8113:W84.

Abstracts of journal articles and other post-1970 publications on the mental health of women. Arranged by subject -- abortion, aging, motherhood, etc. -- with an author index.

Faunce, Patricia Spencer. Women and Ambition: A Bibliography. Metuchen, NJ: Scarecrow, 1980.   Z7961. HQ1206.   016.30141.

An exhaustive bibliography of materials written between 1960 and 1976 on all aspects of female ambition. Arranged by topic; not annotated.

Maccoby, Eleanor E., and Jacklin, Carol N. The Psychology of Sex Differences. Stanford, CA: Stanford University Press, 1974.   BF692.   155.3.

Bibliography: pp. 395-627. Lists reports of research on sex differences, arranged by author's name. The annotations follow a set format, describing the subjects, measures, and results of each study. For an earlier listing complementing this one, see Roberta Oetzel's bibliography (below).

Oetzel, Roberta M. "Annotated Bibliography." In: The Development of Sex Differences, edited by Eleanor E. Maccoby, pp. 223-351. Stanford,CA: Stanford University Press, 1966.   BF692.   155.3308.

An annotated bibliography of empirical studies on sex differences. Abstracts of books and articles are arranged by author. The section titled "Classified Summary of Research" serves as a subject index to the bibliography. For coverage of the topic extending through 1973, see the bibliography in Maccoby and Jacklin (above).

Sherman, Julia A. On the Psychology of Women: A Survey of Empirical Studies. Springfield, IL: C. Thomas, 1971. HQ1206. 155.6.

This book on the psychology of women consists of two parts: a review of the research in the form of a bibliographic essay; and a bibliography proper arranged by author.

Walstedt, Joyce Jennings. The Psychology of Women: A Partially Annotated Bibliography. Pittsburgh: KNOW, 1972. HQ1201.

One of the first widely available guides to writings on the psychology of women. Most of the items listed are books and articles from the 1960s. The compiler annotated the majority of the entries, adding subjective comments on some and highlighting those judged to be classics. Section One of the bibliography is arranged by life stage, from "Infancy and Childhood" to "Old Age." Section Two has a subject arrangement, with sub-sections titled "Cross Cultural," "General Source Material," "Primate Studies," "Minority Group Status, Discrimination," "Psychoanalytic Theories, Mental Health," and "Sexuality and Physiology."

Zukerman, Elyse. Changing Directions in the Treatment of Women: A Mental Health Bibliography. Rockville, MD: National Institute of Mental Health, 1979. RC451.4.W6. 616.8. Sudoc no. HE20.8113:W34.

Focusing on criticism of traditional psychotherapies and descriptions of alternative approaches, this bibliography provides abstracts for over 400 works published between 1960 and 1977. Journal articles predominate, although there are also references to books, parts of books, and conference papers. The subject arrangement permits direct access to pragmatic writings on topics like the psychiatric treatment of minority women or rape crisis counseling, as well as to more theoretical investigations.

INDEXES AND CONTINUING BIBLIOGRAPHIES

Catalog of Selected Documents in Psychology. Washington: American Psychological Association, 1971 to present. BF1. 150.

This quarterly is actually a catalog of writings on psychology which can be ordered from the publisher. The objective is to provide "an intermediate publications outlet between informal communication networks and conventional journals." Recent issues list a number of works on women, often including bibliographies on special topics as well as reports of research.

<u>Child Development Abstracts and Bibliography</u>. Chicago: University of Chicago Press, for the Society for Research in Child Development, 1927 to present.   HQ750.A1. 016.6491.

Published three times a year, this source indexes and abstracts the journal literature on the health, psychology, and education of children. Books are cited and annotated in a separate section. Category arrangement, with a subject index that uses the terms "gender" and "sex," but not "boy" and "girl."

<u>Psychological Abstracts</u>. Arlington, VA: American Psychological Association, 1927 to present.   BF1. 150.

The standard access tool to journal articles in the field of psychology. Each monthly issue groups references in a set topical outline; every article is abstracted. Author and subject indexes are included in the back of each issue and are cumulated every six months. References to articles on the psychology of women are scattered throughout each issue, with a fair number falling into the category "Psychosexual Behavior and Sex Roles." The subject index, which should provide a corrective approach by narrow topic, is rigidly based on a thesaurus of terms and phrases (see below) which does not take women's issues sufficiently into account. The subject heading for women is HUMAN FEMALES. Despite this drawback, <u>Psychological Abstracts</u> remains the single most important tool for literature searches in psychology.

<u>Psychological Index, 1894-1935</u>. Princeton, NJ: Psychological Review, 1895-1936.   42 volumes.   Z7203. 016.15.

The precursor of <u>Psychological Abstracts</u> and the best source for psychological opinion on women in the early years of the twentieth century. The scope of this classified bibliography is international.

Entries are not annotated. The subject categories
varied over the years; the sections labeled
"Individual, Sex and Class Psychology" and "Sex, Age
and Occupational Differences" often included works on
women.

Social Work Research and Abstracts. New York: National
Association of Social Workers, 1965 to present.   HV1.
301.

The scope of this abstracting service extends to
social psychology and psychiatric social work. For a
full annotation, see chapter 9.17, "Sociology."

Thesaurus of Psychological Index Terms. 2nd ed.
Washington: American Psychological Association, 1977.
Z675.1.P7.   025.3.

A guide to the subject terms used to index
Psychological Abstracts (see above). The
"Relationship Section" gives synonymous, broader, and
narrower terms; the "Rotated Alphabetical Terms
Section" is a simple listing of approved terms under
every word in them. This revised edition contains a
number of terms relevant to women's studies,
including FEMINISM, PREMENSTRUAL TENSION, SEX ROLES,
WORKING WOMEN, and FAMILY VIOLENCE.

9.15 RELIGION AND PHILOSOPHY

Central to the theological upheavals of recent years is the raging debate over the role of women in organized religion. Some feminists have renounced the major religions as relentlessly patriarchal. In their place, they have embraced alternative forms of women's spirituality, resurrecting past practices of witchcraft and herbalism and inventing modern rituals. Others have reconciled an abiding faith in traditional religious systems with their emerging feminism, by seeking to reform their organizations from within. The ordination of women as ministers and rabbis and the revision of sexist liturgical language are two focal points for their activism.

Despite the many varieties of religious activity that the women's movement has spurred, academic and religious publishers have lagged in bringing out bibliographies to chronicle the progress. In philosophy, the bibliographical picture is even bleaker. There is, at this writing, no readily-available bibliography pulling together the diverse theories and speculations of feminist philosophers.

In the catalog, the subject entries for works about women and religion are numerous and overlapping. WOMEN AND RELIGION and WOMEN--RELIGIOUS LIFE are applied to both general studies and theoretical writings. Such constructions as WOMEN IN CHRISTIANITY and WOMEN IN BUDDHISM describe the role of women in the major religions, although the inverted headings WOMEN, JEWISH and WOMEN, MUSLIM are also found. WOMEN (IN RELIGION, FOLKLORE, ETC.) covers the image and role of women in folk and primitive religions; WOMAN (THEOLOGY) is a parallel heading. WOMEN IN CHURCH WORK is a broad heading, while both WOMEN CLERGY and ORDINATION OF WOMEN refer to works on women in the ministry. The image of women in sacred writings earns headings such as WOMEN IN THE BIBLE and WOMEN IN THE TALMUD. SEXISM IN RELIGION and FEMINISM--RELIGIOUS ASPECTS are new terms that apply

to many recent works. Additional relevant headings range from MONASTICISM AND RELIGIOUS ORDERS FOR WOMEN to CLERGYMEN'S WIVES.
WOMEN PHILOSOPHERS is the term used in the catalog for women who work in field of philosophy. Some theoretical writings will be entered under FEMINISM--PHILOSOPHY.

GUIDES TO RESEARCH

Bollier, John A. <u>The Literature of Theology: A Guide for Students and Pastors.</u> Philadelphia: Westminster, 1979. Z7751. BR118. 016.23.

DeGeorge, Richard T. <u>The Philosopher's Guide to Sources, Research Tools, Professional Life, and Related Fields.</u> Lawrence: Regents Press of Kansas, 1980. Z7165. 016.1.

Kennedy, James R., Jr. <u>Library Research Guide to Religion and Theology: Illustrated Search Strategy and Sources.</u> Ann Arbor: Pierian Press, 1974. BL41. 200.

Tice, Terrence N., and Thomas P. Slavens. <u>Research Guide to Philosophy.</u> Chicago: American Library Association, 1983. B52. 107.

Wilson, John F., and Thomas P. Slavens. <u>Research Guide to Religious Studies.</u> Chicago: American Library Association, 1982. BL41. 291.

BIBLIOGRAPHIES ON WOMEN

Fischer, Clare B. <u>Breaking Through: A Bibliography of Women and Religion.</u> Berkeley, CA: Graduate Theological Union Library, 1980. Z7963.R45. BL485.R45. 016.2911.

>   Sponsored by Berkeley's Center for Women and Religion, this multidisciplinary bibliography singles out recent feminist scholarship along with more traditional theological writings. Many of the works cited can be found in general women's studies reading lists; the bibliography is largely limited to book-length works; and despite the compiler's attention to cross-cultural studies, the emphasis is on the Jewish and Christian faiths. Nevertheless, this remains a helpful introduction to many facets of the study of women and religion.

Hamelsdorf, Ora, and Sandra Adelsberg. Jewish Women and Jewish Law: Bibliography. Fresh Meadows, NY: Biblio Press, 1980.   Z7963.J4.   HQ1172.   016.3054.

As stated in the preface, this partially annotated bibliography covers "many aspects of recent discussion of Jewish women's role and status within the family, in Jewish courst, in the synagogue, religious identity, obligatory rituals" and "her legal status as daughter, mother, wife, and as divorcee" under traditional Jewish law (halacha). Included are books, periodical articles, unpublished papers, and dissertations. A brief glossary is included, along with addresses for many of the materials cited.

Richardson, Marilyn. Black Women and Religion: A Bibliography. Boston: G. K. Hall, 1980.   Z1361.N39. BR563.N4.   016.2.

Provides access to a varied collection of materials on the religious life of Black American women. Books, articles, works of fiction, musical recordings, and audiovisual materials are cited. Most of the nearly 900 entries are annotated. The arrangement is by type of material, with an author/title index. An appendix lists biographical works and gives brief sketches of seventeen Black women who were active in the church.

CONTINUING BIBLIOGRAPHIES AND INDEXES

The Catholic Periodical and Literature Index. Haverford, PA: Catholic Library Association, 1930 to present. AI3.   011.

An author and subject index to Catholic periodicals and to books by, about, or of interest to Catholics. Issued six times a year, this is a good source of citations on such topics as ABORTION, WOMEN AS PRIESTS, WOMEN IN CHURCH WORK, and RELIGIOUS LIFE FOR WOMEN.

Index to Jewish Periodicals. Cleveland Heights, OH: Index to Jewish Periodicals, 1963 to present.   Z6367.

An author and subject index to articles in Jewish periodicals.   SEX ROLE, WOMEN AS RABBIS, and WOMEN, JEWISH are typical headings.

The Philosopher's Index. Bowling Green, OH: Bowling Green University, 1967 to present. Z7127. 016.105.

Each quarterly issue has three parts: an author index, with full abstracts; an index to book reviews; and a subject index. Look in the subject index under the headings WOMAN, WOMEN'S LIBERATION, FEMINISM, and SEXISM. Two supplements issued in 1978 carry the coverage back to 1940.

Religion Index One: Periodicals. Chicago: American Theological Library Association, 1977 to present. Z7753. BL1. 016.2.

The successor to Index to Religious Periodical Literature, which was issued between 1949 and 1976. Full citations to articles in religious periodicals are arranged by author; abstracts are frequently provided. Book reviews are indexed separately. In the subject index, headings largely follow the established vocabulary of the Library of Congress. Coverage is international, although English-language articles are emphasized. "Church history, biblical literature, theology, history of religions, sociology and psychology of religion and other subject areas in the humanities and current events" come under the umbrella of indexed topics. Issued twice a year in paperback, and four times a year on microfiche.

Religion Index Two: Multi-Author Works. Chicago: American Theological Library Association, 1976 to present. Z7751. BL48. 016.2.

An annual series complementing Religion Index One: Periodicals (see above), this index lists articles in festschriften and other collected works by author, editor, and subject. Not annotated.

Religious and Theological Abstracts. Myerstown, PA: Religious and Theological Abstracts, 1958 to present. BR1. 208.22.

A non-sectarian quarterly that provides short summaries of works in the following sections: biblical; theological; historical; practical. Use the annual subject index to find references under WOMEN, WOMEN--MINISTRY OF, and WOMEN--ROLE OF.

Walters, LeRoy. Bibliography of Bioethics. Detroit: Gale, 1975 to present.   Z6675.E8.   R724.   016.174.

An annual bibliography in the relatively new field of bioethics. Books, essays, journal and newspaper articles, court decisions, bills, laws, films and audio cassettes are included. From a women's studies perspective, this bibliography is most useful for its coverage of the ethical issues surrounding abortion, contraception, and reproductive technologies, but much is also offered on such topics as psychiatric care and death and dying.

9.16 SCIENCE AND TECHNOLOGY

It is hardly surprising that women's studies has made few inroads into scientific and technical fields. These disciplines have traditionally been dominated by men. Moreover, their philosophical foundation -- the logical objectivity of the scientific method -- seems on the surface to rule out any new views of the natural world from a feminist perspective. Nonetheless, some pioneering scholars have rooted out cases of male bias in research design and in the interpretation of findings. In particular, women's studies scholars have exposed the fallacies in theories posited by sociobiologists, theories which point to a genetic basis for women's inferior social and political status.
   To date, however, the greatest impact of women's studies springs from its critique of sex discrimination in the teaching and practice of the sciences. For example, feminists have isolated "math anxiety" as a socialized response in girls, and they have pointed to the dearth of role models for women seeking to enter the pure or applied sciences.
   Hence, subject headings are common in the catalog for books about women in scientific and technical occupations: WOMEN PHYSICISTS, WOMEN ENGINEERS, WOMEN IN SCIENCE, and so forth. Some recent feminist works in biology will appear under the subject WOMEN--PHYSIOLOGY. The broader headings SCIENCE--SOCIAL ASPECTS and TECHNOLOGY--SOCIAL ASPECTS may also be attached to relevant books.

GUIDES TO RESEARCH

Chen, Ching-chih. Scientific and Technical Information Sources. Cambridge, MA: MIT Press, 1977.   Z7401.
Q158.5.   026.

Herner, Saul. **A Brief Guide to Sources of Scientific and Technical Information.** 2nd ed. Arlington, VA: Information Resources Press, 1980.   Q225.5.   507.

Malinowsky, H. Robert, and Jeanne M. Richardson. **Science and Engineering Literature: A Guide to Reference Sources.** 3rd ed. Littleton, CO: Libraries Unlimited, 1980. Z7401.   Q158.5.   016.5.

BIBLIOGRAPHIES ON WOMEN

Chinn, Phyllis Zweig. **Women in Science and Mathematics: Bibliography.** Arcata, CA: Humboldt State University, 1980.   Z7963.S3.   Q130.   016.3314.

> An unannotated list of books, research reports, journal articles, pamphlets, and conference papers. Emphasizing women's roles in science, there are sections for biographies and autobiographies, research on sex differences, and strategies for increasing women's participation in scientific fields, among other topics.

Biological Woman - The Convenient Myth. Edited by Ruth Hubbard, Mary Sue Henifin, and Barbara Fried. Cambridge, MA: Schenkman, 1982.   HQ1206.   305.4.

> This anthology contains an extensive bibliography (pp. 289-376), covering scientific ideas about the sexes, particular issues in the lives of women (including reproduction and motherhood, illness, psychology, rape), and women's experiences in science and health fields.

INDEXES AND CONTINUING BIBLIOGRAPHIES

Applied Science and Technology Index. New York: H. W. Wilson, 1913 to present.   Z7913.   016.6.

> Published eleven times a year and cumulated annually, this index was called **Industrial Arts Index** until 1958. It is useful for locating articles on women in scientific and technical occupations. In addition to the generalized entry WOMAN there are such entries as WOMEN AS ENGINEERS and WOMEN IN THE MINING INDUSTRY.

Biological Abstracts. Philadelphia: Biological
Abstracts, 1926 to present.   QH301. 570.5.

This semimonthly index, with semiannual cumulations, is useful for researching female physiology. More than 5,000 periodicals from 90 countries are covered. Abstracts are arranged in broad categories, with several indexes. The biosystematic index and the generic index can both be used if you are familiar with scientific names, while the concept index groups references in broad topical areas. The subject index is based on keywords in the titles of abstracted articles, so one must check under both WOMAN and WOMEN and also under more specific subject words.

General Science Index. New York: H. W. Wilson, 1978 to present.   Z791.   016.6.

For the nonspecialist, this is an excellent guide to periodical articles in English in all areas of the traditional scientific disciplines, as well as food and nutrition, the environment, health, and psychology. WOMEN appears as a subject term, alone and with modifiers. A recent issue cited articles on toxic shock syndrome, occupational hazards to women, the effect of oral contraceptives on vitamin requirements, and the experience of women with specific diseases such as breast cancer and alcoholism. Also indexed are numerous articles profiling women working in scientific fields. Published ten times a year, with an annual cumulation.

Science Citation Index. Philadelphia: Institute for Scientific Information, 1961 to present.   Z7401. 016.5.

The precursor of Social Sciences Citation Index and Arts & Humanities Citation Index (both described in chapter 8.2), this bimonthly index enables the researcher to find recent writings by known authors or studies which build on earlier research with which one is familiar. For women's studies students, however, the "Permuterm Subject Index" (a keyword index) may be the most useful feature. Science Citation Index is international and interdisciplinary, covering all the sciences, medicine, agriculture, technology, and the behavioral sciences.

9.17 SOCIOLOGY

The discipline of sociology applies orderly research and rigorous theory to a wide range of current social issues. Women constitute a visible group in society, and sub-groups -- Black women, college-educated women, employed women, married women, and so on -- are also identifiable. In studying how groups of women behave and how they interact with other groups and social institutions, sociologists tackle a multitude of concerns, ranging from domestic violence to occupational mobility to consumer choices. The links between sociology and women's studies are so strong that nearly a quarter of the books about women end up classified under the broad category of sociology and social problems -- that is, in the HQ's in the Library of Congress scheme or in the 301's in the Dewey system.
   WOMEN--SOCIAL CONDITIONS is the broadest applicable heading in the library catalog, but many more specific headings also exist. Among them are WOMEN--SOCIETIES AND CLUBS for studies of organizations, WOMEN--LANGUAGE for sociolinguistic books, WOMEN--HEALTH AND HYGIENE for works on women's health care, and headings such as WOMEN PRISONERS, AGED WOMEN, and WORKING CLASS WOMEN for writings on sub-groups of women.
   No single bibliography addresses all the topics studied by sociologists, but new sources on particular issues are constantly appearing. A few of the best are listed below. Many of the bibliographies listed in other chapters of this book, particularly the chapter on minority studies, can be mined for references of sociological significance. Specialists in marriage and family studies have also contributed greatly to the knowledge base of women's studies; bibliographies in that field are therefore included in this chapter.

GUIDES TO RESEARCH

Bart, Pauline, and Linda Frankel. The Student Sociologist's Handbook. 3rd ed. Glenview, IL: Scott, Foresman, 1981. HM68. 301.

A research guide unique for its feminist perspective.

McMillan, Patricia, and James R. Kennedy, Jr. Library Research Guide to Sociology: Illustrated Search Strategy and Sources. Ann Arbor: Pierian Press, 1981. HM48. 301.

BIBLIOGRAPHIES ON WOMEN

Borenstein, Audrey. Older Women in 20th-Century America: A Selected Annotated Bibliography. New York: Garland, 1982. Z7164.O4. HQ1064 016.3052.

This cross-disciplinary bibliography focuses on women over forty years of age, citing nearly 900 books, articles, essays, government documents, and conference papers. Scholarly studies, first-person accounts, and fiction are all represented. The chapter titled "Sociological Perspectives on Older Women" covers love and sex, marriage and family, friendship, neighborhood and community relationships, older women alone, and widowhood.

Davis, Nanette J., and Jone M. Keith. Women and Deviance: Issues in Social Conflict and Change: An Annotated Bibliography. New York: Garland, 1984. Z7964.U49. HQ1420. 016.3054.

This selective bibliography describes over 500 publications concerned with various aspects of social deviance by women -- criminal behavior, alcohol and drug abuse, lesbianism, teenage pregnancy, and mental illness, among other concerns. Also covered are forms of deviant behavior that affect women, such as pornography and battering. Interdisciplinary in scope, the bibliography also includes many general works on women's contemporary and historical roles.

Diner, Hasia R. Women and Urban Society: A Guide to Information Sources. Detroit: Gale, 1979. Z7961. HQ1154. 016.30141.

This guide provides abstracts of books, articles, and conference papers on the topic of women living in cities and the impact of urbanization on women's roles and images. The scope is international, although only English-language works appear to be cited. Entries are grouped under six headings, with author, title, and subject indexes.

Kennedy, Susan Estabrook. America's White Working-Class Women: A Historical Bibliography. New York: Garland, 1981.   Z7963.E7.   016.3055.

This annotated bibliography lists over 1,000 works in groupings by broad historical period. The sub-arrangement of citations is by topic: personal; home and family; community; class; employment; historical conditions (such as the suffrage movement and the World Wars). Author and title indexes are furnished.

Muldoon, Maureen. Abortion: An Annotated Indexed Bibliography. New York: E. Mellen, 1980.   Z6671.2.A2. RG734.   016.3634.

A partially annotated bibliography of 3,397 articles and books. The entries are grouped in the following categories: bibliographies; ethical and theological aspects; legal aspects; studies in the states; studies in other countries; collected articles; and symposia proceedings. All sides of the issue are covered, including social implications of abortion.

Rubin, Rick, and Greg Byerly. Incest: The Last Taboo: An Annotated Bibliography. New York: Garland, 1983. HQ72.U53.   306.7.

A selective, interdisciplinary guide to over 400 items, including books, dissertations, audiovisual materials, and articles in both popular and scholarly periodicals.

Wilson, Carolyn F. Violence Against Women: An Annotated Bibliography. Boston: G. K. Hall, 1981.   HV6250.4. 016.3628.

Lists 213 books, articles, and government publications on battered women, rape, sexual abuse of children, and pornography, plus general studies on women and violence. There are lengthy annotations and well written introductions to each section.

BIBLIOGRAPHIES ON MARRIAGE AND THE FAMILY

NOTE: See also the sub-section on family history in chapter 9.6, "History."

Aldous, Joan, and Reuben Hill. International Bibliography of Research in Marriage and the Family, 1900-1972. Minneapolis: University of Minnesota Press, 1967-74. 2 vols. Z7164.M2. 016.30142.

This is a standard source, indispensible for research on women and the family. Volume 1 covers books, articles, and pamphlets from 1900 to 1964; volume 2, from 1965 to 1972. Citations can be found under subject, keyword-in-title, and author. Continued by the annual Inventory of Marriage and Family Literature (St. Paul: Family Social Service, University of Minnesota, 1973/74 to present).

McKenney, Mary. Divorce: A Selected Annotated Bibliography. Metuchen, NJ: Scarecrow, 1975. Z7164.M2. 016.30142.

This bibliography covers all aspects of divorce -- legal, financial, psychological, religious, etc. -- and the impact of divorce on women, men, and children. References are limited for the most part to American books, articles, and pamphlets published before 1973. The selection is objective, but the annotations reflect the compiler's feminist values.

Schlesinger, Benjamin. The One-Parent Family: Perspectives and Annotated Bibliography. 4th ed. Toronto: University of Toronto Press, 1978. HQ535. 301.42.

Reflecting reality, this bibliography cites more studies of single mothers than of single fathers. There are six introductory essays, followed by an annotated bibliography of over 750 items. The bibliography is divided into three parts, covering the years 1930-1969, 1970-1974, and 1975-1978. A list of recommended readings for children is also included.

INDEXES AND CONTINUING BIBLIOGRAPHIES

Human Resources Abstracts. Beverly Hills: Sage
Publications, 1966 to present.   Z7165.U5.   331.

This quarterly publication was called Poverty and
Human Resources Abstracts until 1974. It focuses on
"human, social, and manpower problems and solutions."
Abstracts are grouped in eleven broad categories, one
of which is labelled "Equal Employment Opportunity."
Additional references on topics of interest in
women's studies can be found under WOMEN in the
subject index in each issue.

International Bibliography of Sociology. Chicago:
Aldine, 1952 to present.   Z7161.   016.301.

This annual bibliography is sponsored by Unesco and
covers the world's literature in sociology. Journal
articles, books, pamphlets, and official documents in
numerous languages are included. Author and subject
indexes are provided in both English and French and
reveal many works on women's studies topics.

Population Index. Princeton, NJ: Office of Population
Research, Princeton University, and the Population
Association of America, 1935 to present.   Z7164.D3.
016.312.

This quarterly publication aids in identifying
studies of fertility, contraception, abortion,
marriage, and family life. Part 1, titled "Current
Items," offers articles, news notes, and occasional
bibliographic essays. Part 2, titled "Bibliography,"
is a classified annotated list of books, periodical
articles, statistical publications, and proceedings
of professional meetings and conferences. The scope
is international. Geographic and author indexes
appear in each issue and are cumulated yearly.
Population Index Bibliography (Boston: G. K. Hall,
1971) is a six-volume cumulation of bibliographic
entries from 1935 through 1968.

Sage Family Studies Abstracts. Beverly Hills: Sage
Publications, 1979 to present.   HQ536.   301.42.

Aimed at both academicians and professionals working
with families, this quarterly publication abstracts
about 250 studies in each issue. Citations,

primarily to books and articles, are organized in
seven categories, variously sub-divided: theory and
methodology; lifestyles; life cycles; marital and
family processes; problems, therapy, and counseling;
sex roles; social issues. Works about women can also
be identified through the subject indexes, which
cumulate annually. Typical subject entries include
WOMEN, MARRIED WOMEN, MOTHERING, FATHERING, BATTERED
WOMEN, and WIDOWHOOD.

Social Work Research and Abstracts. New York: National
Association of Social Workers, 1965 to present. HV1.
361.

From 1965 to 1977, this quarterly journal was known
as Abstracts for Social Workers. Now each issue
includes several reports of recent research, in
addition to summaries of writings of interest to
professional social workers. The scope ranges from
public policy to therapeutic techniques. Abstracts
are grouped in the following categories: fields of
service (e.g., alcoholism and drug addiction, or
family and child welfare); social policy and action;
service methods; the profession; history; related
fields (e.g., psychology). The author and subject
indexes in the back of each issue are cumulated
annually. Relevant subject terms include SEXUAL
EQUALITY, SEX ROLES, MOTHERS, and WOMEN.

Sociological Abstracts. New York: Sociological
Abstracts, 1952 to present. HM1. 301.

This abstracting service publishes five issues a
year, with an annual index. In each issue, the first
and largest section is devote to abstracts of journal
articles in sociology and related fields, presented
in a classified arrangment. In recent years,
"Feminist Studies" has been employed as a category.
Supplementary sections abstract papers presented at
conferences. Each section is followed by its own
author and subject indexes. The subject indexing is
based on word roots rather than a strict keyword-in-
title system. For most bibliographic research in
sociology, this is one of the first sources to
consult.

10
Library Catalogs and Guides to Special Collections of Books and Archives

Undergraduate students can usually complete their research for term papers using the resources of their own campus library. Some projects, however, require students to consult materials in other libraries and special collections. Graduate students and faculty are even more likely to need resources held at other institutions.

The reference sources listed in this section are of several types. Some, like <u>Subject Collections</u> and <u>Women's History Sources</u>, serve as indexes to library and repository collections in particular fields. Others, like the <u>Dictionary Catalog</u> of the New York Public Library, are reproductions of local catalogs. Few general collections are represented by published catalogs, but many specialized collections are, including the Schlesinger Library, the finest collection in the United States of printed sources and manuscripts on women's history.

Using the works described in this section, you can quickly determine what resources are available at other libraries. You may be able to borrow books through your library's interlibrary loan service or to obtain photocopies of articles. To use manuscripts or archival materials, however, you'll almost always have to travel to the library that owns them. It's wise to write or telephone in advance. A collection may be restricted -- that is, inaccessible unless certain conditions, such as permission of the donor, are first met. Another collection might be uncataloged, so making an appointment with its curator would be a must.

Many publications beyond those listed here identify manuscript and archive collections of women's materials within a particular nation, region, or state. You can find them listed in the library catalog under the heading WOMEN with the place name added on, e.g., WOMEN--NEW YORK. Examples of such sources are:

Michigan. History Division. **Bibliography of Sources Relating to Women.** Lansing, MI: History Division, 1975. Z7964.M5. 016.30141.

Women in Australia: **An Annotated Guide to Records.** 2 vols. Canberra: Australian Government Publishing Service, 1977. Z7964.A8. 016.30141.

CATALOGS & GUIDES TO WOMEN'S STUDIES COLLECTIONS

The History of Women in America: **Catalogs of the Books, Manuscripts, and Pictures of the Arthur and Elizabeth Schlesinger Library.** Boston: G. K. Hall, 1983. 10 vols. Z7965. 016.30141.

A catalog of books, periodicals, manuscripts, and pictures housed at the Schlesinger Library at Radcliffe -- one of the largest collections of source material on the history of American women from 1800 to the present. The collection is particularly strong in materials on the suffrage movement, social reform movements, women pioneering in men's professions, and women in the labor movement. Nineteenth-century cookbooks, books on domestic science, and etiquette manuals are also well represented. Recent acquisitions document the lives of "anonymous" women, including women of color and working-class women. In addition to books and periodicals, the library is rich in personal papers, family and organizational archives, newsletters, task force reports, microfilms, and oral histories. The published catalog, like a card catalog, may be searched by author, subject, or title.

Sophia Smith Collection. **Catalogs of the Sophia Smith Collection, Women's History Archive, Smith College, Northampton, Massachusetts.** 7 vols. Boston: G.K. Hall, 1975. Z7965. 016.30141.

The Sophia Smith Collection is the nation's oldest archive of women's history materials. The published catalog has four parts: author catalog; subject catalog; manuscript catalog; and guide to photographs. Emphasizing women in American history, the collection covers such topics as birth control and sex reforms, education, fine and applied arts, peace movements and social reforms, women in industry, women in the professions, suffrage and anti-suffrage campaigns, and women's liberation.

North Carolina. University. Women's College, Greensboro. Library. The Woman's Collection. Greensboro, NC: Women's College Library, 1937 to 1955. Z881.

The main volume and supplements list books acquired by the Women's College Library from 1937 to 1955. The catalog is useful as a bibliography because of its subject arrangement. The collection covers a wide range of interests, from homemaking, etiquette, and "women's avocations" (gardening, needlework, etc.) to women workers and the social history of women. More recently, Marda Scott and Elizabeth Power compiled The Woman's Collection: A Checklist of Holdings (Greensboro, NC: Walter Clinton Jackson Library, 1975). While this new listing extends coverage backwards to include some 2,500 pre-1900 imprints, it offers no subject access nor annotations.

Women's History Sources: A Guide to Archives and Manuscript Collections in the United States. Ed. by Andrea Hinding. New York: Bowker, 1978. Z7964.U49. 016.30141.

This important guide identifies more than 18,000 collections, contained in 1,600 libraries and repositories, which document the lives of American women from Colonial times to the present. It is a tremendously valuable tool for locating primary source material on individual women and women's organizations. For each collection listed, the size, the existence of catalog or guides, and any restrictions on access are noted. The contents and scope of the collections are described in annotations. Arrangement is geographic, with a detailed name and subject index.

GENERAL CATALOGS AND GUIDES

Ash, Lee. Subject Collections: A Guide to Special Book Collections and Subject Emphases as Reported by University, College, Public, and Special Libraries and Museums in the United States and Canada. 5th ed. New York: Bowker, 1978. Z731. 026.

This is a guide to libraries having strong or specialized collections on different subjects. Try looking under the general subject WOMEN and more specific concerns such as WOMEN--SUFFRAGE, WOMEN AUTHORS, WOMEN IN THE PROFESSIONS, and so forth.

Under each subject entry, libraries are listed
alphabetically by place. Very brief information is
provided on the content and scope of the collections.

New York Public Library. Research Libraries. Dictionary
Catalog of the Research Libraries of the New York Public
Library, 1911-1971. New York: New York Public Library,
Astor, Lenox, and Tilden Foundations, 1979. 800 vols.
Z881. 019.

New York Public Library. Research Libraries. Dictionary
Catalog of the Research Libraries. New York: New York
Public Library, 1972 to present. Z881. 019.

The first set is a photographic record of cards in
the New York Public Library's catalog as of 1971.
The new set is a computer-generated cumulative record
of all books cataloged at NYPL since 1972. In both
sets, author, title and subject entries are presented
in a single alphabetic (or "dictionary") sequence.
You can use these catalogs as you would your own
library's, to identify books on a chosen topic. Or
you can use them as a general, multidisciplinary
bibliography for verifying references.

U.S. National Historical Publications Commission. A
Guide to Archives and Manuscripts in the United States.
Edited by Philip M. Hamer. New Haven: Yale University
Press, 1961. CD3022. 025.171.

A respected guide to collections of manuscripts and
papers in the U.S. Entries are arranged
alphabetically by state, then city, then name of
repository. The nature and extent of each collection
is briefly described, and any published guides are
cited. There is an index to personal names and
subjects appearing in the text. If you plan to use
manuscripts or archival materials at another library,
you should also consult the Commission's Directory of
Archives and Manuscript Repositories (Washington:
National Historical Publications and Records
Commission, 1978), which provides phones numbers,
hours, etc.

National Union Catalog of Manuscript Collections.
Washington: Library of Congress, 1959 to present.
Z6620.U5. 016.091.

An ongoing inventory of manuscript collections in
repositories throughout the country. Entries are for

sets of papers, rather than for individual items. Data is given on the size, scope, content, and accessibility of each collection. Entries are in random order, so the indexes (issued annually and cumulated periodically) are essential for identifying collections related to persons, institutions, or topics.

Robbins, John Albert, editor. American Literary Manuscripts: A Checklist of Holdings in Academic, Historical, and Public Libraries, Museums, and Authors' Homes in the United States. 2nd ed. Athens, GA: University of Georgia Press, 1977.   Z6620.U5.   016.81.

Arranged alphabetically by author, this handy guide locates the manuscripts of some 3,000 authors in repositories around the country. Materials are distinguished by a code (e.g., M for literary manuscripts, J for journals and diaries, L for letters), and the approximate number of each is noted.

U.S. National Archives and Records Service. Guide to the National Archives of the United States. Washington: U.S. Government Printing Office, 1974.   CD3023.   027.573.

This source describes, in some detail, archival records of federal agencies and offices now deposited in the National Archives in Washington. (At this writing, a separate two-volume guide to women's materials in the National Archives is being prepared, with one volume to cover military records and the other civilian records.)

U.S. Library of Congress. Special Collections in the Library of Congress: A Selective Guide. Compiled by Annette Melville. Washington: Library of Congress, 1980. Z733.U58.   027.5753.

This guide offers descriptions of 269 "thematic" collections housed at the Library of Congress in Washington. The listing includes non-book materials as well as books and pamphlets, although most manuscript collections are excluded.

11
Biographical Sources

The discovery and celebration of forgotten women continues to be a central aspect of women's studies. One can find book-length biographies of most famous women simply by looking in the catalog under their names. The lives of less renowned women, however, are more likely to be detailed in a collective biography, a biographical dictionary, or a magazine article.
This chapter highlights the most useful biographical sourcebooks. With a single exception (Current Biography), these focus solely on women, thus rectifying omissions in standard scholarly and popular reference sources. In addition, research tools that can lead you to biographies, autobiographies, and diaries are described.

COLLECTIVE BIOGRAPHIES

NOTE: This section is organized in rough chronological sequence.

The International Dictionary of Women's Biography. Edited by Jennifer S. Uglow. New York: Continuum, 1982. CT3202. 920.72.

This is a handy source for biographical background on prominent women of all periods and all parts of the world. The entries are brief (usually one or two paragraphs) and frequently end with a single reference to additional published information. A subject index groups the women by their primary fields of activity.

Raven, Susan, and Alison Weir. Women of Achievement:

Thirty-five Centuries of History. New York: Harmony Books, 1981.   HQ1123.   920.72.

The writing is crisp and the illustrations are plentiful in this international collection of biographical sketches. Entries are divided into ten chapters: Politics and Power; Education and Social Reform; Religion; The Written Word; The Performing Arts; The Visual Arts; Science and Medicine; Money and Management; Travel and Exploration; Sport.

Europa Biographical Dictionary of British Women. Edited by Anne Crawford and others. London: Europa, 1983. CT3320.   920.72.
Coverage in this compendium of brief biographies extends from the earliest history of the British Isles to the present. Only deceased women are included. Many of the entries note further sources of information.

Notable American Women, 1607-1950. 3 vols. Cambridge, MA: Belknap Press of Harvard University Press, 1971. CT3260.   920.72.

Notable American Women: The Modern Period. Cambridge, MA: Belknap Press of Harvard University Press, 1980. CT3260.   920.72.

This classic set presents short biographical essays on American women of distinction in all fields. Patterned after the Dictionary of American Biography and its supplements (New York: C. Scribner's Sons, 1928-1981), all of the entries are written by experts and include a short bibliography. The original three-volume work includes only women who died before 1950; the newer volume extends coverage through 1975. Both include subject indexes which can be useed to identify women active in the various professions or involved in certain causes.

Willard, Frances, and Mary Livermore, editors. American Women. 2 vols. New York: Mast, Crowell and Kirkpatrick, 1897. (Reprint: Detroit: Gale, 1973.)   CT3260. 920.72.

A compilation of 1,500 short biographies of nineteenth-century women of the United States. Most entries include a portrait. Philanthropists, abolitionists, authors, suffragists, social reformers, educators, and actresses predominate. The

first edition was published in 1893 with the title A
Woman of the Century.

Contributions of Black Women to America. Edited by
Marianna W. Davis.   2 vols.   Columbia, SC: Kenday Press,
1982.   E185.86.   973.

Volume 1 covers the arts, media, business, law, and
sports. Volume 2 treats civil rights, politics and
government, education, medicine, and the sciences.
Each section was researched and compiled by a
committee of experts; each contains a selective
bibliography and an index to the names of women
mentioned in the text. This last feature makes it
possible to use the volumes as biographical
dictionaries, although the data presented on each
woman's life are not standardized. Many photographs
illustrate the text. To date this is the most wide-
ranging overview of the accomplishments of Black
American women.

Woman's Who's Who of America. New York: American
Commonwealth Company, 1914. (Reprint: Detroit: Gale,
1976.)   CT3260.   920.72.

An invaluable source on American and Canadian women
in the early years of this century, particularly
those involved in the movements for suffrage and
social reform. Gives brief biographical information
for 9,644 women.

American Women: The Official Who's Who Among the Women
of the Nation. Los Angeles: Richard Blank Publishing
Company, 1935-1940. (Reprint: Detroit: Gale, 1981.)
E747.   920.7.

Volumes 1 through 3, all that were ever published,
span the years 1935 to 1940. Coverage grew with each
edition; volume 3 has brief biographies of 10,222
women. Geographical and occupational indexes are
provided, along with some interesting statistical
summaries. (The 1981 edition reprints the final
volume, with unduplicated entries from the first two
volumes appended.)

Who's Who of American Women. Chicago: Marquis Who's Who,
1958 to present.   CT3260.   920.7.

This work includes women listed in Who's Who in

America (Chicago: Marquis, 1899 to present) plus
others chosen for their prominence. The usual
abbreviated data on education, personal life, career,
and achievements are provided. Published biennially.

The World Who's Who of Women. 6th ed. Cambridge,
England: International Biographical Centre, 1982.
HQ1123. 920.72.

Lists over 8,000 women, with photographs and brief
biographical data. The emphasis is on the United
States and Commonwealth nations. Most useful for
minor figures.

Current Biography. New York: H. W. Wilson, 1940 to
present. CT100. 920.

This standard library reference tool, published
monthly, is an excellent source of biographical
background on women currently in the news.
Cumulative indexes make it easy to search past
volumes.

NOTE: Many one-volume collective biographies and
autobiographies have been published in recent years.
Often these focus on women in a particular region or
women active in a certain profession. Examples are Women
in Early Texas, edited by Evelyn M. Carrington (Austin:
Jenkins, 1975), and Women Composers, Conductors, and
Musicians of the Twentieth Century, by Jane Werner LePage
(Metuchen, NJ: Scarecrow, 1980-1983). You can locate
such works in the catalog under subject headings such as
WOMEN--TEXAS--BIOGRAPHY or WOMEN MUSICIANS--BIOGRAPHY.

BIBLIOGRAPHIES AND INDEXES OF BIOGRAPHIES

Biographical Books, 1876-1949. New York: Bowker, 1983.
Z5301. CT104. 016.92.

Biographical Books, 1950-1980. New York: Bowker, 1980.
Z5301. CT104. 016.92.

The keys to a century of biographies published in the
U.S., these volumes together list some 82,000 books.
The main listing is by the names of the subjects of
the books, with indexes by author and title. The
"vocation index" at the front of each volume aids in

identifying writings on women by their occupations, national origins, or other characteristics.

Biography and Genealogy Master Index. 2nd ed. 8 vols. Detroit: Gale, 1980. Z5305.U5. CT214. 920.

This extremely useful reference source indexes biographical data on both women and men in over 350 published works, including current and retrospective biographical dictionaries and who's who publications. It is produced by computer with little or no editing, so a person may be listed in the index under several forms of name if she was listed differently in the original sources. Altogether, over three million entries are indexed.

Biography Index. New York: H. W. Wilson, 1946 to present. Z5301. 016.92.

An ongoing index to biographical articles published in magazines. Entries are alphabetical by name, with an index by occupation. This is an excellent index for people of current interest. It offers good coverage of women's periodicals such as Ladies' Home Journal. Published four times a year.

Ireland, Norma. Index to Women of the World from Ancient to Modern Times. Westwood, MA: F. W. Faxon, 1970. Z7963.B6. 016.92072.

About 13,000 names appear in this index to the biographies of women. Most references are to chapters in such collective biographies as Dames and Daughters of Colonial Days and Little Known Women of the Bible. A few magazines are indexed. References are listed alphabetically by name, with birth and death dates, nationality, and occupation noted.

BIBLIOGRAPHIES AND INDEXES OF AUTOBIOGRAPHIES

Addis, Patricia K. Through a Woman's I: An Annotated Bibliography of American Women's Autobiographical Writings, 1946-1976. Metuchen, NJ: Scarecrow, 1983. Z7963.B6. CT3260. 016.92072.

This volume provides more than 2,000 brief descriptions of published autobiographies, letters, diaries, journals, memoirs, reminiscences, and travel accounts -- all written by American women during a thirty-year period. Citations are arranged alphabetically by the authors' names. There is an index of titles, an "Index by Profession or Salient Characteristic," and an "Index of Narratives by Subject Matter" (including such categories as "Black Woman's.Experience," "Illness/Handicap," and "Travel/Householding Abroad").

American Autobiography 1945-1980: A Bibliography. Edited by Mary Louise Briscoe. Madison: University of Wisconsin Press, 1982.   Z5305.U5.   CT220.   016.92.

This volume supplements Louis Kaplan's classic A Bibliography of American Autobiographies (see below). Although not limited to women, it is a useful source because women authors have been marked with asterisks, a device which facilitates skimming the entries.

First Person Female American: A Selected and Annotated Bibliography of the Autobiographies of American Women Living After 1950.   Edited by Carolyn H. Rhodes. Troy, NY: Whitson, 1980.   Z7963.A8.   HQ1386.   016.92072.

An annotated guide to autobiographical books (including published letters and diaries) by 224 women living in the U.S. after 1950. For each book discussed, there is a summary of the contents, an evaluation of its usefulness for women's studies, and a brief survey of its critical reception. A topical index is provided.

Kaplan, Louis. A Bibliography of American Autobiographies.   Madison: University of Wisconsin Press, 1961.   Z1224.   016.920073.

A bibliography of autobiographical works arranged alphabetically by the authors' names. Although women are not separated out in the subject index, the extremely detailed listing of persons by occupation, region, and other attributes is very helpful. Such headings as NEW ENGLAND--CRIMINALS, DOMESTIC RELATIONS, FACTORY WORKERS, and IMMIGRANTS (with subheadings for countries of origin) are typical.

BIBLIOGRAPHIES AND INDEXES OF DIARIES

Arksey, Laura, Nancy Pries, and Marcia Reed. American Diaries: An Annotated Bibliography of Published American Diaries and Journals. Detroit: Gale, 1983.
Z5305.U5. CT214. 016.92.

> Volume 1 of this set covers 1492 to 1844; volume 2 will cover 1845 to 1980. Over 2,500 diaries are listed in each volume. Citations are organized chronologically. There are name, geographic, and subject indexes; the last includes many entries for women.

Begos, Jane Dupree. Annotated Bibliography of Published Women's Diaries. Pound Ridge, NY: the author, 1977.
Z7963.B6. CT3230. 016.92072.

> A list of published diaries and journals by women, with brief annotations. In addition to diaries issued as books or excerpted in periodicals, the compiler includes bibliographies and anthologies of diaries, works about diary writing, fiction in diary format, poetry that serves as or is based upon diaries, calendars, almanacs, and yearbooks. Not slick, but quite useful.

12
Directories of Organizations and Services

In this chapter you will find listed a number of gudies to orqanizations working on women's issues or providing services to women. These centers and groups can be of assistance in your research. Many maintain clipping files or small specialized libraries; many compile statistics and other data for their own purposes which they may be willing to share; most issue newsletters and leaflets. For additional listings, consult the annual Encyclopedia of Associations (Detroit: Gale, 1961 to present).

Remember, however, that the primary goal of most of these organizations is not to further scholarship, but to help women directly, through counseling, legislative lobbying, education, and other activities. Be sure your requests for information are not unreasonable, and that you write or visit far in advance of your paper's due date.

Also listed in this chapter are a handful of directories of women's studies programs, sources of financial aid, and the like, which may be of immediate practical use.

Directory of Career Resources for Women. Santa Monica, CA: Ready Reference Press, 1979.   HD6095   331.7.

    This directory identifies organizations offering such services as talent banks, internships, job counseling, continuing education, and re-entry programs. Alphabetic arrangement, with geographic and topical indexes.

Doss, Martha Merrill. The Directory of Special Opportunities for Women. Garrett Park, MD: Garrett Park Press, 1981.   HD6058.   331.4.

This guide emphasizes organizational resources for
employment and education. Section I is an
alphabetical list of national groups, programs, and
government agencies. Section II is a state-by-state
list of women's centers, women's studies programs,
women's resource agencies, YWCA programs, private
firms, and individual counselors. Section III covers
women's colleges, and Section IV is a minimal list of
print and nonprint information sources.

Everywoman's Guide to Colleges and Universities. Old
Westbury, NY: The Feminist Press, 1982.   LC1756.   376.

This guide describes some 600 institutions, both
public and private, from two-year schools to those
granting the Ph.D. Attention is focused on facts
omitted from the standard college handbooks. There
is information on women's studies courses, campus
security, child care facilities, health services,
faculty/student gender ratios, and more. Many of the
colleges are also accorded ratings in three areas:
women in leadership positions (students, faculty, and
administrators); women and the curriculum; and women
and athletics.

Guide to Women's Art Organizations and Directory for the
Arts. Compiled by Cynthia Navaretta. 2nd ed. New York:
Midmarch Associates, 1982.   NX504.   700.

A comprehensive guide to organizations and services
in all branches of the fine arts. Included are
galleries, groups, publications, archives, slide
registries, funding sources, artists' colonies, and
other resources. Includes a bibliography.

Harrison, Cynthia Ellen. Women's Movement Media: A
Source Guide. New York: Bowker, 1975.   Z7964.U49
016.30141.

This guide is "a compendium of sources of
information, rather than just a bibliography."
Approximately 550 organizations are described,
including publishers and distributors, libraries and
research centers, national and local women's
organizations, government agencies, and special
interest groups. The address of each is provided,
along with a contact person's name, a statement of
goals, and a list of available publications and
nonprint media. Indexed by place, media title, name

of group, and subject. Some of the data is out-of-date.

Hosken, Fran P. International Directory of Women's Development Organizations. Washington: Agency for International Development, 1977.   HQ1883.

A worldwide directory of women's organizations. Under each country, organizations are listed by size. Address, names of officers, chapters, total membership, date of founding, publications, meetings, activities, and achievements are all noted. A master chart makes it easy to identify groups concerned with similar issues. Data was gathered by questionnaire in 1975, so some information is obsolete.

Index/Directory of Women's Media. Edited by Martha Leslie Allen. Washington: Women's Institute for Freedom of the Press, 1972 to present.   Z7962. HQ1101. 305.4.

This valuable annual combines an index to the bimonthly Media Report to Women with directories of individuals and women's media groups -- including periodicals, publishers, bookstores, libraries, radio shows, news services, and professional and activist organizations. An up-to-date source for names, addresses, and telephone numbers.

Jawin, Ann J. A Woman's Guide to Career Preparation: Scholarships, Grants, and Loans. Garden City, NY: Anchor/Doubleday, 1979.   HF5382.5.U5.   331.7.

This book is intended for women re-entering the workforce or returning to school after several years as a homemaker. In addition to offering advice on such topics as career planning and interviewing for jobs, this guide serves as a directory of employment services, scholarships, and funding and counseling agencies. Especially helpful for its attention to minority women, older women, and working mothers.

Schlachter, Gail A. The Directory of Financial Aids for Women. 2nd ed. Santa Barbara, CA: ABC-Clio, 1982. HQ1381.   362.8.

Includes information on some 700 scholarships, fellowships, loans, grants, internships, awards, and state educational benefits. Excludes awards

available equally to men and women and programs
administered by institutions for their own students.
Each entry includes address, purpose of award,
amount, limits on eligibility, and deadline for
application.

Who's Who and Where in Women's Studies. Old Westbury,
NY: The Feminist Press, 1974. HQ1181.U5. 375.

The most recent separately-published directory of
women's studies programs and feminist scholars.
Lists 4,658 accredited undergraduate and graduate
courses, 885 U.S. institutions of higher education,
and 2,964 teachers. The data on women's studies
programs is updated by a list released annually by
the National Women's Studies Association. The most
recent (albeit incomplete) list of individuals
involved in women's studies is the membership list of
the NWSA, which is organized by region.

Women Helping Women: A State-by-State Directory of
Services. New York: Women's Action Alliance, 1981.
HV1445. 362.8.

Eight categories of services are listed in this
directory: battered women and rape victim services;
career counseling services; displaced homemaker
programs; Planned Parenthood clinics; skilled trades
training centers; women's centers; women's
commissions; and women's health centers. In each
chapter, entries are arranged by state and city, and
provide no data beyond addresses and phone numbers.

Women's Action Alliance. Women's Action Almanac: A
Complete Action Guide. Edited by Jane Williamson, Diane
Winston, and Wanda Wooten. New York: William Morrow,
1979. HQ1115. 362.8.

This handbook presents a wealth of information in an
easy-to-use format. Brief essays, names and
addresses of organizations, and recommended
publications are given for eighty-four issue-oriented
topics. Affirmative action, child care, DES,
ordination of women, and sexual harrassment are just
a few of the subjects covered. An index and a
directory of national women's organizations enhance
the book's utility.

13
Microform Sources

Sooner or later, nearly everyone will use materials published or re-published in a micro-format. Many researchers' first such experience is with older newspapers or magazines. With shelf space at a premium in most libraries, compact microforms are a valuable alternative to bulky bound volumes. Libraries also find it simpler and less expensive to acquire in microform large sets that are in heavy demand and must be updated often; college catalogs and telephone directories are examples. Microforms permit libraries to preserve for posterity texts printed on poor quality paper.

The earliest micro-reproductions were opaque microcards. Transparent microfilm and microfiche are more common nowadays. Although there is some variance in scale of reduction and size of the finished product, all microforms can be viewed on simple-to-operate equipment.

Besides preserving fragile publications, microform publishing also makes possible the wider distribution of out-of-print works. Even materials that were never published, such as manuscripts, archives, and dissertations, can be readily and cheaply obtained in microform.

There are three major microform sets that are of special importance to women's studies scholars:

The Gerritsen Collection of Women's History, 1543-1945. Microfilming Corporation of America, 1976. (microfiche)

> This fascinating collection of books and periodicals was gathered by Aletta Jacobs Gerritsen, a leading feminist and physician in Holland in the late 19th century. The collection's scope is international, concentrating on Western European and American writings. The original private collection was sold in 1903 to the John Crerar Library in Chicago, and transferred again in 1954 to the library of the

University of Kansas, where it resides today. The microform set includes not only the core collection but also materials added since it came to the United States. In addition, publications about women housed in the library of the University of North Carolina at Greensboro are represented. (The latter, formerly part of a separate Woman's Collection, contains mainly American and British writings.) Altogether, the microfiche set includes 4,471 monographic titles (i.e., books and pamphlets) and complete or nearly complete runs for 265 periodicals.

Items in the set are arranged chronologically within fourteen major categories and over 250 subcategories. The major divisions are: Bibliography; Physiology; History and social condition; Biography; Opinions on women, dissertations, satires, proverbs; Woman in the family; Relations between the sexes; Legal status; Feminism; Political and social reform; Education; Employment; Organizations and clubs; Periodicals.

A three-volume guide to the set, edited by Duane R. Bogenschneider, was issued in 1983. The first volume provides full bibliographic entries for all works, grouped by language and indexed by main entry, title, subject, and date. The second volume offers a complex topical outline, based on the categories noted above. The final volume provides detailed catalog records and various indexes to the serials.

<u>Herstory</u>. Women's History Research Center, 1972-76. (microfilm)

The main set and two supplementary sets together reproduce 821 newsletters, journals, and newspapers published by women's liberation groups between 1956 and 1974. The periodicals were collected by the Women's History Research Center in Berkeley; the originals are now preserved at Northwestern University. <u>Herstory</u> records the growth of the women's movement in the late '60s and early '70s and is thus a treasure trove for social historians. Unfortunately, there is no subject index to the periodicals nor to the articles contained in them. Printed reel guides permit the user to locate all issues of a known title. (Full runs are not always filmed together, but rather may be spread across several reels according to dates of publication.)

The Women's History Research Center has also produced two specialized microfilm sets, <u>Women and Law</u> and <u>Women and Health/Mental Health</u>. Each offers clippings, articles, pamphlets, and other documents grouped by topic.

History of Women.   Research Publications, 1976.
(microfilm)

This microfilm set is based largely on two important collections: the Schlesinger Library on the History of Women in America, at Radcliffe; and the Sophia Smith Collection, at Smith College. Selected materials from other academic and public libraries round out the coverage. 80% of the items are in English; the remainder, in other Western European languages.

Five different kinds of materials are reproduced:

Printed books. Nearly 8,500 volumes are included, grouped in fifteen chronological divisions. The cutoff date is 1920.

Pamphlets. Approximately 2,000 pamphlets are arranged by subject, covering such issues as suffrage, employment, education, and health.

Periodicals. 117 titles have been included, with an emphasis on ephemeral and little-known publications not previously microfilmed. Arrangement is alphabetic by title.

Manuscripts. Some 80,000 pages of original sources have been chosen to illustrate a range of topics in women's history. They are presented in 32 categories, by individual, organization, or subject.

Photographs. This sampling of 800 photographs is a unique feature of History of Women. Important people and events are emphasized.

To aid users, the publisher has compiled a Bibliography-Index. The first section is a reel guide, arranged alphabetically by main entry. The second section is an index to subjects and other entries.

In addition to these large, wide-sweeping, and expensive sets, a number of specialized microform editions are available to women's studies scholars. These include the papers of the Women's Trade Union League, the personal papers of Susan B. Anthony, publications and archives on the history of nursing, and Bibliofem, the catalog of the Fawcett Library in London, a library devoted to materials for the study of women. Two sets focus on pamphlets: The Cornell University Collection of Women's Rights Pamphlets; and Pamphlets in American History: Women. Other microform sets, such as the Underground Newspaper Collection and the Columbia University Oral History Collection, can also support women's studies research.

The following publications can aid you in identifying microform sources relevant to your research topic:

Dodson, Suzanne Cates. *Microform Research Collections: A Guide*. Westport, CT: Microform Review, 1978. Z1033.M5. 011.

A selective bibliography of some 200 microform collections. The full descriptions for each set include publisher, date of publication, format, price, reviews, arrangement and bibliographic control, bibliographies and indexes, and scope and content.

Guide to Microforms in Print. Westport, CT: Meckler Publishing, 1961 to present. Z1033.M5. 686.4.

An annual international listing of microform titles -- books, journals, newspapers, government publications, archival material, collections, and other projects -- which are currently available for purchase. In two parts: one lists works by author or title; the other employs a subject classification that has no separate category for women's studies.

National Register of Microform Masters. Washington: Library of Congress, 1965 to present. Z1033.M5. 011.

A guide to master microforms from which copies may be made. Such masters may be in the possession of libraries or of commerical producers. The first ten years (1965-75) have been cumulated in a single alphabetic listing. Consult this set to determine whether a rare publication has been reproduced in microform in the U.S.

Like books, microforms can often be borrowed from distant libraries. If your libary has not invested in all of the major women's studies sets, you may still be able to view selected reels or fiche. Ask a librarian about interlibrary loan policies and procedures.

14
Online Sources

In addition to providing printed bibliographies and indexes, many libraries offer online access to bibliographic information. Most of the major indexing and abstracting services can be searched by computer, including such important sources as the New York Times Information Bank, Magazine Index, Dissertation Abstracts International, the Monthly Catalog of Government Publications, and scores of others.

Depending on the nature of your question, an online data base search may be rewarding and time-saving. Single-subject topics and works by known authors can be effectively researched without resorting to an online session. More complicated questions, however, benefit from the powers of computerized information storage and retrieval.

One of the great advantages of online bibliographic searching is the capacity to generate citations on a precise intersection of topics. You may determine, for instance, that you'd like to have a list of writings about women and mental depression, published since 1980, in English. After discussing your research problem with you, a librarian can formulate a "search statement" (a list of logically related terms) that will instruct the computer to produce a custom-tailored bibliography in a matter of minutes. To achieve the same results without computer assistance, you would have to examine all of the entries under "mental depression" in appropriate printed indexes and pick out the ones that deal with women -- a tedious task indeed.

The computer can also be used to eliminate topics from a search. Sticking with our example, if you had no interest in premenstrual symptoms of depression, the computer could easily be told to ignore articles on that aspect of the subject.

Some bibliographic data bases can be searched by established subject headings; some, by keywords in the titles; and some, by keywords in the abstracts or full texts of the documents. Many data bases permit all three approaches. In addition, you can frequently limit the search by the year of publication and/or by language.

Sounds wonderful, doesn't it? Yet there is a minor catch. Nearly all libraries charge for online searches. The fees can range from a nominal flat charge-per-search to a steep charge reflecting the true costs of computer connect time, online printing, data base royalties, telecommunication charges, staff time, and overhead. Ask for an estimate, or set a limit on the amount you're willing to spend, before having the search run online.

Because the possible ways to structure an efficient online search vary among the many data bases, experienced library staff usually do the searching. You may, therefore, need to make an appointment for this service. Be prepared to state your research problem unambiguously to the librarian who will conduct the search. Spend some time clarifying your thoughts, and perhaps noting down key phrases and terms, before you sit down to jointly plan the search.

Libraries usually access online data bases through vendors. The big three -- Dialog, Bibliographic Retrieval Services (BRS), and System Development Corporation (SDC) -- each offer numerous data bases from a wide range of disciplines, with the convenience of a single search language and procedure. With the proliferation of personal computers, data base vendors are starting to market their services to individuals as well as institutions. Although at this writing most researchers still avail themselves of the expertise offered by trained librarians and search analysts, unmediated access to bibliographic and informational data bases will surely become more common.

At this time, of the hundreds of online files, there is still no single data base for women's studies. Scholars and librarians from across the nation have formed a network to create an interdisciplinary bibliographic file of materials for the study of women, to be enriched with information about ongoing programs and works in progress. However, it may be a long while before such a data base is constructed, tested, and made widely available.

<u>Catalyst Resources for Women</u> is a specialized data base for researching the lives of working women, especially women in the businesses and professions. It records the holdings of the library of Catalyst, Inc., a network of career information centers based in New York City. The data base indexes books, articles, working papers, and clippings on such concerns as dual career marriages, employer childcare, sex discrimination, and alternative work patterns.

Below is a list of selected data bases which can be helpful for women-related research in the disciplines they cover. You may recognize the titles of several of them; most were previously described in their printed versions in the appropriate subject chapters. Note that not every library will offer the full range of data bases listed here.

Data Base	Subject Area
ABI/Inform	Business
America: History and Life	History (U.S. and Canada)
American Statistics Index	Statistics in all fields
Artbibliographies Modern	Fine arts
Arts & Humanities Citation Index	Fine arts and humanities
Catalyst Resources for Women	Employment issues
Congressional Information Service	Congressional publications
Dissertation Abstracts International	Dissertations in all fields
Economics Abstracts International	Economics
ERIC	Education
Family Resources	Marriage and the family
GPO Monthly Catalog	Federal publications in all fields
Historical Abstracts	History (foreign)
Journal of Economic Literature	Economics
Legal Resources Index	Law
MLA Bibliography	Literature and linguistics
Magazine Index	Current news

Data Base	Subject Area
Management Contents	Business
Medline	Medicine and health
National Newspaper Index	Current news
New York Times Information Bank	Current news
PAIS	All social sciences
Philosopher's Index	Philosophy
Population Bibliography	Population research
PsycInfo/Psychological Abstracts	Psychology
Religion Index	Religion
Social Scisearch/Social Science Citation Index	All social sciences
Sociological Abstracts	Sociology
State Publications Index	State publications
US Political Science Documents	Political science

15
Periodicals

Periodical literature is the cutting edge of women's scholarship, feminist theory, and much of women's culture. This chapter lists, in a rough topical order, both scholarly journals and women's movement periodicals. The former are a source of secondary analyses and essays, while the latter serve to document recent events and trends and the feminist response to them. Some of these titles are indexed or otherwise captured in the bibliographic resources listed in the chapter 8.2. Yet because there is always a time lag in indexing, it may be wise to scan recent issues of relevant periodicals in addition to relying on citations found in indexes and bibliographies.
THIS IS NOT A COMPLETE LIST OF PERIODICALS. There are scores more, including literary magazines, regional and local newspapers, and special interest group newsletters, that may prove relevant to your research. The following sources can help you identify additional titles:

The Annotated Guide to Women's Periodicals in the U.S. and Canada. Edited by Terry Mehlman. Richmond, IN: The Women's Program Office, Earlham College, 1982 to present. Z6944.W6.

This slim semiannual listing is topically arranged. Full data is not available for all entries, but nonetheless the comprehensive coverage is welcome, especially of non-academic titles.

The Index/Directory of Women's Media. Edited by Martha Leslie Allen. Washington: Women's Institute for Freedom of the Press, 1972 to present. Z7962. HQ1101. 305.4.

For annotation, see chapter 12, "Directories of Organizations and Services."

Joan, Polly, and Andrea Chesman. Guide to Women's Publishing. Paradise, CA: Dustbooks, 1978. Z278. 070.4.

For annotation, see chapter 16, "Miscellaneous Guides and Handbooks."

Women's Periodicals and Newspapers from the 19th Century to 1981. Edited by James P. Danky and others. Boston: G. K. Hall, 1982. Z7965. HQ1180. 016.3054.

This is the single most important tool for historical research in women's periodicals. It identifies and fully describes 1,461 titles, including feminist, anti-feminist, and apolitical periodicals published by or for women. Several indexes and charts make it easy to discover periodicals published in particular regions or cities, during a given time period, or with a special focus.

GENERAL

Canadian Women Studies/Les Cahiers de la Femme. 1978 to present. 4/year.

Chrysalis: A Magazine of Women's Culture. 1977 to 1980. 4/year.

FS, Feminist Studies. 1972 to present. 3/year.

Feminist Issues. 1980 to present. 2/year.

Feminist Review. 1979 to present. 3/year.

Frontiers: A Journal of Women's Studies. 1975 to present. 3/year.

Hecate: A Women's Interdisciplinary Journal. 1975 to present. 2/year.

International Journal of Women's Studies. 1978 to present. 5/year.

M/F: A Feminist Journal. 1978 to present. 2/year.

Quest: A Feminist Quarterly. 1974 to 1984. 4/year.

Resources for Feminist Research/Documentation sur la Recherche Feministe. (Formerly Canadian Newsletter of Research on Women.) 1972 to present. 4/year.

Signs: Journal of Women in Culture and Society. 1975 to present. 4/year.

Trivia. 1982 to present. 3/year.

Women: A Journal of Liberation. 1969 to present. 3/year.

Women's Studies. 1972 to present. 3/year.

Women's Studies International Forum. (Formerly Women's Studies International Quarterly.) 1978 to present. 6/year.

Women's Studies Quarterly. (Formerly Women's Studies Newsletter.) 1972 to present. 4/year.

ARTS

Camera Obscura: A Journal of Feminism and Film Theory. 1976 to present. 3/year.

Helicon Nine: The Journal of Women's Arts and Letters. 1979 to present. 3/year.

Heresies: A Feminist Publication on Art and Politics. 1977 to present. 4/year.

Hot Wire: A Journal of Women's Music and Culture. 1984 to present. 3/year.

Paid My Dues: Journal of Women and Music. 1974 to 1980. 4/year.

Woman's Art Journal. 1980 to present. 2/year.

Women and Environments. 1976 to present. 3/year.

Women Artists News. 1975 to present. 6/year.

BUSINESS, ECONOMICS, AND EMPLOYMENT

Savvy. 1980 to present. 12/year.

Women at Work. 1977 to present. 2/year.

Working Woman. 1976 to present. 12/year.

CURRENT EVENTS

   Majority Report. 1971 to 1979. Biweekly.

   Ms. 1972 to present. 12/year.

   New Directions for Women. 1972 to present. 6/year.

   New Women's Times. 1975 to present. 11/year.

   off our backs. 1970 to present. 11/year.

EDUCATION

   On Campus With Women. 1971 to present. 4/year.

   Women's Studies Quarterly. (see GENERAL)

HEALTH AND MEDICINE

   Healthsharing: A Canadian Women's Health Quarterly. 1979 to present. 4/year.

   Women and Health. 1976 to present. 4/year.

HISTORY

   Turn-of-the-Century Women. 1984 to present. 2/year.

   Women and History. 1982 to present. 4/year.

LAW

   Harvard Women's Law Journal. 1978 to present. Annual.

   Law and Inequality. 1983 to present. 2/year.

   Women's Rights Law Reporter. 1971 to present. Irregular.

LESBIAN STUDIES

   Common Lives/Lesbian Lives. 1981 to present. 4/year.

   Conditions. 1976 to present. 2/year.

Sinister Wisdom. 1976 to present. 4/year.

LIBRARIES, SPECIAL COLLECTIONS, AND ARCHIVES

Booklegger. 1973 to 1976. 6/year.

Feminist Collections. 1980 to present. 4/year.

WLW [Women Library Workers] Journal. 1976 to present. 4/year.

LINGUISTICS AND COMMUNICATIONS

Media Report to Women. 1972 to present. 6/year.

Women and Language News. 1976 to present. 3/year.

Women's Studies in Communication. 1977 to present. 2/year.

LITERATURE

Concerns: Newsletter of the Women's Caucus of the Modern Languages. 1971 to present. 4/year.

Tulsa Studies in Women's Literature. 1982 to present. 2/year.

Women and Literature. (Formerly Mary Wollstonecraft Journal.) 1972 to 1979. 2/year.

MILITARY SCIENCE

Minerva. 1983 to present. 4/year.

MINORITY STUDIES

Lilith. (see RELIGION AND SPIRITUALITY.)

Sage: A Scholarly Journal on Black Women. 1984 to present. 2/year.

Third Woman. 1981 to present. 2/year.

NATIONAL AND AREA STUDIES

Connexions: An International Women's Quarterly.

1981 to present. 4/year.

ISIS Women's Journal. 1974 to present. 4/year (including supplements).

WIN [Women's International Network] News. 1975 to present. 4/year.

POLITICAL SCIENCE

Women and Politics. 1980 to present. 4/year.

PSYCHOLOGY

Psychology of Women Quarterly. 1976 to present. 4/year.

Sex Roles: A Journal of Research. 1975 to present. 12/year.

Women and Therapy. 1982 to present. 4/year.

RELIGION AND SPIRITUALITY

Journal of Feminist Studies in Religion. 1985 to present. 2/year.

Journal of Women and Religion. 1981 to present. 6/year.
Lilith: The Jewish Women's Magazine. 1976 to present. 4/year.

Woman of Power. 1984 to present. 4/year.

Womanspirit. 1974 to 1983. 4/year.

REVIEWS

Motheroot Journal: A Women's Review of Small Presses. 1979 to present. 4/year.

New Women's Times Feminist Review. (Supplement to New Women's Times) 1975 to present. 6/year.

The Women's Review of Books. 1983 to present. 12/year.

Women's Studies Review. 1979 to present. 6/year.

16
Miscellaneous Guides and Handbooks

This final chapter features a potpourri of information sources that have been compiled to meet the needs of women's studies scholars, activists in the women's movement, and general readers. The sources range from self-help manuals to authoritative reference books, and from works with a serious purpose to those designed for fun and inspiration. Many of these works have counterparts in the standard reference literature.

Many, many such handbooks have been published in recent years. This chapter is highly selective.

Feminist Quotations: Voices of Rebels, Reformers, and Visionaries. Compiled by Carol McPhee and Ann FitzGerald. New York: Crowell, 1979.   HQ1154. 301.41.

> Nearly 1,500 statements from more than 300 English-speaking women are set forth. The quotations are grouped in subject sections "that reflect the fundamental interests of the women's movement: cultural attitudes, the various forms of male oppression, sex, marriage, motherhood, the aims of feminist political activity, self-determination, self-transcendence, and visions of the future." Within each section, entries spanning the past two hundred years are arranged chronologically. The explicit feminist bias of this book distinguishes it from The Quotable Woman (see below).

Joan, Polly, and Andrea Chesman. Guide to Women's Publishing. Paradise, CA: Dustbooks, 1978.   Z278. 070.4.

> A useful but rapidly aging handbook for feminists hoping to break into print. Women publishers, both

small and large, are listed, with notes on the types
of manuscripts they seek and the history of the
presses. Women's journals and newspapers are also
covered. The annotations are well written, conveying
the "feel" of each publication as well as its stated
scope and policies.

Macksey, Joan, and Kenneth Macksey. The Guinness Guide
to Feminine Achievements. Endfield, England: Guinness
Superlatives, 1975.   HQ1123.   920.72.

Women's Book of World Records. Edited by Lois Decker
O'Neill. Garden City, NY: Anchor/Doubleday, 1979.
CT3234.   920.72.

More for fun than scholarly reference, these
illustrated volumes spotlight notable achievements by
women of all countries and all times. Also
recommended is Famous First Facts, by Joseph N. Kane
(4th ed. New York: H. W. Wilson, 1981), a general
source on American "firsts" that contains many
references to accomplishments of women.

Miller, Casey, and Kate Swift. The Handbook of Nonsexist
Writing. New York: Lippincott and Crowell, 1980.
PN218.   808.

A clearly written style manual that will help anyone
avoid sexist phrasing and vocabulary in both written
and spoken communication.

Monaghan, Patricia. The Book of Goddesses and Heroines.
New York: Dutton, 1981.   BL473.5.   291.2.

An intriguing dictionary of goddesses and other
female figures in religion and mythology. Its scope
is worldwide. Unfortunately, the entries offer no
bibliographic references. (See also Barbara Walker's
The Woman's Encyclopedia of Myths and Secrets,
below.)

The Quotable Woman, 1800-1981. Compiled by Elaine
Partnow. New York: Facts on File, 1983.   PN6081.5.
082.

This compendium is an alternative to the standard
quotation dictionaries, in which women are still
severely underrepresented. Words of wisdom are
arranged chronologically. The name index includes

birth and death dates and brief identification; there is also a subject index. The scope is international, although all quotations are given in English.

Sherr, Lynn, and Jurate Kazickas. The American Woman's Gazetteer. New York: Bantam, 1976. HQ1410. 917.3.

One of the nicer products of the Bicentennial publishing boom, this feminist travel guide notes points of interest throughout the United States. Homes, monuments, and graves of famous women are highlighted, as are the locales of important events in women's history. The illustrated entries contain much biographical and historical background.

Walker, Barbara G. The Woman's Encyclopedia of Myths and Secrets. San Francisco: Harper and Row, 1983. BL458. 291.

A compulsively readable tome that blends mythology, anthropology, religion and linguistics to create an overview of cultural origins. Many of the 1,350 entries are names -- gods and goddesses, creatures of myth and folklore, saints and martyrs -- but events, places, customs, and common symbols are also covered. Sources of information are documented, but the compiler's interpretations are often original.

Warren, Mary Anne. The Nature of Woman: An Encyclopedia and Guide to the Literature. Inverness, CA: Edgepress, 1980. HQ1115. 016.3054.

An unusual handbook that surveys ideas about women as expressed by a variety of thinkers and researchers in the past and present. Entries on individual theorists comprise the bulk of the text. The scope is wide, ranging from influential shapers of Western thought such as Aristotle, Darwin, and Freud, to such modern writers as Mary Daly and Norman Mailer. Each entry presents a feminist appraisal of one or more works by that person. Interspersed among the articles on individuals are short essays on selected topics. Again the range is broad, encompassing such subjects as androgeny, the Bible, menstruation, motherhood, and patriarchy.

Weiser, Marjorie P. K., and Jean S. Arbeiter. Womanlist. New York: Antheneum, 1981. HQ1115. 305.4.

Fun for browsing but of questionable reference value, this volume is a remedy for the paltry coverage of women in the immensely popular The Book of Lists (New York: Morrow, 1977).

The Women's Annual: The Year in Review. Edited by Barbara Haber. Boston: G. K. Hall, 1981 to present. HQ1402.   305.4.

This series presents a yearly overview of vital issues affecting women. Each volume includes essays by well-known experts on such topics as domestic life, women and education, women's health, Third World women in the U.S., new scholarship in the humanities, politics and law, popular culture, psychology of women, women and religion, violence against women, and women and work. Each essay is accompanied by lists of publications, organizations, and statistics.

Appendix A: Dewey Decimal Classification System

000 GENERAL WORKS
   010 Bibliography
   020 Library science
   030 General encyclopedias
   040 General collected essays
   050 General periodicals
   060 General societies, museums
   070 Journalism
   080 Collected works
   090 Book rarities

100 PHILOSOPHY
   110 Metaphysics
   120 Metaphysical theories
   130 Branches of psychology
   140 Philosophic system
   150 Psychology
   160 Logic
   170 Ethics
   180 Ancient philosophy
   190 Modern philosophy

200 RELIGION
   210 Natural religion
   220 Bible
   230 Doctrinal theology
   240 Practical theology
   250 Pastoral theology
   260 Ecclesiastical theology
   270 Christian churches history
   280 Christian churces & sects
   290 Non-Christian religions

300 SOCIAL SCIENCES
   310 Statistics
   320 Political science
   330 Economics
   340 Law
   350 Public administration
   360 Social welfare
   370 Education
   380 Commerce
   390 Customs

400 PHILOLOGY
   410 Comparative philology
   420 English language
   430 German
   440 French
   450 Italian
   460 Spanish
   470 Latin
   480 Greek
   490 Other languages

500 PURE SCIENCES
   510 Mathematics
   520 Astronomy
   530 Physics
   540 Chemistry
   550 Earth sciences
   560 Paleontology
   570 Biological sciences
   580 Botany
   590 Zoology

600 APPLIED SCIENCES
    610 Medicine
    620 Engineering
    630 Agriculture
    640 Home economics
    650 Business
    660 Industrial chemistry
    670 Manufacturing
    680 Mechanic trades
    690 Building

700 ARTS AND RECREATION
    710 Landscape/Civic art
    720 Architecture
    730 Sculpture
    740 Drawing
    750 Painting
    760 Prints & print making
    770 Photography
    780 Music
    790 Recreation

800 LITERATURE
    810 American literature
    820 English literature
    830 German literature
    840 French literature
    850 Italian literature
    860 Spanish literature
    870 Latin literature
    880 Greek literature
    890 Other literature

900 HISTORY
    910 Geography & travel
    920 Collective biography
    930 Ancient history
    940 History of Europe
    950 Asia
    960 Africa
    970 North America
    980 South America
    990 Oceania & polar regions

Appendix B:
Library of Congress
Classification System

A	General works.
B	Philosophy. Psychology. Religion.
C	Auxiliary sciences of history.
D	History and topography (except America).
E	American history.
F	United States local history.
G	Geography. Anthropology.
H	Social sciences.
J	Political science.
K	Law.
L	Education.
M	Music.
N	Fine arts.
P	Language and literature.
Q	Science.
R	Medicine.
S	Agriculture.
T	Technology.
U	Military science.
V	Naval science.
Z	Bibliography and library science.

Appendix C:
Review Essays in *Signs*

Signs: Journal of Women in Culture and Society is the leading scholarly journal in women's studies. Since its founding in 1975, this respected quarterly has featured review essays. These bibliographic reviews, written by recognized experts, have addressed such broad areas as anthropology, literature, and sociology, and such specialized concerns as housework, widowhood, and women's studies in Korea. Printed under the running title "The New Scholarship," these critical articles are invaluable jumping-off points for library research.

Vol. 1, no. 1, Autumn 1975
Parlee, Mary Brown. "Psychology." Pp. 119-138.
Chapman, Jane Roberts. "Economics." Pp. 139-146.
Stack, Carol B., et al. "Anthropology." Pp. 147-160.
Boals, Kay. "Political science." Pp. 161-174.
Angrist, Shirley S. "An Overview." Pp. 175-184.
Fox, Karen F. A. "Audiovisual Teaching Materials." Pp. 185-192.

Vol. 1, no. 2, Winter 1975
Showalter, Elaine. "Literary Criticism." Pp. 435-460.
Sicherman, Barbara. "American History." Pp. 461-486.
Pierce, Christine. "Philosophy." Pp. 487-504.
Orenstein, Gloria Feman. "Art History." Pp. 505-525.

Vol. 1, no. 3, Spring 1976
Huber, Joan. "Sociology." Pp. 685-698.
Birdsall, Nancy. "Women and Population Studies." Pp. 699-712.
Vetter, Betty M. "Women in the Natural Sciences." Pp. 713-720.
Todd, Janet M. "The Biographies of Mary Wollstonecraft." Pp. 721-734.

Vol. 1, no. 4, Summer 1976
Glazer-Malbin, Nona. "Housework." Pp. 905-922.
Hayden, Dolores, and Gwendolyn Wright. "Architecture and Urban Planning" Pp. 923-934.
Kilson, Marion. "The Status of Women in Higher Education." Pp. 935-942.
Brugh, Anne E., and Benjamin R. Beede. "American Librarianship." Pp. 943-956.
Verbrugge, Martha H. "Women and Medicine in Nineteenth-Century America." Pp. 957-972.

Vol. 2, no. 1, Autumn 1976
Vaughter, Reesa M. "Psychology." Pp. 120-146.
Jaquette, Jane S. "Political Science." Pp. 147-164.
Lopata, Helena Znaniecki. "Sociology." Pp. 165-176.
Jusenius, Carol L. "Economics." Pp. 177-189.

Vol. 2, no. 2, Winter 1976
Arthur, Marilyn B. "Classics." Pp. 382-403.
Kolodny, Annette. "Literary Criticism." Pp. 404-421.
Moulton, Janice. "Philosophy." Pp. 422-433.
Driver, Anne Barstow. "Religion." Pp. 434-442.

Vol. 2, no. 3, Spring 1977
Lamphere, Louise. "Anthropology." Pp. 612-627.
Lougee, Carolyn C. "Modern European History." Pp. 629-650.
Lee, Susan Dye. "Audiovisual Teaching Materials." Pp. 651-663.

Vol. 2, no. 4, Summer 1977
Fitzpatrick, M. Louise. "Nursing." Pp. 818-834.
Kennard, June A. "The History of Physical Education." Pp. 835-842.
Almquist, Elizabeth M. "Women in the Labor Force." Pp. 843-855.
Barrett, Carol J. "Women in Widowhood." Pp. 856-868.

Vol. 3, no. 1, Autumn 1977 - no review essays

Vol. 3, no. 2, Winter 1977
Eichler, Margrit. "Sociology of Feminist Research in Canada." Pp. 409-422.
Albin, Rochelle Semmel. "Psychological Studies of Rape." Pp. 423-435.
Ballou, Patricia K. "Bibliographies for Research on Women." Pp. 436-450.

Vol. 3, no. 3, Spring 1978
Greenblat, Cathy Stein, and Joan Gaskill Baily. "Sex Role Games." Pp. 622-637.
Kramer, Cheris, Barrie Thorne, and Nancy Henley. "Perspectives on Language and Communication." Pp. 638-

651.
Kahne, Hilda. "Economic Research on Women and Families." Pp. 652-665.

Vol. 3, no. 4, Summer 1978
English, Jane. "Philosophy." Pp. 823-831.
Marks, Elaine. "Women and Literature in France." Pp. 832-842.

Vol. 4, no. 1, Autumn 1978
Aldrich, Michele L. "Women in Science." Pp. 126-135.
Mandelbaum, Dorothy Rosenthal. "Women in Medicine." Pp. 137-145.

Vol. 4, no. 2, Winter 1978
Harrison, James B. "Men's Roles and Men's Lives." Pp. 324-336.

Vol. 4, no. 3, Spring 1979
Rapp, Rayna. "Anthropology." Pp. 497-513.
Kaplan, Sydney Janet. "Literary Criticism." Pp. 514-527.
Tuchman, Gayle. "Women's Depiction by the Mass Media." Pp. 528-542.

Vol. 4, no. 4, Summer 1979
Shanley, Mary Lyndon. "The History of the Family in Modern England." Pp. 740-750.
Yoon, Soon Young. "Women's Studies in Korea." Pp. 751-762.

Vol. 5, no. 1, Autumn 1979
Navarro, Marysa. "Research on Latin American Women." Pp. 111-120.
Parlee, Mary Brown. "Psychology and Women." Pp. 121-133.

Vol. 5, no. 2, Winter 1979
Brown, Linda Keller. "Women and Business Management." Pp. 266-288.
Carroll, Berenice A. "Political Science, Part I: American Politics and Political Behavior." Pp. 289-306.
Hayler, Barbara. "Abortion." Pp. 307-323.
Norton, Mary Beth. "American History." Pp. 324-337.

Vol. 5, no. 3, Spring 1980
Carroll, Berenice A. "Political Science, Part II: International Politics, Comparative Politics, and Feminist Radicals." Pp. 449-458.
Gould, Meredith. "The New Sociology." Pp. 459-467.
Russell, H. Diane. "Art History." Pp. 468-481.

Vol. 5, no. 3, Supplement, Spring 1980
Wekerle, Gerda R. "Women in the Urban Environment." Pp. S188-S214.

Vol. 5, no. 4, Summer 1980

Friedman, Richard C., et al. "Behavior and the Menstrual Cycle." Pp. 719-738.
Goodman, Madeleine. "Toward a Biology of Menopause." Pp. 739-753.
Leifer, Myra. "Pregnancy." Pp. 754-765.
Weisskopf, Susan (Contratto). "Maternal Sexuality and Asexual Motherhood." Pp. 766-782.
Miller, Patricia Y., and Martha R. Fowlkes. "Social and Behavioral Constructions of Female Sexuality." Pp. 783-800.

Vol. 6, no. 1, Autumn 1980
Baker, Susan W. "Biological Influences on Human Sex and Gender." Pp. 80-96.
Dye, Nancy Schrom. "History of Childbirth in America." Pp. 97-108.
Ross, Ellen. "'The Love Crisis': Couples Advice Books of the Late 1970s." Pp. 109-122.

Vol. 6, no. 2, Winter 1980
Green, Rayna. "Native American Women." Pp. 248-267.
Register, Cheri. "Literary Criticism." Pp. 268-282.
Wood, Elizabeth. "Women in Music." Pp. 283-297.

Vol. 6, no. 3, Spring 1981 - no review essays.

Vol. 6, no. 4, Summer 1981
Speizer, Jeanne J. "Role Models, Mentors, and Sponsors: The Elusive Concepts." Pp. 692-712.

Vol. 7, no. 1, Autumn 1981
Hirsch, Marianne. "Mothers and Daughters." Pp. 200-222.

Vol. 7, no. 2, Winter 1981 - no review essays.

Vol. 7, no. 3, Spring 1982
Boxer, Marilyn J. "For and About Women: The Theory and Practice of Women's Studies in the United States." Pp. 661-695.

Vol. 7, no. 4, Summer 1982
McGaw, Judith A. "Women and the History of American Technology." Pp. 798-828.

Vol. 8, no. 1, Autumn 1982
Krieger, Susan. "Lesbian Identity and Community: Recent Social Science Literature." Pp. 91-108.

Strobel, Margaret. "African Women." Pp. 109-131.

Vol. 8, no. 2, Winter 1982
Atkinson, Jane Monnig. "Anthropology." Pp. 236-258.
Baca Zinn, Maxine. "Mexican-American Women in the Social Sciences." Pp. 259-272.
Ferber, Marianne A. "Women and Work: Issues of the 1980s." Pp. 273-295.

Vol. 8, no. 3, Spring 1983
Breines, Wini, and Linda Gordon. "The New Scholarship on Family Violence." Pp. 490-531.

Vol. 8, no. 4, Summer 1983 - no review essays.

Vol. 9, no. 1, Autumn 1983
Chown, Linda C. "American Critics and Spanish Women Novelists, 1942-1980." Pp. 91-107.

Vol. 9, no. 2, Winter 1983 - no review essays.

Vol. 9, no. 3, Spring 1984
Gerson, Mary-Joan, Judith L. Alpert, and Mary Sue Richardson. "Mothering: The View from Psychological Research." Pp. 434-453.

Vol. 9, no. 4, Summer 1984
Zimmerman, Bonnie. "The Politics of Transliteration: Lesbian Personal Narratives." Pp. 663-682.

Author Index

Addis, Patricia K., 199
Adelsberg, Sandra, 175
Aldous, Joan, 186
Allen, Martha Leslie, 205, 215
Anderson, Philip B., 134
Arbeiter, Jean S., 223
Arksey, Laura, 201
Armour, Robert A., 86
Arntzen, Etta, 81
Ash, Lee, 191
Astin, Helen S., 94, 102, 168

Bachmann, Donna G., 82
Backer, Thomas E., 95
Backscheider, Paula, 134
Baer, Helen, 168
Bakerman, Jane S., 132
Ballou, Patricia K., 37, 38
Barrow, Margaret, 149
Bart, Pauline, 184
Bass, Dorothy, 112
Batty, Linda, 88
Batz, Wilmer H., 142
Baxter, Pam M., 167
Beere, Carole A., 168
Begos, Jane Dupree, 201
Benjamin, Jules R., 112
Bergstrom, Len V., 43
Berry, Dorothea M., 101
Bettison, Margaret, 159
Bickner, Mei Liang, 94
Bitner, Harry, 120
Block, Adrienne Fried, 84
Bock, Ulla, 150
Bogenschneider, Duane R., 208
Bollier, John A., 174
Borenstein, Audrey, 184
Brigham, Clarence Saunders, 62

Briscoe, Mary Louise, 200
Brock, Clifton, 161
Bryer, Jackson R., 134
Buhle, Mari Jo, 162
Bullough, Vern, 120
Buvinic, Mayra, 97
Byerly, Greg, 185
Byler, Mary Gloyne, 140
Bysiewicz, Shirley R., 120

Cabello-Argandona, Roberto, 140
Cantor, Aviva, 140
Cardinale, Susan, 47
Carrington, Evelyn M., 198
Chaff, Sandra L., 108
Chalfant, H. Paul, 168
Chen, Ching-chih, 179
Chesman, Andrea, 216, 221
Chiarmonte, Paula L., 82
Chinn, Phyllis Zweig, 180
Christian Science Monitor. See
  Index to the Christian Science
  Monitor
Cismaresco, Francoise, 102
Cohen, Aaron I., 84
Cohen, Morris L., 119
Cohen-Stuart, Bertie A., 153
Common Women Collective, 113
Congressional Information Service.
  See CIS/Index
Conway, Jill, 113
Coven, Brenda, 89
Cowan, Belita, 108
Crawford, Anne, 196
Cromwell, Phyllis, E., 169
Cruikshank, Margaret, 123

Daims, Diva, 131, 132

235

Daniells, Lorna, 94
Danky, James P., 216
Davis, Lenwood G., 141
Davis, Marianna W., 197
Davis, Nanette J., 184
Dawson, Bonnie, 87
DeCaro, Francis A., 77
De Courtivron, Isabelle, 131
DeGeorge, Richard T., 174
DeMarr, Mary Jean, 132
Diner, Hasia R., 184
Dodson, Suzanne Cates, 210
Dorris, Michael A., 140
Doss, Martha Merrill, 203
Drinker, Sophie H., 114
Druesedow, John E., Jr., 84
Duckles, Vincent, 84
Duke, Maurice, 134
Dweck, Susan, 94, 102

Educational Resources Information Center (ERIC), 105, 213
Een, JoAnn Delores, 44
Eichler, Margit, 158
Elwell, Ellen Sue Levi, 141
English Association, 136
Equal Rights Amendment Project, 120
ERIC. See Educational Resources Information Center
Evans, Mary, 41

Fairbanks, Carol, 134, 156
Famera, Karen, 84
Fan, Kok Sim, 147
Farmer, Helen S., 95
Farr, Sidney Saylor, 157
Faunce, Patricia Spencer, 169
Feinberg, Renee, 94, 102
Fenichel, Carol, 108
Fenster, Valmai Kirkham, 130
Fischer, Clare B., 174
Fishburn, Katherine, 91
Fisher, Anne, 168
Fitch, Nancy Elizabeth, 162
FitzGerald, Ann, 221
Frankel, Linda, 184
Franklin, Margaret Ladd, 112
Frantz, Charles, 77
Frasier, James, 85
Frey, Linda, 115, 150
Frey, Marsha, 115, 150
Frick, Elizabeth, 112
Fried, Barbara, 180

Friedman, Leslie J., 91
Froschl, Merle, 102

Gohdes, Clarence, 130
Goodwater, Leanna, 116
Granger, Edith, 133
Green, Rayna, 141
Gregory, Winifred, 62
Grier, Barbara, 124
Grimes, Janet, 131, 132

Haber, Barbara, 42, 224
Haimbach, Ruth, 108
Hamelsdorf, Ora, 175
Hamer, Philip M., 192
Harrison, Cynthia Ellen, 113, 204
Henifin, Mary Sue, 180
Henley, Nancy, 126
Hennessee, Don, 85
Herner, Saul, 180
Hill, Reuben, 186
Hirschfelder, Arlene B., 140
Hixon, Don L., 85
Holden, Miriam Y., 114
Holler, Frederick, 161
Hosken, Fran P., 205
Hubbard, Ruth, 180
Hughes, Marija Matich, 120

Inge, M. Thomas, 134
International Repertory of Music Literature, 86
Ireland, Norma, 199

Jacklin, Carol N., 169
Jacobs, Sue-Ellen, 78
Jacobstein, J. Myron, 119
Janeway, Elizabeth, 59
Jarrard, Mary E. W., 125
Jawin, Ann J., 205
Joan, Polly, 216, 221
Jones, Lois B., 82

Kane, Joseph N., 222
Kanner, Barbara, 150, 151
Kaplan, Louis, 200
Kazickas, Jurate, 223
Keith, Jone M., 184
Kelly, David H., 103
Kelly, Gail P., 103
Kelly, Joan, 116, 151
Kemmer, Elizabeth Jane, 120
Kennedy, James R., Jr., 102, 174, 184

Kennedy, Susan Estabrook, 185
King, Betty, 132
Klotman, Phyllis Rauch, 142
Knaster, Meri, 153
Koh, Hesung Chun, 147
Kowalski, Rosemary R., 87
Kramarae, Cheris, 126
Kratochvil, Laura, 146
Krichmar, Albert, 42, 114

Landrum, Larry N., 91
Lapidus, Gail, 149
Leavitt, Judith A., 95
Leonard, Eugenie A., 114
LePage, Jane Werner, 198
Lerner, Gerda, 114
Levenson, Edward R., 141
Levenson, Rosaline, 162
Li, Christine, 164
Library of Congress, 49-50, 193
Light, Beth, 157
Livermore, Mary, 196
Loeb, Catherine, 142
Lynn, Naomi B., 38

MacCann, Richard Dyer, 88
Maccoby, Eleanor E., 169
McCoy, Florence N., 112
McFeely, Mary Drake, 95
McInnis, Raymond G., 167
McKenney, Mary, 186
Macksey, Joan, 222
Macksey, Kenneth, 222
McMillan, Patricia, 184
McPhee, Carol, 221
Mainiero, Lina, 130
Malinowsky, H. Robert, 180
Manning, Beverley, 163
Marovitz, Sanford E., 130
Matasar, Ann B., 38
Meggett, Joan M., 84
Meghdessian, Samira Rafidi, 155
Mehlman, Terry, 215
Melnyk, Peter, 94
Melville, Annette, 193
Merritt, Richard L., 161
Mersky, Roy M., 119
Milden, James Wallace, 117
Miller, Casey, 222
Miller, Wayne Charles, 140
Milner, Anita Cheek, 61
MLA. See Modern Language Association of America

Modern Humanities Research Association, 136
Modern Language Association of America (MLA), 126, 136
Monaghan, Patricia, 222
Morgan, David, 41
Morton, Leslie Thomas, 108
Muehsam, Gerd, 82
Muldoon, Maureen, 185

Nelson, Barbara A., 163
Neuls-Bates, Carol, 84
Newman, Joan E., 132
New York Public Library, 90, 192
New York Times, 59-60
Nicolas, Suzanne, 95
Nims, Marion R., 112
Nordquist, Joan, 42
Nussbaum, Felicity, 134

Oakes, Elizabeth H., 43
Oakley, Ann, 30, 31
Oetzel, Roberta M., 169
O'Neill, Lois Decker, 222

Parelman, Allison, 168
Parker, Betty June, 103
Parker, Franklin, 103
Partnow, Elaine, 222
Patterson, Margaret C., 130
Patterson-Black, Gene, 157
Patterson-Black, Sheryll, 157
Perry, Edward S., 88
Phelps, Ann T., 95
Piland, Sherry, 82
Pool, Jeannie G., 85
Poulton, Helen J., 112
Price, Miles O., 120
Pries, Nancy, 201
Public Affairs Information Service. See PAIS Bulletin
Pyszka, Gloria J., 161

Qazzaz, Al-, Ayad, 155

Raccagni, Michelle, 155
Rainwater, Robert, 81
Rakowski, Cathy A., 97, 146, 154
Randall, Phyllis R., 125
Raven, Susan, 195
Reardon, Joan, 131
Reed, Jeffrey G., 167
Reed, Marcia, 201

Resnick, Margery, 131
Rhodes, Carolyn H., 200
Richardson, Jeanne M., 180
Richardson, Marilyn, 139, 175
Riesner, Dieter, 130
Rihani, May, 97
Ritchie, Maureen, 37, 38
Robbins, John Albert, 193
Roberts, J. R., 124
Roper, Brent S., 168
Rosenberg, Marie Bavoric, 38
Rosenberg-Dishman, Marie B., 43, 44
Rowbotham, Sheila, 163
Rubin, Rick, 185

Sakala, Carol, 148
Sapiro, Virginia, 162
Saulniers, Suzanne Smith, 97, 146, 154
Schlachter, Gail A., 38, 140, 205
Schlesinger, Benjamin, 186
Schneider, Joanne, 115, 150
Schuster, Mel, 87
Schweik, Robert C., 130
Shafer, Robert Jones, 112
Shaughnessy, Marlene, 94
Shaw, Shauna, 146
Sheahan, Eileen, 87
Sheldon, Kathleen E., 43
Sherif, Carolyn, 168
Sherman, Julia A., 170
Sherr, Lynn, 223
Sims, Janet, 142
Skowronski, JoAnn, 85
Slavens, Thomas P., 174
Smith, Sophia, Collection, 190
Soliday, Gerald L., 116
Soltow, Martha Jane, 96
Stanwick, Kathy, 164
Steiner-Scott, Elizabeth, 112
Stephenson, Marylee, 158
Stern, Susan, 85
Sternberg, Robert J., 168
Stewart-Green, Miriam, 84
Stineman, Esther, 44, 164
Strong-Boag, Veronica, 157, 158
Sullivan, Kaye, 87
Summers, Anne, 159
Sundberg, Sara Brooks, 156
Suniewick, Nancy, 94, 102
Sveistrup, Hans, 151
Swift, Kate, 222

Terris, Virginia R., 44
Thorne, Barrie, 126
Thorsen, Kristine A., 131
Tice, Terrance N., 174
Tingley, Donald F., 115
Tingley, Elizabeth, 115
Tufts, Eleanor, 82
Turabian, Kate, 12

Uglow, Jennifer S., 195
UNESCO. See United Nations
United Nations, 45, 66, 102
U.S. Air Force Academy, 96
U.S. National Archives and Records Service, 193
U.S. National Historical Publications Commission, 192
U.S. Office of Education, 96, 103

Vicinus, Martha, 150, 151
Vose, Clement, E., 161

Wagle, Elizabeth Pearce, 112
Walker, Barbara G., 223
Walstedt, Joyce Jennings, 170
Walters, LeRoy, 177
Warren Mary Anne, 223
Wei, Karen T., 148
Weir, Alison, 195
Weiser, Marjorie P. K., 223
Wery, Mary K., 96
Westmoreland, Guy T., 140
Whalon, Marion K., 89
Wheeler, Helen R., 45
White, Barbara Anne, 135
Wilkins, Kay S., 104
Willard, Frances, 196
Williams, Ora, 142
Williamson, Jane, 37, 39, 102, 206
Wilson, Carolyn F., 185
Wilson, John F., 174
Witych, Barbara, 150
Women's Action Alliance, 206
Woodbury, Marda, 102
Woodside, Nina B., 108
Wren, Christopher G., 120
Wren, Jill Robinson, 120
Writers Program, 87

Yogev, Sara, 31

Zahn-Harnack, Agnes, 151
Zaimont, Judith Lang, 84
Zukerman, Elyse, 170

Title Index

ABC Pol Sci, 164
Abortion: An Annotated Indexed Bibliography (Muldoon), 185
Abortion Bibliography, 107
Abstracts for Social Workers. See Social Work Research and Abstracts
Abstracts in Anthropology, 78
Abstracts of English Studies, 135-136.
Abstracts of Popular Culture, 92
Access, 53
Adolescent Female Portraits in the American Novel, 1961-1981 (Bakerman & DeMarr), 132
Africa, 147
African Bibliographic Center, 146
African Women: A Select Bibliography (Kratochvil & Shaw), 146
Alternative Press Index, 14, 53
America: History and Life, 114, 117
American Autobiography 1945-1980: A Bibliography (Briscoe, ed.), 200
American Bibliography of Russian and East European Studies. See American Bibliography of Slavic and East European Studies
American Bibliography of Slavic and East European Studies, 152
American Black Women in the Arts and Social Sciences: A Bibliographic Survey (Williams), 142-143
American Diaries: An Annotated Bibliography of Published American Diaries and Journals (Arksey et al.), 201
American Literary Manuscripts: A Checklist of Holdings in Academic, Historical, and Public Libraries, Museums, and Authors' Homes in the United States (Robbins, ed.), 193
American Literary Scholarship, 136
American Newspapers, 1821-1936: A Union List of Files Available in the United States and Canada (Gregory, ed.), 62
American Political Women: Contemporary and Historical Profiles (Stineman), 164
American Popular Culture: A Guide to Information Sources (Landrum), 91
American Statistics Index, 64, 213
American Woman's Gazetteer, The (Sherr & Kazickas), 223
American Women (Willard & Livermore, eds.), 196-197
American Women: The Official Who's Who Among the Women of the Nation, 197
American Women and Politics: A Bibliography and Guide to the Sources (Nelson), 163
American Women and the Labor Movement, 1825-1974: An Annotated Bibliography (Soltow & Wery), 96
American Women Artists, Past and

Present: A Selected Bibliographic Guide (Tufts), 82-83
American Women Dramatists of the Twentieth Century: A Bibliography (Coven), 89
American Women in Church and Society, 1607-1920: A Bibliography (Bass), 112-113
American Woman in Colonial and Revolutionary Times, 1565-1800, The: A Syllabus with Bibliography (Leonard et al.), 114
American Women Writers: A Critical Reference Guide from Colonial Times to the Present (Mainiero, ed.), 130
American Women Writers: An Annotated Bibliography of Criticism (White), 135
American Women Writers: Bibliographical Essays (Duke et al., eds.), 134
America's White Working-Class Women: A Historical Bibliography (Kennedy), 185
"Annotated Bibliography" (Oetzel), 169
Annotated Bibliography of Published Women's Diaries (Begos), 201
Annotated Bibliography of Twentieth-Century Critical Studies on Women and Literature, 1660-1800, An (Backscheider et al.), 134
Annotated Guide to Reference Books on the Black American Experience, An (Westmoreland), 140
Annotated Guide to Women's Periodicals in the U.S. and Canada, The (Mehlman, ed.), 215
Annual Bibliography of English Language and Literature (Modern Humanities Research Assn.), 136
Anthologies By and About Women: An Analytical Index (Cardinale), 47
Anthropological Literature, 78-79
Appalachian Women: An Annotated

Bibliography (Farr), 157
Applied Science and Technology Index, 180
Artbibliographies Modern, 83
Art Documentation Supplement. See Women Artists: A Resource and Research Guide
Art Index, 83
Art Research Methods and Resources: A Guide to Finding Art Information (Jones), 82
Arts and Humanities Citation Index, 57, 213
Audiovisuals for Women (Nordquist), 42-43

Bibliofem, 209
Bibliographical Guide to Conference Publications, 70
Bibliographic Guide to Dance (N.Y. Public Library), 90
Bibliographic Guide to Educational Research, A (Berry), 101
Bibliographic Guide to Government Publications-Foreign, 64
Bibliographic Guide to Government Publications-U.S., 64
Bibliographic Guide to Studies on the Status of Women: Development and Population Trends, 41, 96
Bibliographic Guide to Theatre Arts (N.Y. Public Library), 90
Bibliographic Guide to the Study of the Literature of the U.S.A. (Gohdes & Marovitz), 130
Bibliography in the History of American Women (Lerner), 114-115
Bibliography in the History of European Women (Kelly), 116, 151
Bibliography of American Autobiographies, A (Kaplan), 200
Bibliography of Asian Studies, 148-149
Bibliography of Bioethics (Walters), 177
"Bibliography of Materials on Canadian Women Pertinent to the Social Sciences and Published Between 1950 and 1975, A" (Eichler), 158
Bibliography of Prostitution, A

(Bullough et al.), 120
Bibliography of Sources Relating to Women (Michigan), 190
Bibliography on the History of Medicine, 109
Bibliography on Women Workers (1861-1965) (Nicholas), 95
Biographical Books, 1876-1949/1950-1980, 198-199
Biography and Genealogy Master Index, 199
Biography Index, 199
Biological Abstracts, 181
Biological Woman - The Convenient Myth (Hubbard et al., eds.), 180
Black Family and the Black Woman, The: A Bibliography (Klotman & Batz), 142
Black Lesbians: An Annotated Bibliography (Roberts), 124
Black Woman in American Society, The: A Selected Annotated Bibliography (Davis), 141
Black Women and Religion: A Bibliography (Richardson), 139, 175
Booklegger, 219
Book of Goddesses and Heroines, The (Monaghan), 222
Books in Print, 48
Books in Print Supplement, 48-49
Breaking Through: A Bibliography of Women and Religion (Fischer), 174
Brief Guide to Sources of Scientific and Technical Information (Herner), 180
British Humanities Index, 152
Broadsheet, 159
Business Index, The, 98
Business Information Sources (Daniells), 94
Business Periodicals Index, 98

Camera Obscura: A Journal of Feminism and Film Theory, 217
Canadian Newsletter of Research on Women. See Resources for Feminist Research
Canadian Periodical Index/Index de periodique canadiens, 158
Canadian Women Studies/Les

Cahiers de la Femme, 216
Case for Women Suffrage, The: A Bibliography (Franklin), 112
Catalog of Selected Documents in Psychology, 170-171
Catalogs of the Sophia Smith Collection, Women's History Archive, Smith College, Northampton, Massachusetts, 190
Catalyst Resources for Women, 212, 213
Catholic Periodical and Literature Index, The, 175
Changing Directions in the Treatment of Women: A Mental Health Bibliography (Zukerman), 170
Chicago Tribune, The: Newspaper Index, 60
"Chicana, La: A Bibliographic Survey" (Loeb), 142
Chicana, The: A Comprehensive Bibliographic Study (Cabello-Argandona), 140
Chicano Periodical Index: A Cumulative Index to Selected Chicano Periodicals Between 1967 and 1978, 143
Chicano Periodical Index: A Cumulative Index to Selected Periodicals, 1979-1981, With Selected Serials Indexed Retrospectively, 143
Child Development Abstracts and Bibliography, 171
Chrysalis: A Magazine of Women's Culture, 216
CIS/Index, 64-65, 213
CIS U.S. Serial Set Index, 65
Columbia University Oral History Collection, 209
Common Lives/Lesbian Lives, 218
Comprehensive Bibliography for the Study of American Minorities (Miller), 140
Comprehensive Dissertation Index, 1861-1972, 73, 74
Concerns: Newsletter of the Women's Caucus of the Modern Languages, 219
Conditions, 218
Connexions: An International Women's Quarterly, 219-220
Contemporary Concert Music by Women: A Directory of Composers

and Their Works (Zaimont & Famera), 84
Contributions of Black Women to America (Davis, ed.), 197
Cornell University Collection of Women's Rights Pamphlets, The, 209
"Cousin Cinderella: A Guide to Historical Literature Pertaining to Canadian Women" (Strong-Boag), 158
Cumulated Dramatic Index, 1909-1949, 89-90
Cumulated Fiction Index, 133
Cumulative Book Index, 49
Cumulative Subject Index to the Monthly Catalog of United States Government Publications, 1900-1971, 66
Current Bibliography on African Affairs, A (African Bibliographic Center), 146
Current Biography, 162, 195, 198
Current Contents: Social and Behavioral Sciences, 53-54
Current Index to Journal in Education, 104

Development as if Women Mattered: An Annotated Bibliography With a Third World Focus (Rihani), 97
Development of Sex Differences, The (Maccoby, ed.), 169
Dictionary Catalog of the Research Libraries (N.Y. Public Library), 192
Dictionary Catalog of the Research Libraries of the New York Public Library, 1911-1971, 192
Directory of Archives and Manuscript Repositories (U.S. National Historical Publications Commission), 192
Directory of Career Resources for Women, 203
Directory of Financial Aids for Women, The (Schlachter), 205-206
Directory of Published Proceedings. Series SSH: Social Sciences/Humanities, 70
Directory of Special Opportunities for Women, The (Doss), 203-204
Dissertation Abstracts International, 32, 73, 74, 211, 213
Divorce: A Selected Annotated Bibliography (McKenney), 186

Economics: Bibliographic Guide to Reference Books and Information Sources (Melnyk), 94
Educational Documentation and Information. See "Education and Training of Women"; "Education of Women in Developing Countries"
"Education and Training of Women" (Cismaresco), 102
Education Index, 104
"Education of Women in Developing Countries" (Kelly & Kelly), 103
Effective Legal Research (Price et al.), 120
Encyclopedia of Associations, 203
Equal Rights Amendment, The: A Bibliographic Study (ERA Project), 120
Essay and General Literature Index, 47-48
Europa Biographical Dictionary of British Women (Crawford et al., eds.), 196
Everywoman's Guide to Colleges and Universities, 204

Family in Past Time, The: A Guide to the Literature (Milden), 117
Famous First Facts (Kane), 222
Far Eastern Quarterly, 149
Farm Women on the Prairie Frontier: A Sourcebook for Canada and the United States (Fairbanks & Sundberg), 156-157
F & S Index Europe. See Predicasts F & S Index United States
F & S Index International. See Predicasts F & S Index United States
Female Experience in Eighteenth- and Nineteenth-Century America, The: A Guide to the Study of the History of American Women (Conway), 113
Feminist Collections, 219
Feminist Issues, 216

Feminist Periodicals: A Current
  Listing of Contents, 33, 51-52
Feminist Quotations: Voices of
  Rebels, Reformers, and Vision-
  aries (McPhee & Fitzgerald,
  comps.), 221
Feminist Resources for Schools
  and Colleges: A Guide to
  Curricular Materials (Froschl
  & Williamson), 102-103
Feminist Review, 216
Femmes, Les: Guide Bibliograph-
  ique, 150
Fiction Catalog, 133
Film: A Reference Guide
  (Armour), 86
Film Index (Writers Program),
  87-88
Film Literature Index, 88-89
Films For, By, and About Women
  (Sullivan), 87
First Person Female American: A
  Selected and Annotated Bibli-
  ography of the Autobiographies
  of American Women Living After
  1950 (Rhodes, ed.), 200
Forthcoming Books, 49
Frauenfrage in Deutschland, Die:
  Bibliographie; Band 10, 1931-
  1980, 150
Frauenfrage in Deutschland, Die:
  Stroemungen und Gegenstroem-
  ungen, 1790-1930 (Sveistrup &
  Zahn-Harnack), 151
Frontiers: A Journal of Women's
  Studies, 142, 216
FS, Feminist Studies, 216
Fundamentals of Legal Research
  (Jacobstein & Mersky), 119

General Science Index, 181
Gerritsen Collection of Women's
  History, The, 1543-1945, 207-
  208
Girls Are People Too! A Bibliog-
  raphy of Nontraditional Female
  Roles in Children's Books
  (Newman), 132-133
Granger's Index to Poetry, 133
Guide to American Literature
  (Fenster), 130
Guide to Archives and Manu-
  scripts in the United States,
  A (U.S. National Historical

Publications Commission), 192
Guide to Basic Information
  Sources in the Visual Arts
  (Muehsam), 82
Guide to Historical Method, A
  (Shafer), 112
Guide to Library Sources in
  Political Science, A: American
  Government (Vose), 161-162
Guide to Microforms in Print,
  210
Guide to Published Works on
  Women and Politics II
  (Sapiro), 162-163
Guide to Research on North Ameri-
  can Indians (Hirschfelder et
  al.), 140
Guide to Social Science Resources
  in Women's Studies (Oakes &
  Sheldon), 43
Guide to Sources of Educational
  Information, A (Woodbury), 102
Guide to the Literature of Art
  History (Arntzen & Rainwater),
  81-82
Guide to the National Archives
  of the United States (U.S.
  National Archives and Records
  Service), 193
Guide to the Performing Arts, 90
Guide to Women's Art Organiza-
  tions and Directory for the
  Arts, 204
Guide to Women's Publishing
  (Joan & Chesman), 216, 221-222
Guinness Guide to Feminine
  Achievements, The (Macksey &
  Macksey), 222

Handbook of Latin American
  Studies, 154
Handbook of Nonsexist Writing,
  The (Miller & Swift), 222
HAPI: Hispanic American Periodi-
  cals Index, 143, 154
Harvard Women's Law Journal, 218
Healthsharing: A Canadian Women's
  Health Quarterly, 218
Hecate: A Women's Interdisci-
  plinary Journal, 159, 216
Helicon Nine: The Journal of
  Women's Arts and Letters, 217
Heresies: A Feminist Publication
  on Art and Politics, 217

Herstory, 208
Her Story: Australian Women in Print, 1788-1975 (Bettison & Summers), 159
Historian's Handbook, The: A Descriptive Guide to Reference Works (Poulton), 112
Historical Abstracts, 117-118, 213
History and Bibliography of American Newspapers, 1690-1820. Additions and Corrections (Brigham), 62
History of the Family and Kinship: A Select International Bibliography (Soliday, ed.), 116-117
History of Women, 209
History of Women in America, The: Catalogs of the Books, Manuscripts, and Pictures of the Arthur and Elizabeth Schlesinger Library, 190
Hot Wire: A Journal of Women's Music and Culture, 217
How to Use a Medical Library (Morton), 108
Humanities Index, 32, 56
Human Resources Abstracts, 187

Incest: The Last Taboo: An Annotated Bibliography (Rubin & Byerly), 185
Index/Directory of Women's Media (Allen, ed.), 205, 215-216
Index Medicus, 109
Index of Economic Articles in Journals and Collective Volumes, 1886/1924--, 98
Index to American Women Speakers, 1828-1978 (Manning), 163
Index to Current Urban Documents, 65
Index to Jewish Periodicals, 175
Index to Legal Periodicals, 121
Index to Periodical Articles By and About Blacks, 143
Index to Periodical Articles Relating to Law, 121
Index to Religious Periodical Literature. See Religion Index One: Periodicals

Index to Scientific and Technical Proceedings, 71
Index to Social Science and Humanities Proceedings, 70-71
Index to the Christian Science Monitor, 60
Index to Women of the World from Ancient to Modern Times (Ireland), 199
Information Sources of Political Science, The (Holler), 161
International African Bibliography, 147
International Bibliography of Books and Articles on the Modern Languages and Literatures (MLA), 126-127, 136-137
International Bibliography of Economics, 99
International Bibliography of Political Science, 164-165
International Bibliography of Research in Marriage and the Family, 1900-1972 (Aldous & Hill), 186
International Bibliography of Social and Cultural Anthropology, 79
International Bibliography of Sociology, 187
International Dictionary of Women's Biography, The (Uglow, ed.), 195
International Dictionary of Women's Development Organizations (Hosken), 205
Internationale Bibliographie der Zeitschriftenliteratur aus allen Gebieten des Wissens/ International Bibliography of Periodical Literature Concerning All Fields of Knowledge, 152-153
International Encyclopedia of Women Composers (Cohen), 84-85
International Index, 56
International Index to Film Periodicals, 88
International Index to Periodicals, 56
International Journal of Women's Studies, 216
International Nursing Index, 109

International Political Science
    Abstracts, 165
ISIS Women's Journal, 220

Jewish Woman, The, 1900-1980:
    Bibliography (Cantor), 140-141
Jewish Women and Jewish Law:
    Bibliography (Hamelsdorf &
    Adelsberg), 175
Jewish Women's Studies Guide,
    The (Elwell & Levenson, eds.),
    141-142
Journal of Asian Studies, 149
Journal of Feminist Studies in
    Religion, 220
Journal of Family History, 116
Journal of Women and Religion,
    220
"Judging the professional woman:
    changing research, changing
    values" (Yogev), 31-32

Keyboard Music by Women Com-
    posers: A Catalog and Bib-
    liography (Meggett, comp.), 84
Korean and Japanese Women: An
    Analytic Bibliographic Guide
    (Koh), 147-148

Language, Gender, and Society
    (Thorne et al., eds.), 126
Language and Sex: Difference and
    Dominance. See Language, Gen-
    der, and Society
Law and Inequality, 218
LCSH. See Library of Congress
    Subject Headings, The
Legal Research in a Nutshell
    (Cohen), 119
Legal Research Manual, The: A
    Game Plan for Legal Research
    and Analysis (Wren & Wren),
    120
Legal Resources Index, 121-122,
    213
Lesbian in Literature, The: A
    Bibliography (Grier), 124
Lesbian Periodicals Index, 123
Lesbian Studies: Present and
    Future (Cruikshank, ed.),
    123-124
Library of Congress Subject
    Headings, The, 23-24, 34, 122
Library Research Guide to Edu-

cation: Illustrated Search
    Strategy and Sources (Kennedy),
    102
Library Research Guide to His-
    tory: Illustrated Search
    Strategy and Sources (Frick),
    112
Library Research Guide to Music:
    Illustrated Search Strategy
    and Sources (Druesedow), 84
Library Research Guide to Reli-
    gion and Theology: Illustrated
    Search Strategy and Sources
    (Kennedy), 174
Library Research Guide to Soci-
    ology: Illustrated Search
    Strategy and Sources
    (McMillan & Kennedy), 184
Library Use: A Handbook for
    Psychology (Reed & Baxter), 167
Lilith: The Jewish Women's Maga-
    zine, 219, 220
Literary Research Guide (Patter-
    son), 130
Literature of Political Science,
    The: A Guide for Students,
    Libraries, and Teachers
    (Brock), 161
Literature of Theology, The: A
    Guide for Students and Pastors
    (Bollier), 174
LLBA: Language and Language Be-
    havior Abstracts, 126
LOMA: Literature on Modern Art.
    See Artbibliographies Modern
Los Angeles Times, The: News-
    paper Index, 60

Magazine Index, 54, 211, 213
Majority Report, 218
Management Contents, 33, 99, 214
Manual for Writers of Term
    Papers, Theses, and Disserta-
    tions (Turabian), 12
Mary Wollstonecraft Journal.
    See Women and Literature
Media Report to Women, 219. See
    also Index/Directory of Women's
    Media
Medical Subject Headings. See
    Index Medicus
M/F: A Feminist Journal, 216
Microform Research Collections:
    A Guide (Dodson), 210

Middle East, The: Abstracts and Index, 155-156
Mideast File, 156
Minerva, 219
Minorities and Women: A Guide to Reference Literature in the Social Sciences (Schlachter), 38-39, 140
Modern Arab Woman, The: A Bibliography (Raccagni), 155
Modern Language Association International Bibliography, 33, 213
Monthly Catalog of Government Publications, The, 14, 32, 211
Monthly Catalog of U.S. Government Publications, 65-66, 213
Monthly Checklist of State Publications, 66
More Women in Literature: Criticism of the Seventies (Fairbanks), 134-135
Motheroot Journal: A Women's Review of Small Presses, 220
Motion Picture Performers. See Women and Film: A Bibliography
Moving Pictures: An Annotated Guide to Selected Film Literature with Suggestions for the Study of Film (Sheahan), 87
Ms., 218
Music Index, 86
Music Reference and Research Materials (Duckles), 84

National Register of Microform Masters, 210
National Union Catalog, 49
National Union Catalog of Manuscript Collections, 192-193
Native American Women: A Contextual Bibliography (Green), 141
Nature of Woman, The: An Encyclopedia and Guide to the Literature (Warren), 223
New Career Options for Women: A Selected Annotated Bibliography (Phelps et al.), 95
New Directions for Women, 218
New Feminist Scholarship: A

Guide to Bibliographies (Williamson), 39
New Film Index, The: A Bibliography of Magazine Articles in English, 1930-1970 (MacCann & Perry), 88
New Jersey Women, 1770-1970 (Steiner-Scott & Wagle), 112
New Orleans Times-Picayune, The: Newspaper Index, 60
NewsBank, 61
NewsBank Index, 61
Newspaper Indexes: A Location and Subject Guide for Researchers (Milner), 61-62
Newspapers in Microform, 62
New Women's Times, 218. See also New Women's Times Feminist Review
New Women's Times Feminist Review, 220
New York Times Index, 60-61
New York Times Information Bank, 211, 214
Nineteenth Century Readers' Guide to Periodical Literature, 1890-1899, With Supplementary Indexing, 1900-1922, 54
Notable American Women, 9
Notable American Women, 1607-1950, 196
Notable American Women, The Modern Period, 196
Nursing and Allied Health Index, 109-110

off our backs, 218
Older Women in 20th-Century America: A Selected Annotated Bibliography (Borenstein), 184
On Campus With Women, 218
One-Parent Family, The: Perspectives and Annotated Bibliography (Schlesinger), 186
On the Psychology of Women: A Survey of Empirical Studies (Sherman), 170

Paid My Dues: Journal of Women and Music, 217
PAIS Bulletin, 32, 55, 214
Pamphlets in American History: Women, 209
Paperbound Books in Print, 49

Performing Arts Research: A
  Guide to Information Sources
  (Whalon), 89
Philosopher's Guide to Sources,
  Research Tools, Professional
  Life, and Related Fields, The
  (DeGeorge), 174
Philosopher's Index, The, 176
Play Index, 90
Poetry by American Women, 1900-
  1975: A Bibliography
  (Reardon & Thorsen), 131
Political Participation of
  Women in the United States,
  The: A Selected Bibliography
  1950-1976 (Stanwick & Li),
  164
Poole's Index to Periodical
  Literature, 1802-1881, 1st-
  5th Supplements, 1882-1907,
  54
Popular Periodical Index, 54
Population Index, 187
Population Index Bibliography,
  187
Poverty and Human Resources
  Abstracts. See Human Re-
  sources Abstracts
Predicasts F & S Index United
  States, 99
Progress of Afro-American Women,
  The: A Selected Bibliography
  and Resource Guide (Sims), 142
Psychological Abstracts, 33,
  171, 214
Psychological Index, 1894-1935,
  171-172
Psychology of Sex Differences,
  The (Maccoby & Jacklin), 169
Psychology of Women, The: A
  Partially Annotated Bibliog-
  raphy (Walstedt), 170
Psychology of Women Quarterly,
  31, 220

Quest: A Feminist Quarterly,
  216
Quotable Woman, The, 1800-1981
  (Partnow, comp.), 222-223

Rape and Rape-Related Issues:
  An Annotated Bibliography
  (Kemmer), 120
Readers' Guide to Periodical

Literature, 14, 30-31, 32, 55
  Supplement, 56
Recently Published Articles, 118
Reference Sources in English and
  American Literature: An Anno-
  tated Bibliography (Schweik &
  Riesner), 130
Religion Index One: Periodicals,
  176
Religion Index Two: Multi-Author
  Works, 176
Religious and Theological Ab-
  stracts, 176
Research Guide for Psychology
  (McInnis), 167
Research Guide in Women's
  Studies (Lynn et al.), 38
Research Guide to Philosophy
  (Tice & Slavens), 174
Research Guide to Religious
  Studies (Wilson & Slavens),
  174
Research in Education. See
  Resources in Education
Researching and Writing in His-
  tory: A Practical Handbook for
  Students (McCoy), 112
Resources for Feminist Research/
  Documentation sur la Recherche
  Feministe, 43, 158, 217
Resources in Education, 104-105
Resources in Women's Educational
  Equity (U.S. Office of Educa-
  tion), 103
Retrospective Index to Film
  Periodicals, 1930-1971 (Batty),
  88
RILA, Repertoire International
  de la Litterature de l'Art,
  83
RILM Abstracts of Music Litera-
  ture, 86

Sage: A Scholarly Journal on
  Black Women, 219
Sage Family Studies Abstracts,
  187-188
Sage Race Relations Abstracts,
  143-144
Savvy, 217
Science and Engineering Litera-
  ture: A Guide to Reference
  Sources (Malinowsky & Richard-
  son), 180

Science Citation Index, 181
Scientific and Technical Information Sources (Chen), 179
Sex Roles: A Journal of Research, 220
Sex Roles: A Research Bibliography (Astin et al.), 168
Sex Role Stereotyping in the Mass Media: An Annotated Bibliography (Friedman), 91
Sexual Barrier, The: Legal, Medical, Economic and Social Aspects of Sex Discrimination (Hughes), 120-121
Short Story Index, 133-134
Signs: Journal of Women in Culture and Society, 217, 229-233
Sinister Wisdom, 219
Social and Behavioral Aspects of Female Alcoholism: An Annotated Bibliography (Chalfant & Roper), 168-169
Social Science Index, 32, 56, 214
Social Sciences and Humanities Index, 56
Social Sciences Citation Index, 56
Social Work Research and Abstracts, 172, 188
Sociological Abstracts, 188, 214
Sociology of Housework, The (Oakley), 30-31
Special Collections in the Library of Congress: A Selective Guide (Library of Congress), 193
Status of the Arab Woman, The: A Select Bibliography (Meghdessian), 155
Status of Women: A Select Bibliography (UN), 45
Student Anthropologist's Handbook, The: A Guide to Research, Training, and Career (Frantz), 77
Student Political Scientist's Handbook, The (Merritt & Pyszka), 161
Student Sociologist's Handbook, The (Bart & Frankel), 184
Student's Guide to History, A (Benjamin), 112
Studies on Women Abstracts, 52

Subject Catalog (Library of Congress), 50
Subject Collections: A Guide to Special Book Collections and Subject Emphases as Reported by University, College, Public, and Special Libraries and Museums in the United States and Canada (Ash), 191-192
Subject Guide to Books in Print, 48
Subject Guide to Forthcoming Books, 49
Suffer and Be Still: Women in the Victorian Age (Vicinus, ed.), 150

Thema Frau: Bibliographie der deutschsprachigen Literatur zur Frauenfrage 1949-1979 (Bock & Witych), 150
Thesaurus of ERIC Descriptors (ERIC), 105
Thesaurus of Psychological Index Terms, 172
Third Woman, 219
Through a Woman's I: An Annotated Bibliography of American Women's Autobiographical Writings, 1946-1976 (Addis), 199-200
Times (London) Index, The, 60
Topical Bibliography (Selectively Annotated) on the Psychology of Women (Baer & Sherif), 168
Toward a Feminist Tradition: An Annotated Bibliography of Novels in English by Women, 1891-1920 (Daims & Grimes), 131, 132
Trivia, 217
True Daughters of the North: Canadian Women's History: An Annotated Bibliography (Light & Strong-Boag), 157
Tulsa Studies in Women's Literature, 219
Turn-of-the-Century Women, 218

Underground Newspaper Collection, 209
UNDOC: Current Index, 66-67
United States Political Science Documents, 165, 214

Violence Against Women: An
  Annotated Bibliography
  (Wilson), 185

Wall Street Journal Index, 61
Washington Post: Newspaper
  Index, 61
Western Women in History and
  Literature (Patterson-Black &
  Patterson-Black), 157-158
Who's Who and Where in Women's
  Studies, 206
Who's Who of American Women,
  197-198
Widening Sphere, A: Changing
  Roles of Victorian Women
  (Vicinus), 151
WIN (Women's International Network) News, 220
WLW (Women Library Workers)
  Journal, 219
Womanhood Media: Current Resources About Women and Supplement (Wheeler), 45
Womanlist (Weiser & Arbeiter),
  223-224
Woman of Power, 220
Woman's Art Journal, 217
Woman's Collection, The (N.C.),
  191
Women's Encyclopedia of Myths
  and Secrets, The (Walker),
  223
Woman's Guide to Career Preparation, A: Scholarships, Grants,
  Loans (Jawin), 205
Womanspirit, 220
Woman's Who's Who of America,
  197
Women: A Bibliography of Bibliographies (Ballou), 38
Women: A Bibliography of Special
  Periodical Issues, 52
Women: A Bibliography on Their
  Education and Careers (Astin
  et al.), 94, 102
Women: A Journal of Liberation,
  217
Women, Education, and Employment:
  A Bibliography of Periodical
  Citations, Pamphlets, Newspapers, and Government Documents (Feinberg), 94, 102
Women, 1870-1928: A Select Guide
  to Printed and Archival Sources
  in the United Kingdom (Barrow),
  149
Women, 1965-1975, 59
Women: Their Changing Roles
  (Janeway, ed.), 59-60
Women and Ambition: A Bibliography (Faunce), 169
Women and Deviance: Issues in
  Social Conflict and Change: An
  Annotated Bibliography (Davis &
  Keith), 184
Women and Environments, 217
Women and Feminism in American
  History: A Guide to Information
  Sources (Tingley & Tingley),
  115
Women and Film: A Bibliography
  (Kowalski), 87
Women and Folklore: A Bibliographic Survey (DeCaro), 77-78
Women and Health, 218
Women and Health/Mental Health,
  208
Women and History, 218
Women and Language News, 219
Women and Law, 208
Women and Literature, 219
Women and Literature: An Annotated Bibliography of Women
  Writers, 131-132
Women and Mental Health: A Bibliography (Cromwell), 169
Women and Politics, 220
Women and Society: A Critical
  Review of the Literature with
  a Selected Annotated Bibliography (Rosenberg-Dishman &
  Bergstrom), 43-44
Women and Society, Citations 3601
  to 6000: An Annotated Bibliography (Een & Rosenberg-Dishman), 44
Women and the American Economy
  (U.S. Air Force Academy), 96
Women and the American Left: A
  Guide to Sources (Buhle), 162
Women and the Health System:
  Selected Annotated References,
  108
Women and Therapy, 220
Women and Urban Society: A Guide
  to Information Sources (Diner),
  184-185

Women and Women's Issues: A Handbook of Tests and Measures (Beere), 168
Women and World Development: An Annotated Bibliography (Buvinic), 97
Women Artists: An Historical, Contemporary and Feminist Bibliography (Bachmann & Piland), 82
Women Artists: A Resource and Research Guide (Chiarmonte, ed.), 82
Women Artists News, 217
Women at Work, 217
Women at Work: An Annotated Bibliography (Bickner); Volume II (Bickner & Shaughnessy), 94
Women Composers: A Checklist of Works for the Solo Voice (Stewart-Green), 84
Women Composers: A Discography (Frasier), 85
Women Composers: A Handbook (Stern), 85-86
Women Composers, Conductors, and Musicians of the Twentieth Century (LePage), 198
Women Helping Women: A State-by-State Directory of Services, 206
Women in America: A Guide to Books, 1963-1975 (Haber), 42
Women in America: A Guide to Information Sources (Terris), 44-45
Women in American History: A Bibliography (Harrison, ed.), 113-114, 117
Women in American Music: A Bibliography (Skowronski), 85
Women in American Music: A Bibliography of Music and Literature (Block & Neuls-Bates), 84
Women in Antiquity: An Annotated Bibliography (Goodwater), 116
Women in Australia: An Annotated Guide to Records, 190
Women in Canada (Stephenson, ed.), 158
Women in China: A Selected and Annotated Bibliography (Wei), 148
Women in Early Texas (Carrington, ed.), 198
Women in Government and Politics: A Bibliography of American and Foreign Sources (Levenson), 162-163
Women in Literature: Criticism of the Seventies (Fairbanks), 134-135
Women in Management: An Annotated Bibliography and Sourcelist (Leavitt), 95
Women in Medicine: A Bibliography of the Literature on Women Physicians (Chaff et al., comps.), 108
Women in Music: A Bio-bibliography (Hixon & Hennessee), 85
Women in Music History: A Research Guide (Pool), 85
Women in Non-Traditional Occupations--A Bibliography (U.S. Office of Education), 96
Women in Perspective: A Guide for Cross-Cultural Studies (Jacobs), 78
Women in Politics: The United States and Abroad; A Select Annotated Bibliography, 1970-Oct. 1980 (Fitch), 162
Women in Popular Culture: A Reference Guide (Fishburn), 91
Women in Science and Mathematics: Bibliography (Chinn), 180
Women in Southeast Asia: A Bibliography (Fan), 147
Women in Soviet Society (Lapidus), 149
Women in Spanish America: An Annotated Bibliography from Pre-Conquest to Contemporary Times (Knaster), 153-154
Women in the Caribbean: A Bibliography (Cohen-Stuart), 153
Women in the Development Process: A Select Bibliography on Women in Sub-Saharan Africa and Latin America (Saulniers & Rakowski), 97, 146, 154
Women in the Middle East and North Africa: An Annotated Bibliography (Al-Qazzaz), 155

Women in the War: A Bibliography (Nims), 112
Women in U.S. History: An Annotated Bibliography (Common Women Collective), 113
Women in Western European History: A Select Chronological, Geographical, and Topical Bibliography from Antiquity to the French Revolution (Frey et al.), 115-116, 150
Women of Achievement: Thirty-five Centuries of History (Raven & Weir), 195-196
Women of England, The: From Anglo-Saxon Times to the Present; Interpretive Bibliographic Essays (Kanner, ed.), 151-152
"Women of England in a Century of Social Change, The, 1815-1914: A Select Bibliography" (Kanner), 150
"Women of England in a Century of Social Change, The, 1815-1917: A Select Bibliography, Part II" (Kanner), 151
Women of South Asia: A Guide to Resources (Sakala), 148
Women of the Future: The Female Main Character in Science Fiction (King), 132
Women's Action Almanac: A Complete Guide (Women's Action Alliance), 8, 206
Women's Annual, The: The Year in Review (Haber, ed.), 8, 224
Women's Book of World Records (O'Neill, ed.), 222
Women's Education - A World View, Vol. 2: Annotated Bibliography of Books and Reports (Parker & Parker), 103
Women's Education in the United States: A Guide to Information Sources (Wilkins), 104
Women's Films in Print: An Annotated Guide to 800 Films by Women (Dawson), 87
Women's Health Care: Resources, Writings, Bibliographies (Cowan), 108

Women's History Sources: A Guide to Archives and Manuscript Collections in the United States, 111, 191
Women's Liberation and Revolution: A Bibliography (Rowbotham), 163
Women's Movement in the Seventies, The: An International English-Language Bibliography (Krichmar), 42, 114
Women's Movement Media: A Source Guide (Harrison), 204-205
Women Speaking: An Annotated Bibliography of Verbal and Nonverbal Communication, 1970-1980 (Jarrard & Randall), 125-126
Women's Periodical and Newspapers from the 19th Century to 1981 (Danky et al., eds.), 216
Women's Review of Books, The, 220
Women's Rights Law Reporter, 218
Women's Rights Movement in the United States, The, 1848-1970: A Bibliography and Sourcebook (Krichmar), 42, 114
Women's Studies, 217
Women's Studies: A Checklist of Bibliographies (Ritchie), 38
Women's Studies: A Recommended Core Bibliography (Stineman), 44
Women's Studies in Communication, 219
Women's Studies International Forum, 217
Women's Studies International Quarterly. See Women's Studies International Forum
Women's Studies Newsletter. See Women's Studies Quarterly
Women's Studies Quarterly, 217
Women's Studies Review, 220
Women Studies Abstracts, 14, 31-32, 52-53
Women's Work in Britain and America from the Nineties to World War I: An Annotated Bibliography (McFeely), 95
Women Writers in Translation: An Annotated Bibliography,

1945-1982 (Resnick & De Courtivron), 131
Working Woman, 217
Work on Women: A Guide to the Literature (Evans & Morgan), 41-42
World Who's Who of Women, The, 198

Writings on American History, 118
Writing the Psychology Paper (Sternberg), 168

Year's Work in English Studies, The (English Assn.), 136
Year's Work in Modern Language Studies, The, 137

Subject Index

Abortion, 107, 115, 185
Abstracts, 14, 30, 31-32, 33, 34, 52. See also specific subjects and topics
Action groups, 15. See also Organizations and services directories
Africa, 41, 97, 117, 137, 146-147, 155
Aging, 184. See also Health and medicine
Alcoholism, 168-169, 181, 184
American Indians, 39, 133, 139, 140, 141
Annotation, 31
Anthologies, 8, 9, 47, 98, 151
Anthony, Susan B., 209
Anthropology, 77-79, 223. See also Linguistics; National and area studies; Social anthropology
Appalachia, 157
Arab region, 41. See also Middle East
Archives. See Library catalogs
Armed forces. See History; Minerva (in Title Index)
Arts. See Film; Music; Popular culture; Theater; Visual Arts
Asia, 41, 117, 131, 137, 147-149
Asian Americans, 39, 139
Audiovisual materials, 11, 29, 42, 44, 45, 103
Australia, 159, 190
Authors. See Literature
Autobiographies, 199-200

Bangladesh, 148
Battered women, 12, 184, 185
Bibliographic Retrieval Services (BRS), 212
Bibliographies, 11, 12, 19, 29-34, 36
 classified, 33
 continuing, 33
 general, 41-45
 multidisciplinary, 47-57, 59-67, 69-71, 73-74
 reference, 37-39
 topical, 9-10, 13, 75-188
 See also specific disciplines and subjects
Bioethics, 177
Biography, 9, 44, 54, 195-201
 library arrangement, 27
 subject headings, 21
 special subject, 82, 84-85, 89, 99, 108, 109, 130, 143, 162, 164
 See also National and area studies
Black women, 39, 124, 133, 139, 140, 141, 142-143, 197, 219
Books, 44, 45, 47-50
 as research tool, 9, 13, 14, 29
 See also Card catalog
Bookstores, 15
BRS. See Bibliographic Retrieval Services
Brunei, 147
Burma, 147
Business, 93-96, 98-99, 217

Call number, 17-18, 25-27

Canada, 43, 62, 65, 85-86, 113-114, 156-158, 191, 215, 217, 218
Card catalog, 17-27
  advantages and disadvantages, 9
  alphabetization, 24-25
  alternate forms, 17
  author, 17, 18, 19-20
  dictionary, 17
  subject, 12, 13-14, 17, 20-24
  title, 17, 18, 19-20
  See also Library catalogs; Serials catalogs
Careers. See Labor force participation
Caribbean, 153
Catholic women, 175
Chicanas. See Latinas
China, 148
Church, women in, 112-113. See also Religion and philosophy
College and university directories, 204, 206
Computerized sources. See Online sources
Computer print-out holdings, 17, 192
Conference proceedings, 14, 19, 69-71
Copyright date, 33
Corporate authorship, 19
Criminology. See Law and criminology
Cross-cultural surveys, 7, 78, 102

Databases, 213-214. See also Online sources
Demographic features, 41. See also National and area studies
Development. See Economic development
Dewey decimal system, 25-26, 225-226
Dialog, 212
Diaries, 199, 200, 201. See also Literature; Manuscript inventories
Directories, 15, 45, 70, 84, 192, 203-210
Discographies, 29, 85
Dissertations, 73-74, 95, 96, 103

Divorce. See Family and home life; Sociology

Eastern Europe, 41, 152
Economic development, 41, 93, 96-97, 103
Economics, 93-96, 98-99
Edition information, 18
Education, 41, 94, 101-105, 218
Encyclopedias, 8
Equal Rights Amentment (ERA), 33, 120. See also Law and criminology
ERA. See Equal Rights Amendment

Family and home life, 41, 97, 186-187. See also History; Housework; Minority women; National and area studies; Psychology
Fawcett Library (London), 209
Feminist publishers, 15, 220
Fiction, 44. See also Literature; Science fiction
Filing. See Card catalog, alphabetization
Film, 86-89, 217
Filmographies, 29, 87
Folklore, 223
Footnotes, 11
Foreign-language materials, 32, 55, 64, 99, 116, 131, 150, 151, 152-153

Genealogy, 199
Gerritsen, Aletta Jacobs, 207
Girls' clubs, 151
Government Printing Office, 63
Government publication sources, 14, 32, 44, 63-67, 94, 103
  library arrangement, 27, 63
Great Britain. See United Kingdom

Handbooks, 8, 221-224
Harvard University. See Tozzer Library
Health and medicine, 107-110, 180, 181, 208, 209, 218. See also Psychology
Hispanic American women. See Latinas
History, 111-118, 207-209, 218, 223

History (continued)
of medicine, 109
of newspapers, 62
See also Biography; Library catalogs; National and area studies
Housework, 30-31

Imprint. See Publisher Information
Incest, 185
Indexes, 14, 19, 30, 32, 34. See also specific subjects and topics
India, 148
Indonesia, 147
Interlibrary loan, 35, 62
International African Institute, 147
International Standard Book Number (ISBN), 18(fig.), 19
ISBN. See International Standard Book Number

Japan. See Asia
Jewish women, 139, 140, 141, 175, 220
Journals, 44-45, 47, 51-57, 215-220, 229-233
interlibrary loan, 35
library arrangement, 27
as research tools, 10, 13, 14, 29, 32
tables of contents, 33
topical, 88, 94, 95, 96, 98, 104. See also chapter subheading. Indexes and Continuing Bibliographies
See also Popular magazines; Serials catalog

Keyword searching, 20, 34, 74
Korea. See Asia

Labor force participation, 41, 91, 93-99, 185, 217. See also Health and medicine; History; Law and criminology; Minority women; Organizations and services directories; Political science; Religion and philosophy; Science and technology
Labor movement. See Trade unions

Latin America, 41, 97, 137, 146, 153-154
Latinas, 39, 139, 140, 142, 143
Law and criminology, 119-122, 151, 184, 208, 218
Lesbian studies, 123-124, 184, 218-219
Letters, 199, 200. See also Literature
Library catalogs, 189-193, 219
Library of Congress, 21, 23, 49, 50, 193
classification system, 25, 26-27, 227
Linguistics, 125-127, 219, 222, 223
Literature, 129-137, 217, 219. See also Manuscript inventories; National and area studies

Malaysia, 147
Manuscript inventories, 29, 192-193, 209
Marriage. See Family and home life; Sociology
Medicine. See Health and medicine
Mental health. See Psychology
Mexican-American women. See Latinas
Michigan, 190
Microfiche, 17, 61, 207
Microfilm, 17, 62, 73, 98, 121, 207, 208-210
Microform. See Microfiche; Microfilm
Middle East, 117, 155-156
Military science. See Minerva
Minority women, 38-39, 94, 115, 124, 133, 139-144, 175, 219, 220
Music, 84-86, 198, 217
Myths, 223

National and area studies, 145-159, 219-220
National Women's Studies Association, 139, 206
Native Americans. See American Indians
Nepal, 148
Newspapers, 59-62, 94, 95, 98, 216
underground, 209

New York Times, 60-61, 98
New Zealand, 159
Non-print information. See
    Audiovisual materials
North Carolina, 191
Nursing. See Health and medicine

Oceania, 159
Online sources, 14, 17, 20, 34,
    211-214
Oral history, 209
Organizations and services
    directories, 203-210

Pakistan, 148
Pamphlets, 15, 94, 96, 209
Periodicals. See Journals; News-
    papers
Philippines, 147
Philosophy. See Religion and
    philosophy
Political science, 161-165,
    217, 220
Popular culture, 91-92, 218
Popular magazines, 14, 53, 54,
    55-56
Preliminary research, 8-11, 37-
    39
Professional women, 31-32. See
    also Labor force participa-
    tion
Prostitution. See Law and
    criminology
Psychology, 167-172, 220
Publisher information, 18

Quotations, 221, 222. See also
    Speeches

Rape. See Law and criminology;
    Sociology
Religion and philosophy, 139,
    140-141, 173-177, 220
Resource people, 15
Reviews, 8, 220, 229-233

Schlesinger, Arthur and Eliza-
    beth, Library, 190, 209
Scholarships, grants, and
    loans, 205-206
Science and technology, 179-181
Science fiction, 132
SDC. See System Development
    Corporation

Serials catalogs, 20
Series information, 18
Sexual discrimination. See Law
    and criminology; Sociology
Singapore, 147
Smith College, 190, 209
Social anthropology, 7, 78-79
Social sciences, 34, 43-44, 53,
    56, 70, 158. See also specific
    disciplines
Sociology, 183-188
Soviet Union, 149, 152
Special collections. See Library
    catalogs
Speeches, 163, 164, 221, 222
Sri Lanka, 148
State government documents, 66
Statistics, 64
Stereotyping. See Popular cul-
    ture; Psychology
SuDoc (Superintendent of Docu-
    ments) numbers, 63, 66
Suffrage, 151. See also History
Survey texts, 8
Symposia papers, 14, 19, 69-71.
System Development Corporation
    (SDC), 212

Temperance movement, 9, 151
Term paper writing guides, 12,
    168
Texas, 198
Thailand, 147
Theater, 89-90
Thesaurus, 33-34
Third World. See Economic de-
    velopment; Minority studies;
    National and area studies
Toxic shock, 12, 181
Tozzer Library (Harvard) collec-
    tion, 78
Tracings, 18(fig.), 19
Trade unions, 96, 151
Travel guide, 223

Union catalog, 17, 49, 62, 192
United Kingdom, 41, 95, 149, 150-
    152, 196
United Nations Decade for Women
    (1975-1985), 145
United States, 41, 42, 44, 62,
    85-86, 156-157
University Microfilms Interna-
    tional, 73

University of Kansas, 208
University of North Carolina, 191, 208
Urbanization, 184-185

Vertical files, 10-11, 14
Victorian women, 150-151
Visual arts, 81-83, 204, 217

Wall Street Journal, 61, 98
WCTU. See Women's Christian Temperance Union
Western Europe, 41, 85-86, 99, 115-117, 131, 137, 149-153

Willard, Frances, 9
Women's Christian Temperance Union (WCTU), 9
Women's College Library (N.C.), 191, 208
Women's History Research Center, 208
Women's movement, 42, 114, 204-205, 207-209. See also Handbooks; History; Minority women
Women's Trade Union League, 209
Works Progress Administration, 87-88
Writers. See Literature

Ref Z 7961 .S42 1985
Searing, Susan E.
Introduction to library
 research in women's studies

DEC 2 6 1985